Avenues

Alfredo Schifini
Deborah J. Short
Josefina Villamil Tinajero

Erminda García
Eugene E. García
Else Hamayan
Lada Kratky

SMBSD

HAMPTON-BROWN

Grades 3–5 Curriculum Reviewers

Fran Alcántara
Bilingual Support Teacher
Cicero Public Schools District 99
Cicero, Illinois

Santina Y. Buffone, Ed.D.
Coordinator
Bilingual/Compensatory Education
Dearborn Public Schools
Dearborn, Michigan

Anastasia Colón
Bilingual Teacher
Buhrer Elementary
Cleveland Municipal School District
Cleveland, Ohio

Kelley E. Crockett
Team Leader, Language Center
Meadowbrook Elementar
Fort Worth Independent School
 District
Fort Worth, Texas

Lily Pham Dam
Former Administrator
Dallas Independent School District
Dallas, Texas

Marian Evans
Teacher
Ault Elementary
Cypress-Fairbanks Independent
 School District
Houston, Texas

David Garcia
Bilingual/ESL Teacher
Winston Elementary
Edgewood Independent School
 District
San Antonio, Texas

Sue Goldstein
*Bilingual Education Coordinator
 and Program Teacher*
Regional Multicultural Magnet School
New London, Connecticut

Sandra Guerra
Assistant Principal
Chapa Elementary
La Joya Independent School District
La Joya, Texas

Ruth Henrichs
ESL Teacher
Fleetwood Elementary
East Ramapo Central School District
Spring Valley, New York

Linda Hoste, M.Ed.
ESL Specialist
Birdville Independent School District
Fort Worth, Texas

Virginia Jama
ESL Coordinator, K–12
New York City Board of Education
Brooklyn, New York

Liliana Jaurrieta
Teacher
Lujan-Chavez Elementary
Socorro Independent School District
El Paso, Texas

Clara Levy
Teacher
Mesita Elementary
El Paso Independent School District
El Paso, Texas

Dr. Mark R. O'Shea
Professor of Education
Institute for Field-Based Teacher
 Education
California State University,
 Monterey Bay
Monterey, California

Raul Ramirez, Jr.
Bilingual/GT Teacher
Royalgate Elementary
South San Antonio
 Independent School District
San Antonio, Texas

Christa A. Wallis
*Elementary Program Specialist
 English Learners*
San Bernardino City Unified School
 District
San Bernardino, California

Acknowledgments

Every effort has been made to secure permission, but if any omissions have been made, please let us know. We gratefully acknowledge the following permissions:

Cover Design and Art Direction: Pronk&Associates.

Cover Illustration: Shelly Shinjo.

Boyds Mills Press, Inc.: *"Puddle"* from Storm Coming! by Audrey Baird. Text copyright © 2001 by Audrey Baird. Illustrations copyright © 2001 by Patrick O'Brien. Published and reprinted with the permission of Boyds Mills Press, Inc.

Acknowledgments continue on page 500.

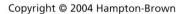

Hampton-Brown
P.O. Box 223220
Carmel, California 93922
800-333-3510
www.hampton-brown.com

Printed in the United States of America

ISBN 0-7362-1709-6

05 06 07 08 09 10 11 12 9 8 7 6 5 4 3

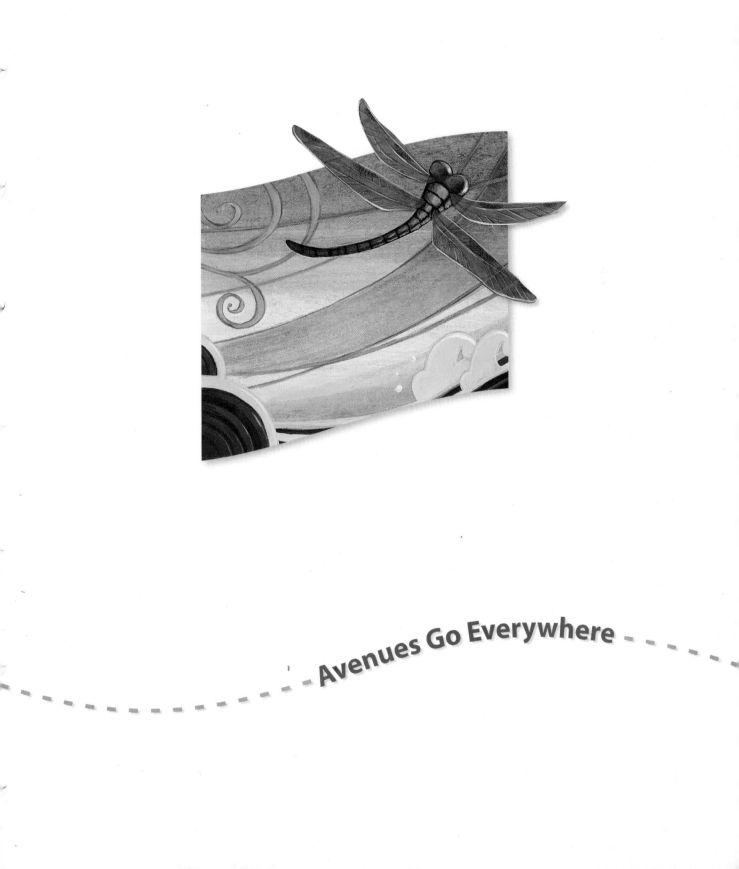

Avenues Go Everywhere

Native Land

Social Studies
- Native North America
- Regions

Once Upon
a Storm

Science
▪ Weather
▪ Safety

Fiction
Adventure Story

Nonfiction
News Article

Unit 4

Watery World

Science
- Animal Adaptations
- Ocean Ecosystem

Cultural Ties

Social Studies
- Culture
- Immigration

Unit 6

THIS STATE OF MINE

Social Studies
- State History
- Regions

What's It Worth?

Social Studies
- Free Enterprise
- Trade

Unit 8

Rocky Tales

Science
- Rocks, Soil, Minerals
- Earth Systems

TO: Gary Soto

Subject: Itch

Dear Mr.

If the   me of the time
for m   ut it or
Late   tiful dre
Steph
that I w

This
wo

Online with Gary Soto

I got a bea...
it made ...
er fri...

Make a Graph

1. Show your favorite book. Name the author. Tell why you like the author.
2. Take turns with your classmates.
3. Then make a graph. Show the favorite authors in your class.

Favorite Authors

Tomie De Paola	The Popcorn Book by Tomie DePaola	Helga's Dowry by Tomie DePaola	Strega Nona by Tomie DePaola	Strega Nona by Tomie DePaola
Gail Gibbons	Sharks by Gail Gibbons	Whales by Gail Gibbons	Sharks by Gail Gibbons	
Gary Soto	Too Many Tamales by Gary Soto	Chato's Kitchen by Gary Soto	Too Many Tamales by Gary Soto	Too Many Tamales by Gary Soto / Chato's Kitchen by Gary Soto
E. B. White	Stuart Little by E. B. White	Charlotte's Web by E. B. White		

Communication Tools

letter

▲ Use the mail to send a package or a letter to someone.

Use a telephone to hear someone's voice. ▶

e-mail message

▲ Use e-mail to send a message on the computer.

▲ Use a cell phone to call from anywhere.

◀ Use a fax machine to send written messages quickly.

message

message

Use a pager to send or get a message from someone. ▶

The World Wide Web

The World Wide Web is part of the Internet, a large computer network. The Web is a huge collection of documents stored on computers all over the world.

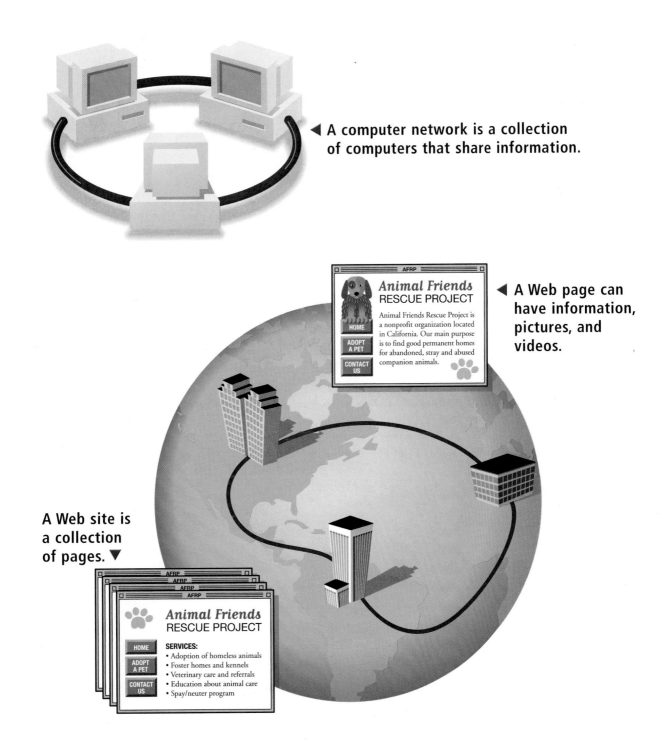

◀ A computer network is a collection of computers that share information.

◀ A Web page can have information, pictures, and videos.

A Web site is a collection of pages. ▼

BACK TO SCHOOL SALE!

9AM-9PM
Friday through Sunday

Have you **outgrown** your old clothes?

Are you tired of wearing your cousin's **hand-me-down** clothes?

Then come to Clothes Mart for **brand-new** clothes.

People will **notice** your great **style**!

Walk **proudly** when you go back to school.

We don't **mind** if you stay all day!

We **refuse** to let you leave without something you love!

CLOTHES MART

If the Shoe Fits

by Gary Soto

illustrated by Terry Widener

Read a Story

Genre

A **humorous fiction** story tells about funny events. In this story, a boy learns to care about more than what he looks like.

Characters

Rigo

Uncle Celso

Story Problem

Rigo is the youngest child in a large family. He always gets hand-me-downs from his brothers. Rigo wants brand new clothes instead.

▲ Rigo's family

Selection Reading

1

Rigo wants some new clothes. Find out if he gets them.

Rigo had three brothers and one sister, and when you counted his parents and Uncle Celso, who lived with them, his home was as crowded as a bus.

He didn't really **mind** the noisy house. What Rigo minded most were his **hand-me-down** clothes.

His oldest brother, Hector, **passed his shirts and pants down to Manuel**, who passed them to Carlos, who passed them to Rigo.

Rigo **passed** them into the garbage can.

---

passed his shirts and pants down to Manuel gave his clothes that were too small to the next younger brother, Manuel,

passed put

"Mom, I need some new clothes!" Rigo cried one day when he put on a jacket that Carlos had **outgrown**.

Two buttons were missing and the **fabric was faded**.

"*Mi'jo*, new clothes cost money," his mother said.

When Rigo started to **pout**, Uncle Celso brought out his old wallet and handed Rigo a five-dollar bill.

"Let me help you," Uncle said.

Rigo **refused** the money. He didn't want to tell his uncle that new clothes cost more than that.

---

fabric was faded color was not bright anymore

Mi'jo My son (in Spanish)

pout look sad and angry

But for Rigo's ninth birthday, his mom bought him a pair of **brand-new** shoes. They were called loafers. They were the **fanciest** shoes Rigo had ever owned. They didn't even have laces to drag in the dirt.

"Put a penny in them," Rigo's sister, Theresa, said. "That's the **style**."

But instead of **worthless** pennies, Rigo pushed in nickels.

---

fanciest best
worthless unimportant

"There," he said. He **slipped into** his new shoes
and **clicked** his heels together.

That day Rigo marched down the street,
grinning **proudly** at his shoes. He liked
how the nickels **glinted** in the sunlight.

---

slipped into put on
clicked made a sound by hitting
glinted shone, sparkled

Before You Move On

1. **Cause/Effect** Is Rigo proud
   of his new loafers? Why?

2. **Inference** Why doesn't Rigo
   want to tell his uncle how
   much new clothes cost?

Find out why Rigo won't wear his new shoes anymore.

At the corner playground some kids were throwing water balloons at each other. Rigo wanted to join them but was afraid he might **ruin his shoes**.

Suddenly, Angel sneaked up from behind and yelled, "Hey, **how come you got** nickels in your shoes? You **ain't** rich!"

"It's the style," Rigo answered.

"There **ain't no** style like that!" Angel growled. "Nobody wears those kind of stupid shoes!"

Then Angel demanded the nickels from Rigo's shoes.

---

ruin his shoes get his shoes all wet
how come you got why do you have
ain't aren't (slang)
ain't no isn't any (slang)

"**Nah**, Angel!" Rigo begged. "I don't want to **mess up my new loafers**. It was hard to put the nickels in."

"Forget your loafers!" Angel **snapped**. And he **ripped** the nickels from the slots.

Rigo went home and threw his shoes into the closet.

Nah No (slang)

mess up my new loafers make my new shoes look bad

snapped said in an angry way

ripped grabbed

But at the end of summer he changed his mind. He had received an invitation to a birthday party. It was from Kristie Hernandez. No girl had ever invited him to a birthday party before.

On the day of the party, Rigo brushed his teeth extra hard and combed his hair four different ways. He **settled on slicking his hair back**. He felt **suave**. Next he put on his newest-looking hand-me-downs, and finally he got his fancy loafers from the closet.

"Come on," he grunted, trying to **cram** his feet into the shoes.

---

settled on slicking his hair back decided to comb his wet hair straight back

suave very grown up and good-looking

cram push

When he stood up, he knew the shoes were too tight. Pain **stabbed** the top of his feet as he took a step. He took off the **torture shoes** and stretched them, yanking on the leather. He put on his thinnest socks, even though they had holes in the heels.

---

stabbed hurt
torture shoes shoes that hurt his feet

Rigo left the house walking **stiffly**. After three painful blocks, he wished he were crawling instead of walking. But lucky for him, he discovered that his feet didn't hurt so much if he walked backwards. He walked like that all the way to the party.

"Nice shoes," Kristie said, greeting him at the door.

"Thanks," said Rigo, trying to smile. He didn't want to tell her that they were **killing his feet**. He was sure that he had **blood blisters** and one of his little toes had fallen off. "But if you don't mind, I'm going to take them off."

"Why?" Kristie asked.

---

stiffly very slowly and carefully
killing his feet hurting his feet a lot
blood blisters small skin sores

29

Rigo's mind **whirled for** an answer.

He clicked his fingers and said, "To play soccer!"

When he scored two goals, his feet felt better.

---

whirled for quickly tried to find

Before You Move On

1. **Cause/Effect** Why does Rigo throw his shoes in the closet?

2. **Motive** Why does Rigo wear his shoes to the party?

31

Rigo gives a gift to Uncle Celso. Find out why.

Over dinner that night, Rigo told his family that Kristie's party was great. "Everyone was there! José-Luis, Julie, Debbie, Joey, Carolina, Lupe, Rachel, Sofia, Martin, Jaime, Lily, Maya, and Maya's little sister, I forgot her name, plus some little cousins of Kristie's who were still in their diapers . . ."

"*¡Híjole!* That's a lot of kids to feed!" Uncle Celso **remarked**.

"Yeah, but a party's more fun with lots of kids," Rigo said.

"Next year, *mi'jo*, we can have a party for you like that," his uncle said. "And you know why?"

Rigo shook his head.

"Because I have a new job as a waiter!" Uncle announced. "I'll make a lot of money—*¡mucho dinero!*"

¡Híjole! Wow! (in Spanish)
remarked said
¡mucho dinero! a lot of money! (in Spanish)

After dinner, Uncle Celso began to gather the dirty plates from the table. Rigo's father **protested**, "Leave them for the kids."

"No, *hombre*, I have to practice being a waiter," Uncle said.

"I'll help with the dishes," said Rigo. He liked to be with Uncle and listen to his stories about Mexico.

Rigo rolled up the sleeves of his sweatshirt.

As the two worked side by side, Rigo **noticed** that he was **slightly** taller than Uncle.

He noticed that Uncle's pants were too loose for him and that his shirt had **flecks** of paint on it. He looked at Uncle's shoes.

---

protested argued
hombre man (in Spanish)
slightly a little
flecks small pieces

The next morning Rigo brought his loafers to the couch, where Uncle slept.

"*¿Qué es esto?*" Uncle asked, opening one eye. "What's this?"

"A present for you. **Kind of used**, but try them on!"

Uncle sat up and took the shoes.

"These are the most beautiful shoes I've ever had," he said. He **patted** Rigo's cheek.

"You don't mind if they're hand-me-downs?" Rigo asked.

¿Qué es esto? What is this? (in Spanish)
Kind of used I have used them a few times
patted softly touched

"**Hand-me-downs, nothing**!" Uncle said. "These are brand-new! I can go to work in style!" He tapped on the soles and then put them on. He **squinted an eye** at his nephew. "Are you sure you want to give them to me?"

"Yeah, I'm sure," Rigo said. "To tell you the truth, Uncle, I like them, but they hurt my feet. I grew a little."

Hand-me-downs, nothing! Of course I don't mind!

squinted an eye closed one eye halfway and looked

Uncle reached for his front pocket.

"These coins are older than I am," Uncle said. He held up two *centavos*, brown as his own skin, and smiled. "They're kind of like hand-me-downs, too."

When Rigo took the old Mexican coins, he knew what to do with them—fit them into the slots of his new loafers, if he ever got any. Next time around he would wear them no matter what people like Angel said.

---

centavos Mexican pennies (in Spanish)

Before You Move On

1. **Cause/Effect** Why does Rigo decide to give the loafers to Uncle Celso?

2. **Character** How does Rigo feel about used clothes now? Why?

Meet the Illustrator

Terry Widener

AWARD WINNER

Terry Windener always dreamed of illustrating children's books, but he started work as a graphic designer. Fourteen years later he got to illustrate his first picture book.

"I've got three kids, so I know all about hand-me-downs," Mr. Widener says. "My wife comes from a large family, too." Mr. Widener used his experiences to create the crowded feeling of Rigo's house. Most readers agree that Mr. Widener's art helps make *If the Shoe Fits* so much fun to read.

Think and Respond

Strategy: Analyze Character

A character's feelings affect what the character does. To understand a character, look for:

- ✔ what happens to the character
- ✔ how the character feels about what happens
- ✔ what the character does as a result.

Make a character chart for Rigo.

If the Shoe Fits

Events →	Rigo's Feelings →	Rigo's Actions
Rigo gets new shoes for his birthday.	Rigo feels happy and proud.	Rigo puts nickels in his shoes and wears them proudly.
Angel tells Rigo that his shoes are stupid.		
Rigo gets an invitation to a party.		
Rigo sees that his uncle's clothes are old.		

Retell the Story

Use your chart to retell the story to a partner. How do Rigo's feelings change? Does your partner agree?

Talk It Over

 1 Personal Response Do you think this story is funny? Why or why not?

 2 Conclusion What did Rigo learn from his uncle? Tell how you know.

3 Comparison Compare Rigo and Uncle Celso. How are they alike? How are they different?

4 Personal Experience Tell about a time you got something you really wanted. Did it make you happy? Why or why not?

Compare Characters

Compare Rigo with a character in another story. How do their feelings affect their actions?

Content Connections

Make a Celebration Scrapbook

large group

Make a page for a class scrapbook. Show how your family celebrates a special event. Tell who comes to the event, where it happens, and when. Share your celebration and learn about others.

Family Fiesta

When: Grandparents' Day in September

Where: in our back yard

Who: my parents, cousins, aunts, and uncles

How: We have a fiesta. We barbecue and bring presents.

Create a Shopping List

Internet

partners

Pretend Rigo gets $100 for his next birthday. Find prices of things he might buy. Write the cost of each item. Add 5% sales tax. What can Rigo buy for $100?

Rigo's Shopping List

Item	Cost
	$20
	$25

Role-Play a Conversation

partners

List people Rigo could talk to about Angel, the bully. Role-play a conversation between Rigo and another person. Rigo explains the problem. The other person tells Rigo what to do.

Mr. Lee, could you help me, please?

Write to Entertain

on your own

What clothes do you like to wear most? Write something to tell why. Choose the best form to entertain:

- a story
- a limerick
- a song

Be sure to use colorful words in your writing.

I once had a bright purple shirt.
It went with my pink flowered skirt.
I wore them to play on one rainy day,
and now they're all covered with dirt!

Use Context Clues

Context clues can help you figure out the meaning of a word you don't know. Context clues are the other words and sentences in the story or article.

To **use context clues** :

✔ Read the sentence again.
✔ Look for clues, or hints, about the word's meaning.
✔ Read the sentences that come before and after to find more clues.
✔ Use the clues to guess a meaning for the word.
✔ Try that meaning in the sentence.

Try the strategy.

from

But for Rigo's ninth birthday, his mom bought him a pair of brand-new shoes. They were called loafers. They were the fanciest shoes Rigo had ever owned. They didn't even have laces to drag in the dirt.

When I read the sentences before and after the word loafers, I can figure out that loafers are fancy shoes.

Practice

Take this test and **use context clues** to understand words in "If The Shoe Fits."

Read each item. Choose the best answer.

1 **Read the passage.**

> Pain stabbed the top of his feet as he took a step. He took off the torture shoes and stretched them, <u>yanking</u> on the leather. He put on his thinnest socks, even though they had holes in the heels.

What does the word <u>yanking</u> mean?

A   pulling

B   hurting

C   stepping

D   standing up

2 **Read the passage.**

> Suddenly, Angel <u>sneaked up</u> from behind and yelled, "How come you got nickels in your shoes?"

Which word helps you know what sneaked up means?

A   suddenly

B   yelled

C   nickels

D   shoes

> ✔ **Test Strategy**
>
> Try to answer the question without reading the answer choices. Then compare your answer to the choices.

Vocabulary

I Reply

I want to write a book,
And if you ask me why,
"To **publish** my **experience** ."
That's how I **reply** .

I want to write a book
That will **communicate**
My **imagination** through
The stories I create.

I want to write a book
And include the things we do,
To **remind** me of the happy times
That I have spent with you!

—S. A. Costigan

Tune: "The Farmer in the Dell"

46

Key Words

publish

experience

reply

communicate

imagination

remind

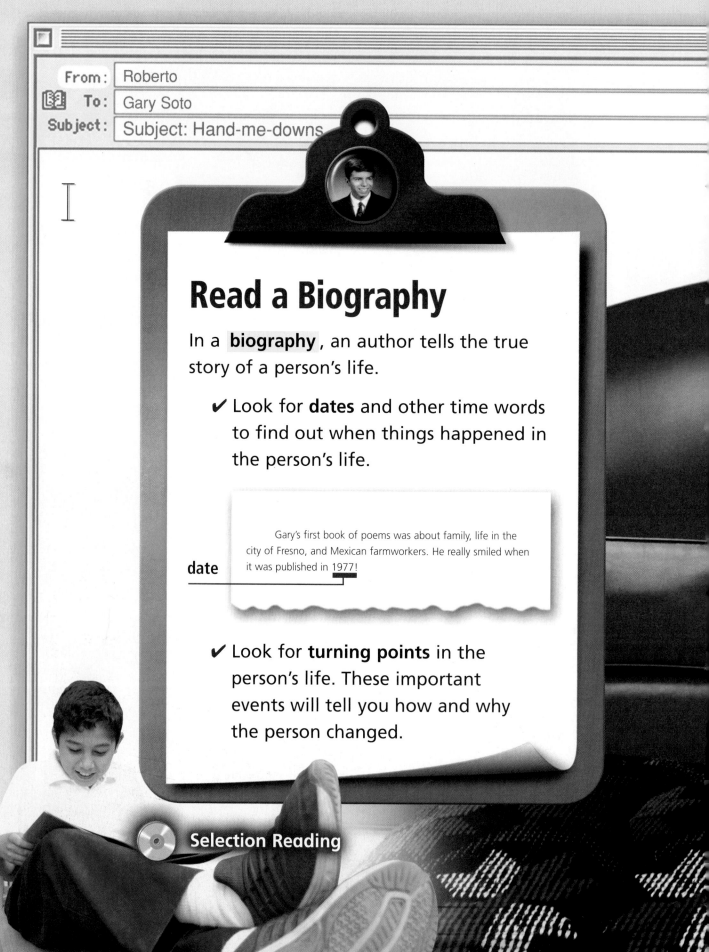

From: Roberto
To: Gary Soto
Subject: Subject: Hand-me-downs

Read a Biography

In a **biography**, an author tells the true story of a person's life.

✔ Look for **dates** and other time words to find out when things happened in the person's life.

> Gary's first book of poems was about family, life in the city of Fresno, and Mexican farmworkers. He really smiled when it was published in 1977!

date

✔ Look for **turning points** in the person's life. These important events will tell you how and why the person changed.

Selection Reading

In Gary Soto's Shoes

by Shirleyann Costigan

Something to Smile About

Gary Soto has changed a lot since he was a kid, but one thing about him hasn't changed a bit. He still has his great smile. When he was young, though, Gary didn't have much to smile about. He lived in a poor neighborhood in Fresno, California. His father was killed in an accident in 1957 when Gary was five years old. His mother had to work at two jobs while his big brother, Rick, **looked after** Gary and his little sister.

Yet, when he thinks about his childhood, he remembers happy times. He remembers playing baseball with Rick. He remembers looking for gardening jobs in the neighborhood so he could buy **crisp**, new shirts. These things made him smile.

Gary in kindergarten ▶

---

looked after took care of
crisp fresh

When he was a kid, no one **expected much from Gary Soto**, not even Gary. He had no plans for his future. He quit high school in 1969, a year before graduation. Then he ran away to Glendale, near Los Angeles, California.

---

expected much from Gary Soto thought Gary Soto would do anything important

▲ Rick, Gary, and Debrah Soto in 1956

◀ Mr. Soto as an adult

Before You Move On

1. **Plot** Tell about the important events in Mr. Soto's childhood.

2. **Inference** How does Mr. Soto feel about his childhood?

In Glendale, Gary got a job at a tire factory. The job was awful. Black dust covered his skin. **Toxic fumes** from the hot rubber filled his lungs. He returned home without a plan. He knew that he wanted a better job, but what could he do?

The first thing he did was finish high school. After that, he went to college to study geography. Then one day in the library he **found his future**.

Toxic fumes Dangerous air

found his future discovered what he wanted to do

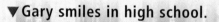

▼**Gary smiles in high school.**

52

What Gary really found was a book of **modern poems**. The poems were about the kinds of feelings Gary had. They seemed to **communicate** his sadness and fears. These writers felt like he did, and they wrote about it! "Wow!" he thought. "I want to do this, too!" So, Gary began to write poetry and study **literature**.

▲ Many of Gary Soto's books for children and adults have won awards.

Gary's first book of poems was about family, life in the city of Fresno, and Mexican farmworkers. He really smiled when it was **published** in 1977!

Mr. Soto still has a lot to smile about today. Through his books, he communicates the feelings that all people can have. Read them and say, "Wow!"

---

modern poems poems written not long ago
literature stories and poems

Before You Move On
1. **Motive** Why does Mr. Soto decide to finish high school?
2. **Inference** What topics does Mr. Soto write about? Why?

E-mails to El Paso

Gary Soto loves communicating with kids through his books. Sometimes he communicates in other ways, too. Here are some e-mails he has received from third- and fourth-grade students in El Paso, Texas.

FROM: Roberto
TO: Gary Soto

SUBJECT: Hand-Me-Downs and Bullies

Dear Mr. Soto,

Your story, *If the Shoe Fits*, is **incredible!** My family and I liked the part when the brothers passed the clothes to each other, then to Rigo, and he had to throw them in the garbage can. We laughed because I am the oldest brother, and I have to pass my clothes on to my little brother. **:-)**

I did not like the part where Angel took the nickels away from Rigo. I can only **imagine** how Rigo must have felt when that happened. Was this something that happened to you?

Sincerely,

Roberto

---

incredible great
:-) computer symbol for "I'm smiling."
imagine guess

54

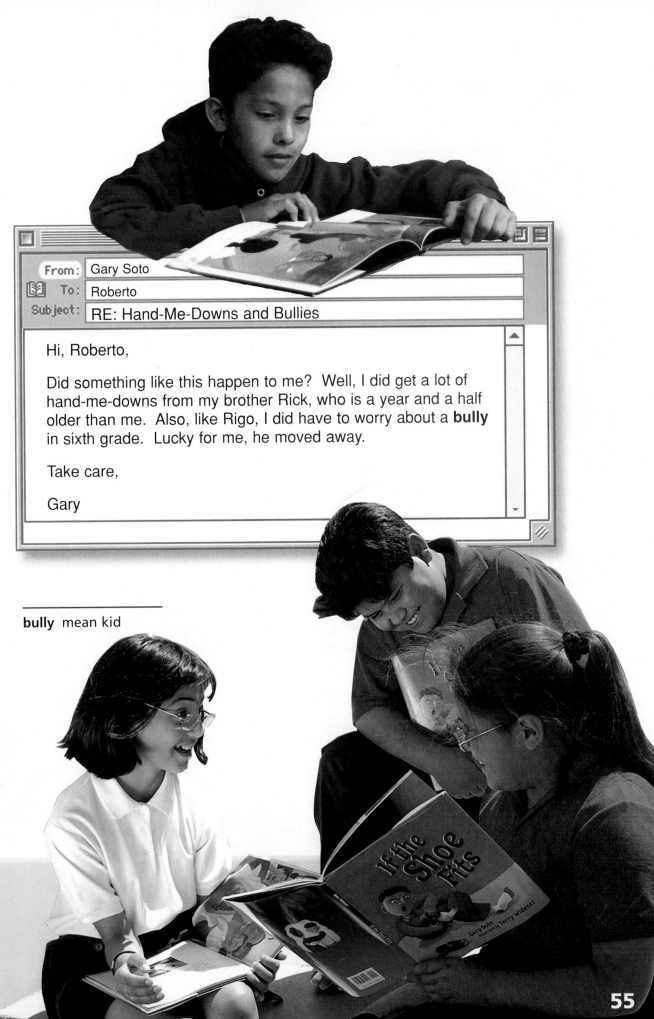

From: Gary Soto
To: Roberto
Subject: RE: Hand-Me-Downs and Bullies

Hi, Roberto,

Did something like this happen to me? Well, I did get a lot of hand-me-downs from my brother Rick, who is a year and a half older than me. Also, like Rigo, I did have to worry about a **bully** in sixth grade. Lucky for me, he moved away.

Take care,

Gary

---

bully mean kid

FROM: Adriana
TO: Gary Soto

BJECT: Itchy Dress

Dear Mr. Soto,

If the Shoe Fits **reminds** me of the time I got a beautiful dress for my birthday, but every time I put it on, it made my back itch. Later, my mother gave my beautiful dress to her friend's daughter Stephanie. Stephanie **was embarrassed**. I guess she thought that I was going to laugh at her.

This story also reminds me of my pretty sandals that I always wore, except with my pants. One day, my sister Lucy was cleaning the closet, and she threw my pretty sandals away.

Sincerely,

Adriana

From: Gary Soto
To: Adriana
Subject: RE: Itchy Dress

Dear Adriana,

An itchy dress? Pretty sandals? You lost them both. How sad **:-(**, but I'm glad to know that you didn't laugh at Stephanie. It shows **your maturity** and care for others. César Chávez, the great labor leader, was always poor, but who would dare to laugh at him? Nobody. There is more to a person than his or her clothes.

You take care. I hope to meet you sometime in El Paso.

Gary

---

was embarrassed felt like people were laughing at her

:-(computer symbol for "I'm sad."

your maturity that you can act grown-up

FROM: Lilia
TO: Gary Soto

SUBJECT: What Happened to the Shoes?

Dear Mr. Soto,

I want to ask you something about your book, *If the Shoe Fits.* I want to know what the uncle did after the shoes Rigo gave him didn't fit him anymore. I hope you can **reply**. I'm always going to wonder whatever happened to those shoes.

Your friend,

Lilia

From: Gary Soto
To: Lilia
Subject: RE: What Happened to the Shoes?

Hello, Lilia,

I can reply because *If the Shoe Fits* is a story from my **imagination**. The uncle took the shoes and wore them out. Then the shoes went in the trash, I guess.

Keep asking questions,

Gary

SUBJECT: Being the Only Boy

Dear Mr. Soto,

Your book, *If the Shoe Fits*, reminds me of when my sister Claudia passes her clothes to me. Last time, she passed me three dresses and some shorts and skirts. I still have them, and I don't mind if they **are faded or torn.** Well, there is this sweater I don't like. It's old, super old, and rough. Every time I wear it, I say "EEEEWWWW!"

This book also reminds me of my friend Alex who is the only boy in his family. He has four sisters, just like the boy in your book. I wonder what it feels like to be the only boy or girl in the family.

Sincerely,

Areli

From: Gary Soto
To: Areli
Subject: RE: Being the Only Boy

Dear Areli,

Yes, I would like to know how it feels to be the only boy in a family, too. I have one daughter. She is 23 years old now. She got a lot of attention when she was little because she was an only child.

Thank you for writing,

Gary

_____
are faded or torn have lost some of their color or have holes in them

FROM: David
TO: Gary Soto

SUBJECT: Spanish

Dear Mr. Soto,

My favorite part in your book is when you wrote words in Spanish because it sounded funny. **<LOL>**

Sincerely,

David

From: Gary Soto
To: David
Subject: RE: Spanish

¡Hola! David,

You like the Spanish words? Good. I like to read and write in Spanish. My favorite poet is Pablo Neruda, a great poet from Chile who writes in Spanish and won the Nobel Prize in 1971. Ask your teacher what the Nobel Prize is.

Take care,

Gary

<LOL> computer symbol for "I'm laughing out loud."

¡Hola! Hello! (in Spanish)

FROM: Laura
TO: Gary Soto

SUBJECT: Shoe Art

Dear Mr. Soto,

Your story reminds me of when **my little niece**, Sandra, got a brand-new pair of shoes as white as milk. As soon as she got home, she got a bright idea and **wrote a huge scribble** on her shoes. I guess she thought they would look nicer.

Sincerely,

Laura

From: Gary Soto
To: Laura
Subject: RE: Shoe Art

Hi, Laura!

Sometimes I wonder what gets into our heads when we do silly things like what your little niece did. These are events that can turn into great stories!

Thanks for writing,

Gary

---

my little niece the young daughter of my sister or brother

wrote a huge scribble made a big mark with a pen or marker

FROM: Nicole
TO: Gary Soto

SUBJECT: What About Rigo's Sister?

Dear Mr. Soto,

I really liked your book. It reminds me of when my brother gets new shoes and says, "I'm running so fast I could win the Olympics!" I answer him, "Sure you can, Angel." My brother seems to think that shoes make him run faster.

I think hand-me-downs are wonderful. My brother Angel gives them to my cousin and they fit. My aunt, who is in high school, gives me her clothes. I love them. **<gg>**

BTW, I'm wondering why Rigo's sister did not have an exciting part in the story.

Nicole

From: Gary Soto
To: Nicole
Subject: RE: What About Rigo's Sister?

Hi, Nicole,

You know, I had the opposite **experience**. When I was a boy, I used to think that if I wore old shoes, I could run faster. Then again, I felt that if I ran barefoot, I would run even faster.

As far as Rigo's sister goes, maybe she deserves her own book. So, why don't you write a story about her?

Take care,

Gary

<gg> computer symbol for "I'm grinning or smiling."
BTW By the way
As far as Rigo's sister goes To answer your question about Rigo's sister

Before You Move On

1. **Details** What are most of the e-mails to Mr. Soto about?

2. **Conclusion** Describe two ways Mr. Soto gets ideas for his stories.

Think and Respond

Strategy: Analyze Information

Some stories tell about important events that change a character or person. These are called turning points. Make a turning point map of Gary Soto's life. Show what happened before and after each turning point.

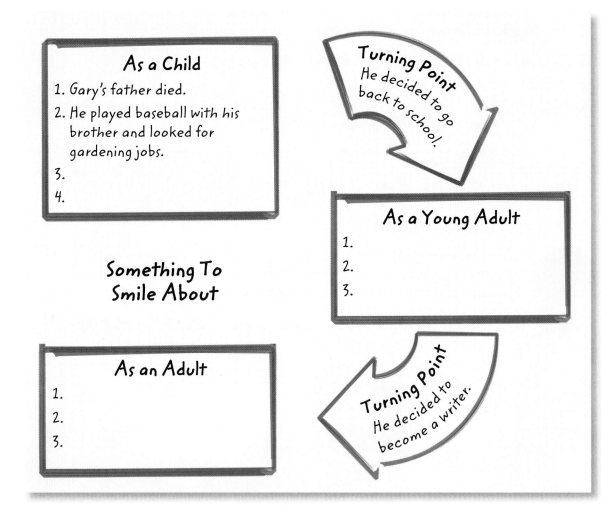

As a Child
1. Gary's father died.
2. He played baseball with his brother and looked for gardening jobs.
3.
4.

Turning Point
He decided to go back to school.

As a Young Adult
1.
2.
3.

Something To Smile About

As an Adult
1.
2.
3.

Turning Point
He decided to become a writer.

Express Opinions

Would you like to meet Mr. Soto? Why or why not? Talk about it with a partner.

Talk It Over

 Personal Response Which e-mail do you think is the most interesting? Why?

2 **Inference** Why do you think no one expected very much from Mr. Soto when he was young?

3 **Generalization** What is one lesson you learned from Mr. Soto's life?

4 **Opinion** Do you think the job of an author is important? Why or why not?

Compare Genres

The biography and the e-mails give you two views of Mr. Soto. Compare what you learned from each one.

> The biography gave facts about Mr. Soto. The e-mails showed me how funny he can be.

Content Connections

large group

Ask the Author

Invite an author to talk to your class.

1. Write questions you want to ask.

2. Ask the author your questions.

3. Listen to the answers. Take notes.

After the author's visit, talk about the most interesting thing you learned.

> Do you always write about your own life?

ART

Design a Book Cover

partners

Look at the covers of Gary Soto's books on page 53. Which cover makes you want to read the book? Tell your partner why. Then choose a book you know. Design a new cover for it. Does your partner want to read it?

Too Many Tamales
Gary Soto

Give a Demonstration

Internet

People use many different tools to communicate. Find out about the right way to communicate with one tool. Show your group how to use it.

How to Use Symbols Online

:)   1. Shows you are happy.
     2. Means you hope the other person likes something you said.

:(1. Shows you are sad.
     2. Means you don't like something.

Write a Biography

partners

Interview a partner. Ask questions about his or her life. What important events were turning points? Make a time line. Then write a biography of your partner's life.

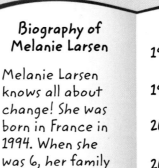

Biography of Melanie Larsen

Melanie Larsen knows all about change! She was born in France in 1994. When she was 6, her family moved to Georgia.

1994 —— born in France

1995 ——

2000 —— moved to Georgia

2003 ——

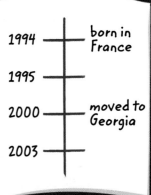

Sentences

Listen and chant.

Chant

EVERY AUTHOR

Every author has a story.
Kids like you have stories, too.
Not all stories are the same.
Some are fiction. Some are true.

What is the story in your mind?
Is it fiction? Is it true?
Write or tell someone your story.
You will be an author, too!

—Jane Zion Brauer

How Language Works

There are different kinds of sentences.
Use the kind that fits your purpose.

Statements	Questions

■ Use a statement to give information. In a statement, the <u>subject</u> often comes before the **verb**.
 	
Examples:
   <u>**Alex writes**</u> a story.
   <u>**He tells**</u> about his family.
	■ Use a question to ask for information. In a question, the **verb** usually comes before the <u>subject</u>.
	
	Examples:
	   Is <u>**his story**</u> good?
	   Are <u>**the pictures**</u> nice?

Practice with a Partner

Copy the words onto cards. Put them in the correct order.
Then read the sentence.

1.	big?	Is	family	your	
2.	two	I	brothers.	have	
3.	your	is	house?	Where	
4.	live	by	school.	the	We
5.	with	us.	uncle	lives	My

Put It in Writing

Write about your family. Use statements and questions. Put the words in the right order.

Five people are in my family.
We have a cat, too.
What is your family like?

Show What You Know

Talk About the Author

In this unit, you read a story by Gary Soto, a biography about him, and e-mails he wrote to some readers. Look back at this unit. Choose one idea about communication. Write the idea on an index card. Trade cards with a partner. Talk about the ideas.

Make a Mind Map

Talk with a partner about why Gary Soto writes. Make a mind map to show what you learned.

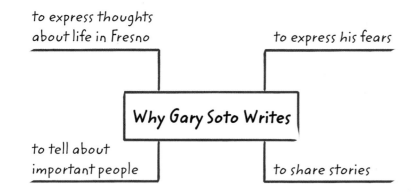

to express thoughts about life in Fresno

to express his fears

Why Gary Soto Writes

to tell about important people

to share stories

Think and Write

Why is it important for people to communicate with each other? Write a paragraph. Add this writing to your portfolio. Include other work from this unit that shows what you learned about communication.

Read and Learn More

Leveled Books

Good News
by Suzy Blackaby

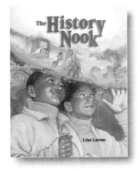

The History Nook
by Lisa Lerner

Theme Library

**The Old Man
and His Door**
by Gary Soto

**Snapshots from
the Wedding**
by Gary Soto

Internet
Go to: www.hbavenues.com
Meet the Authors
Young Writers
E-mail Language for Kids

Native Land

Design a Home

1. With your group, gather materials all around you.
2. Use what you find to build a home.
3. Talk about your home with other groups.

Native Life in North America Long Ago

Fishing

▲ Fishing was and is an important source of food to people in the Northwest Coast.

Shelter

▲ People in California often lived in homes made of grass and leaves.

Crafts

▲ Intermountain people made and still make baskets and blankets.

Agriculture

▲ People in the Southwest were among the first to grow corn.

Native American Regions Long Ago

Chinook
Willamette
Yakima
Nez
Perce
Klamath
Tahoe
Mojave
Cheyenne
Omaha
Pueblo
Yuma
Navaho
Comanche
Delaware
Cherokee
Seminole

Key
- Northwest Coast
- California
- Intermountain
- Southwest
- Plains
- Eastern Woodlands

Hunting

▲ People of the Plains hunted buffalo for food, shelter, and clothing.

Gathering

▲ In the Eastern Woodlands, people gathered berries.

Vocabulary

Chant

LISTEN NOW!

Listen now.
The **Chief** calls to his people,
"Prepare the **village** for a feast!"

Listen now.
The drums send out the **signal**,
"Come to the village for a feast!"

Listen now.
The **tribe** retells a story,
Their arms **push up** the sky.

Listen now.
The crow calls to the people.
Hear his noisy cry.

"Are we **agreed**, my brothers?
This feast is my idea!"

pole

Key Words

chief

village

signal

tribe

push up

agreed

pole

75

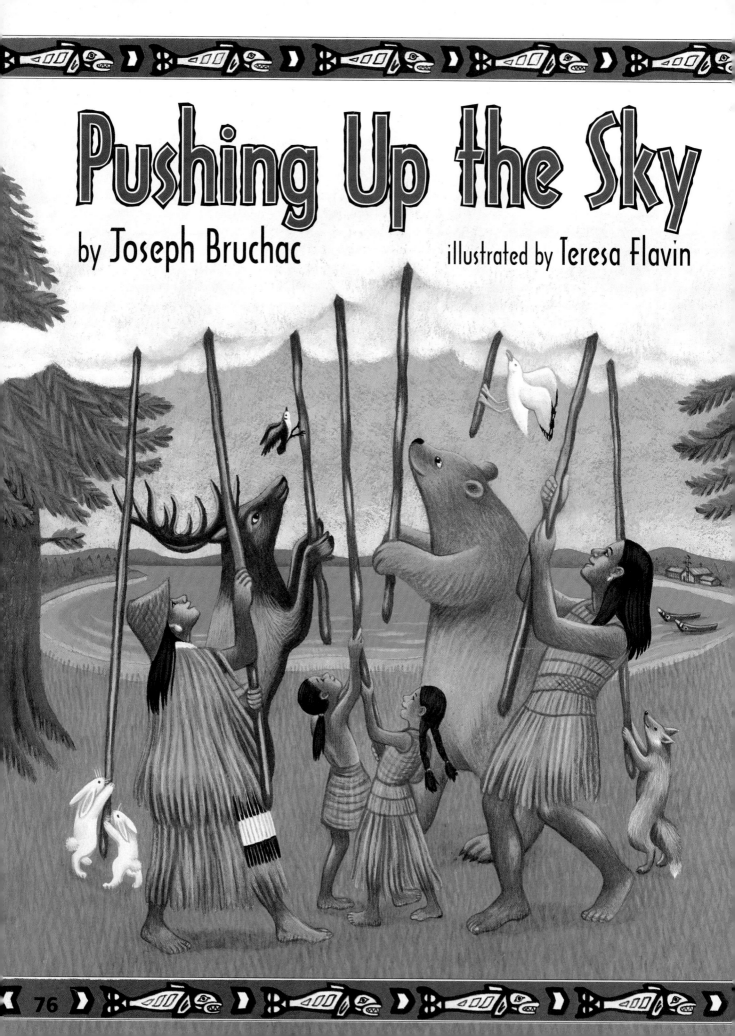

Pushing Up the Sky

by Joseph Bruchac

illustrated by Teresa Flavin

Read a Play

Genre

A **play** is a story that is acted out. A **script** is the written form of a play. This play tells a story about why people see stars in the sky.

Characters

The People

Chiefs

Birds and Animals

Setting

The story takes place long ago in a forest in the Pacific Northwest.

▲ **Pacific Northwest**

Selection Reading

The Snohomish people live in the area of the Pacific Northwest that is now known as the state of Washington, not far from Puget Sound. They fished in the ocean and gathered food from the shore. Their homes and many of the things they used every day, such as bowls and canoe paddles, were carved from trees. Like many of the other peoples of the area, they also carved totem poles, which recorded the history and stories of their nation.

▼ Snohomish Chief William Shelton carves a story pole.

This story is one that was carved into a story pole by Chief William Shelton.

▼ Chief Shelton's pole now stands in Olympia, the capital of Washington.

Olympia, Washington

The sky is too close to Earth. Find out why this is a problem.

Scene I: A Village Among Many Tall Trees

Tall Man, Girl, Mother, Boy stand onstage.

Narrator: Long ago the sky was very close to the earth. The sky was so close that some people could jump right into it. Those people who were not good jumpers could climb up the tall fir trees and step into the sky. But people were not happy that the sky was so close to the earth. Tall people kept bumping their heads on the sky. And there were other problems.

Tall Man: Oh, that hurt! I just hit my head on the sky again.

Girl: I just threw my ball and it landed in the sky, and I can't get it back.

Mother: Where is my son? Has he climbed a tree and gone up into the sky again?

Boy: Every time I shoot my bow, my arrows get stuck in the sky!

All: THE SKY IS TOO CLOSE!

Before You Move On

1. **Genre** Name the characters that speak in Scene I.

2. **Problem** Why do the People think the sky is too close? Give three reasons.

What do you think the People will do about the sky?

Scene II: The Same Village

The seven **chiefs** *stand together onstage.*

Narrator: So people decided something had to be done. A great meeting was held for all the different **tribes**. The seven **wisest** chiefs got together to talk about the problem.

First Chief: My people all think the sky is too close.

Second Chief: The Creator did a very good job of making the world.

---

wisest smartest

Third Chief: That is true, but the Creator should have put the sky up higher. My tall son keeps hitting his head on the sky.

Fourth Chief: My daughter keeps losing her ball in the sky.

Fifth Chief: People keep going up into the sky when they should be staying on the earth to help each other.

Sixth Chief: When mothers look for their children, they cannot find them because they are up playing in the sky.

Seventh Chief: We are **agreed** , then. The sky is too close.

All: WE ARE AGREED.

Second Chief: What can we do?

Seventh Chief: I have an idea. Let's **push up** the sky.

Third Chief: The sky is heavy.

Seventh Chief: If we all push together, we can do it.

Sixth Chief: We will ask the birds and animals to help. They also do not like it that the sky is so close.

Second Chief: The elk are always getting their **antlers** caught in the sky.

Fourth Chief: The birds are always hitting their wings on it.

First Chief: We will cut tall trees to make **poles**. We can use those poles to push up the sky.

Fifth Chief: That is a good idea. Are we all agreed?

All: WE ARE ALL AGREED.

---

antlers large horns

Before You Move On

1. **Inference** Why do the chiefs make the decision about what to do?

2. **Cause/Effect** Why do the chiefs think the birds and animals will help?

The People and Animals try to push up the sky. Can they do it?

Scene III: The Same Village

*All the People, except Seventh Chief, are gathered together. They hold long poles. The Birds and Animals are with them. They all begin **pushing randomly, jabbing their poles into** the air. (The sky can be imagined as just above them.)*

Girl: It isn't working!

Boy: The sky is still too close.

Fifth Chief: Where is Seventh Chief? This was his idea!

Seventh Chief *(entering)***:** Here I am. I had to find this long pole.

First Chief: Your plan is not good! See, we are pushing and the sky is not moving.

Seventh Chief: Ah, but I said we must push together.

Fifth Chief: We need a **signal** so that all can push together. Our people speak different languages.

---

pushing randomly, jabbing their poles into
pushing and poking the poles at different times and in different places

Seventh Chief: Let us use YAH-HOO as the signal. Ready?

All: YES!

Seventh Chief: YAH-HOO.

At the signal, everyone pushes together.

All: YAH-HOO!

Seventh Chief: YAH-HOO.

Again everyone pushes together.

All: YAH-HOO!

Tall Man: We are doing it!

Mother: Now my son won't be able to hide in the sky!

Seventh Chief: YAH-HOO!

Again everyone pushes together.

All: YAH-HOO!

Boy: It will be too high for my arrows to stick into it.

Seventh Chief: YAH-HOO.

Again everyone pushes together.

All: YAH-HOOOO!

First Chief: We have done it!

Narrator: So the sky was pushed up. It was done by everyone working together. That night, though, when everyone looked **overhead**, they saw many stars in the sky. The stars were shining through the holes poked into the sky by the poles of everyone who pushed it up higher.

No one ever bumped his head on the sky again. And those stars are there to this day.

overhead up

Before You Move On

1. **Solution** Do the People solve the problem? How?

2. **Cause/Effect** Why can the People see the stars at the end of the story?

Meet the Playwright

Joseph Bruchac

AWARD WINNER

Joseph Bruchac loves stories. He travels all over the world to hear the stories of others and to share his own. His writing ideas often come from the stories told by his Native American ancestors, the Abenaki tribe.

In Native American cultures, stories always have lessons. Mr. Bruchac says his stories have simple messages. "We have to listen to each other and to the Earth. We have to respect each other and the Earth." In "Pushing Up the Sky," the people need to respect each other and work together to solve their problem.

Think and Respond

Strategy: Problem and Solution

Some stories, like "Pushing Up the Sky," tell how characters solve a problem. In these stories, look for:

✔ the problem
✔ the events
✔ the solution.

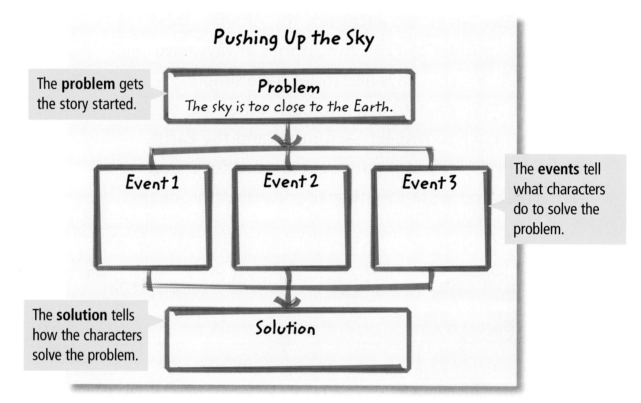

Pushing Up the Sky

The **problem** gets the story started.

Problem
The sky is too close to the Earth.

Event 1

Event 2

Event 3

The **events** tell what characters do to solve the problem.

The **solution** tells how the characters solve the problem.

Solution

Make a problem-and-solution chart for "Pushing Up the Sky."

Interview a Character

Pretend you are a character from the play. Have your partner ask you questions such as, "What was the problem in your village? How did the chiefs solve the problem?" Then switch roles.

Talk It Over

 Personal Response What do you like best about the play? Why?

 Judgment Is the Seventh Chief a good leader? Why or why not?

 Prediction What do the People learn? How do you think they will solve problems in the future?

4 **Mood** Is this story funny or serious? Explain your answer.

Compare Themes

Rigo learned a lesson in "If the Shoe Fits." What did the People learn in "Pushing Up the Sky"? Are the lessons alike? How?

Content Connections

Listen to a Story

large group

Listen to a story from Sri Lanka. Talk about how it is like or unlike "Pushing Up the Sky." How was the sky a problem in each story? Who solved each problem?

In both stories, people had problems with the sky.

Research Star Patterns
Internet

partners

Patterns in the stars are called constellations.

1. Use the Internet or science books to find a constellation.

2. Draw it on black paper.

3. Make a hole for each star.

4. Shine a light through the paper.

5. Tell about the constellation.

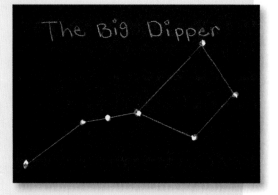

The Big Dipper

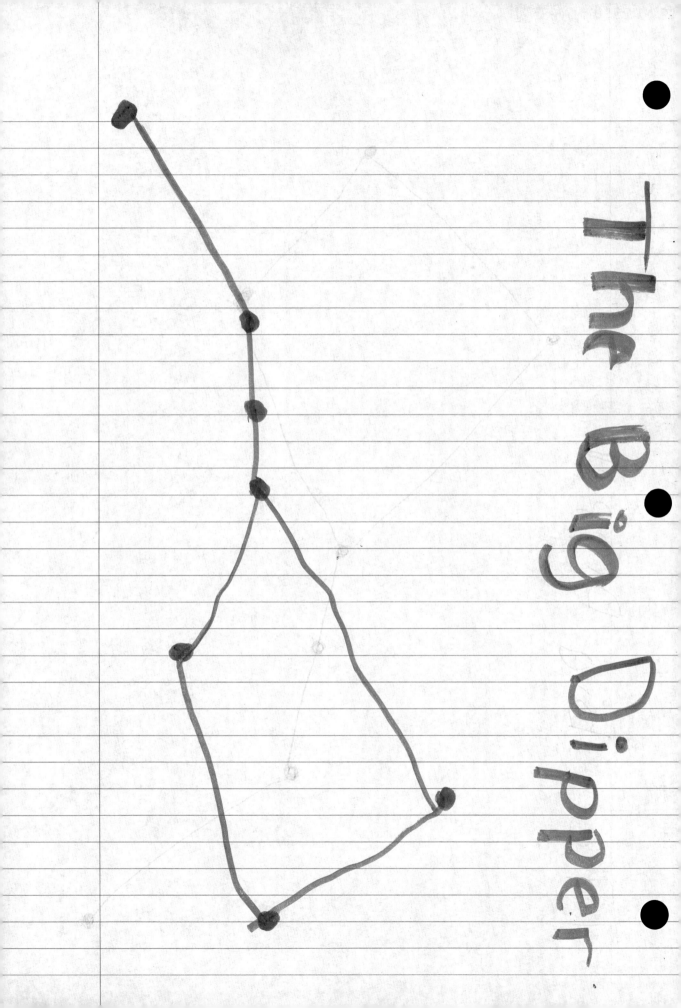

The Big Dipper

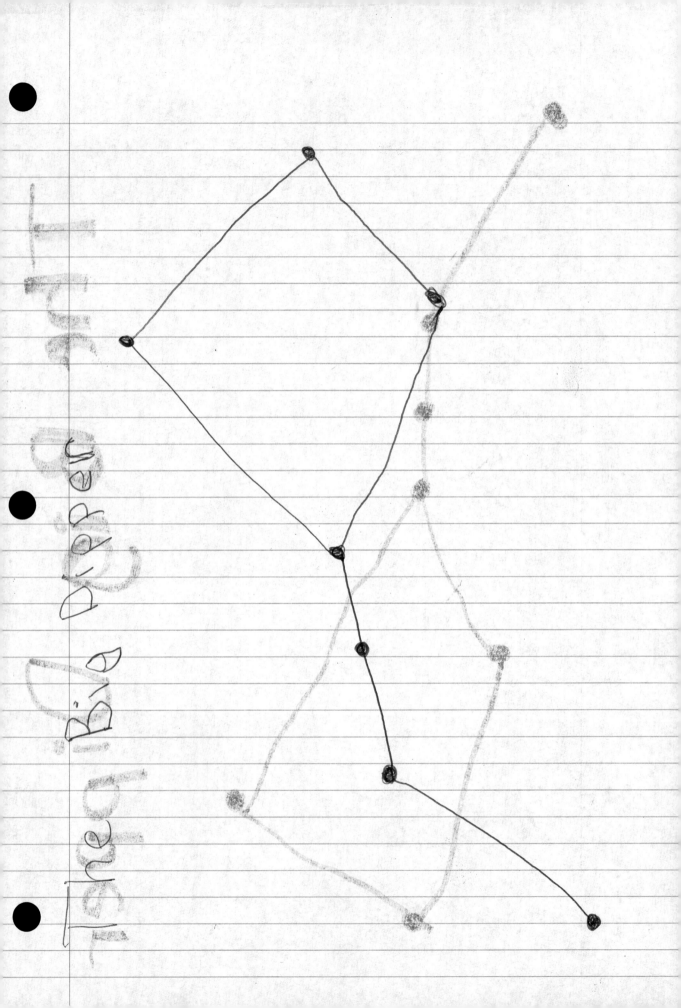

The Big Dipper

Make a Totem Pole

on your own

Native peoples make totem poles to tell their family's history and stories. Make a totem pole about your family's history or stories. Tell the class about your totem pole. Why did you choose each event? Why is each important to you?

Write New Dialogue

small group

Create two new characters for the play. What problems would they have with the sky? Write dialogue for the new characters, and read it to your group. Compare the new characters with the ones in "Pushing Up the Sky."

Flying Duck: I need to land, but I can't see the lake through the clouds.

Dancing Girl: I can't kick high because clouds get in my way.

Identify Main Idea and Details

The **main idea** is the most important idea of a story or article. **Supporting details** give more information about the main idea. To identify the main idea and supporting details:

✔ Read carefully.
✔ Think about the most important idea.
✔ Look for details that tell more about the main idea.

Try the strategy.

Many Uses for Trees

The Native peoples of the Pacific Northwest found many ways to use cedar trees from the forests. They made canoes from huge cedar logs. First they burned the inside of the log, and then they carved out the burned wood. They also made homes from cedar planks. The roof, floors, and walls were all made from cedar. They even used trees for crafts.

The main idea is the Native peoples of the Pacific Northwest used cedar trees for many things. One supporting detail is that they used cedar logs to make canoes.

Practice

Take this test and **identify the main idea and supporting details**.

Read the article. Then read each item. Choose the best answer.

The ocean is important to many Native peoples of the Pacific Northwest. Many live near the ocean. They go to sea to catch much of their food: seals, sea lions, salmon, and cod. In the past, they also traveled by sea because it was easier than traveling on land over the tall mountains. Native peoples once traveled along the coast to trade crafts, such as woodcarvings and blankets.

1　**The main idea is —**

   A   The ocean has seals, sea lions, salmon, and cod.

   B   It was easier to travel by sea than on land.

   C   Native peoples once traveled along the coast to trade crafts.

   D   The ocean is important to many Native peoples of the Pacific Northwest.

2　**Which detail does *not* support the main idea?**

   A   They traveled by sea.

   B   They lived by the ocean.

   C   They traded wood carvings and blankets.

   D   They ate seals, sea lions, salmon, and cod.

✔ **Test Strategy**

Look for words like *best* and *not*. They will help you find the correct answer choice.

HOUSE TALK

▲ A stone house in Peru

▲ People build the **frame** of a wood house in Kenya.

People often make homes from **material** that is easy to find. In a **region** with many rocks, people build stone houses. In a place with many trees, people build homes with wood.

▲ Houseboats in India

Houseboats are **temporary**. They can stay in one place for a short time. Mud houses are **permanent**. They last for a long time.

Key Words

material

region

frame

temporary

permanent

Native peoples

nation

traditional

Many **Native peoples** build homes the way the people of their **nation** have for thousands of years.

▲ A **traditional** mud house in the U.S.

Read Social Studies

A **social studies article** is nonfiction. It gives facts. Many social studies articles tell about how and where people live.

✔ Look for **section headings**. They tell what each section is mostly about.

section heading

Homes in North America

Thousands of years before the United States or Canada were countries, hundreds of groups of people lived throughout North America. These were North America's first peoples. They are known as Native peoples or Native Americans.

✔ Read the **captions, labels,** and **diagrams** to understand how and where people live.

Selection Reading

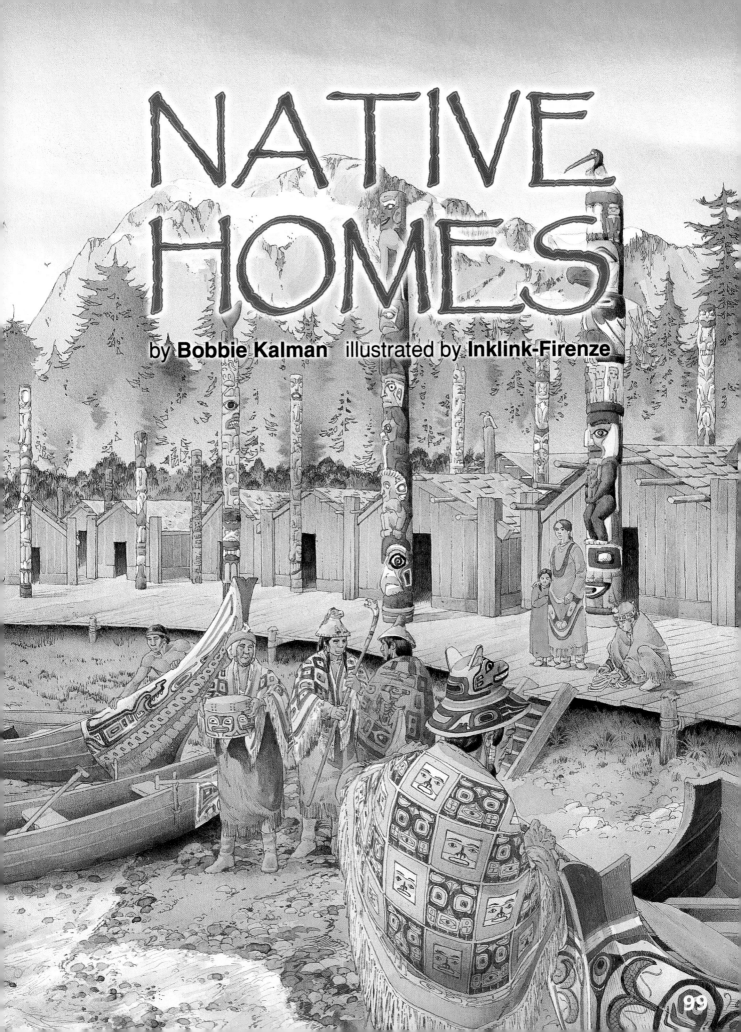

NATIVE HOMES

by **Bobbie Kalman**   illustrated by **Inklink-Firenze**

Set Your Purpose

Read to learn how and why Native Americans built different homes.

Homes in North America

Thousands of years before the United States or Canada were countries, hundreds of groups of people lived throughout **North America**. These were North America's first peoples. They are known as **Native peoples**, or Native Americans.

In the past, Native people built **traditional** homes, or lodges, that **suited** their surroundings, lifestyles, and the climate of the areas in which they lived. Wherever they lived, people always built their homes from natural **materials** of their **region**.

North America the area that today includes Canada, the United States, and Mexico

suited went well with

Temporary and Permanent Homes

In areas with **poor soil** or little water, Native bands, or groups, had to hunt to survive. These **nomadic people** followed animal herds and lived in **temporary** camps. They made shelters of **animal hides**, grass, tree bark, and fur. These materials were **ideal** for traveling because they were easy to pack up and move.

People who lived in areas with rich soil and a good water supply usually stayed in one place. They grew crops such as corn, beans, and pumpkins, but they also made short hunting and fishing trips. They built **permanent** homes.

---

poor soil bad ground for growing food

nomadic people people who moved from place to place to find food

animal hides dried animal skins

ideal perfect

▼ **North America's first people lived in different kinds of homes.**

Before You Move On

1. **Viewing** Which homes in the picture are permanent? Temporary?

2. **Details** Why did some Native peoples stay in one place?

Materials from Nature

In the cool **wooded areas** such as in the Northeast and the West, people built large permanent homes using tree trunks. In the Great Plains and the Southwest, there were not many trees, so people made homes using grass, mud, and stone. Some built simple wooden **frames** and covered them with animal hides. In warm, wet areas such as the Southeast, homes were often made of **woven plants**.

This article tells about many kinds of Native homes in different regions. You will find out what life was like in each kind of home.

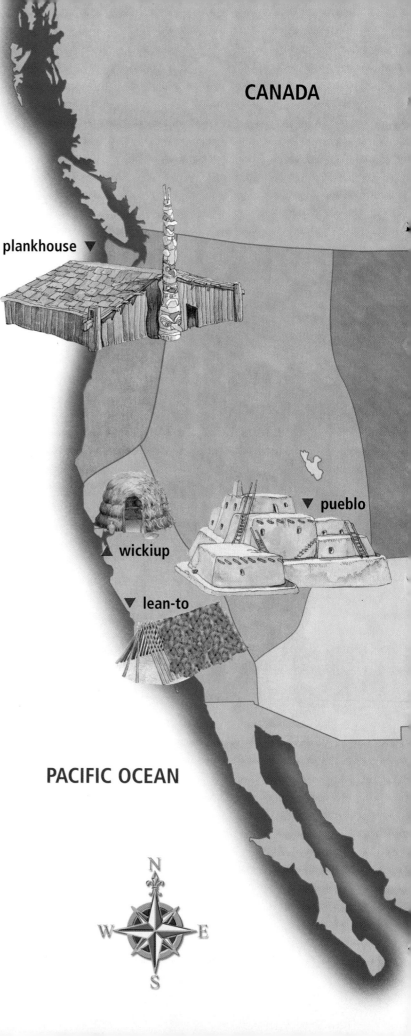

CANADA

plankhouse ▼

▲ wickiup

▼ pueblo

▼ lean-to

PACIFIC OCEAN

N
W E
S

---

wooded areas forests

woven plants plant parts put together tightly

102

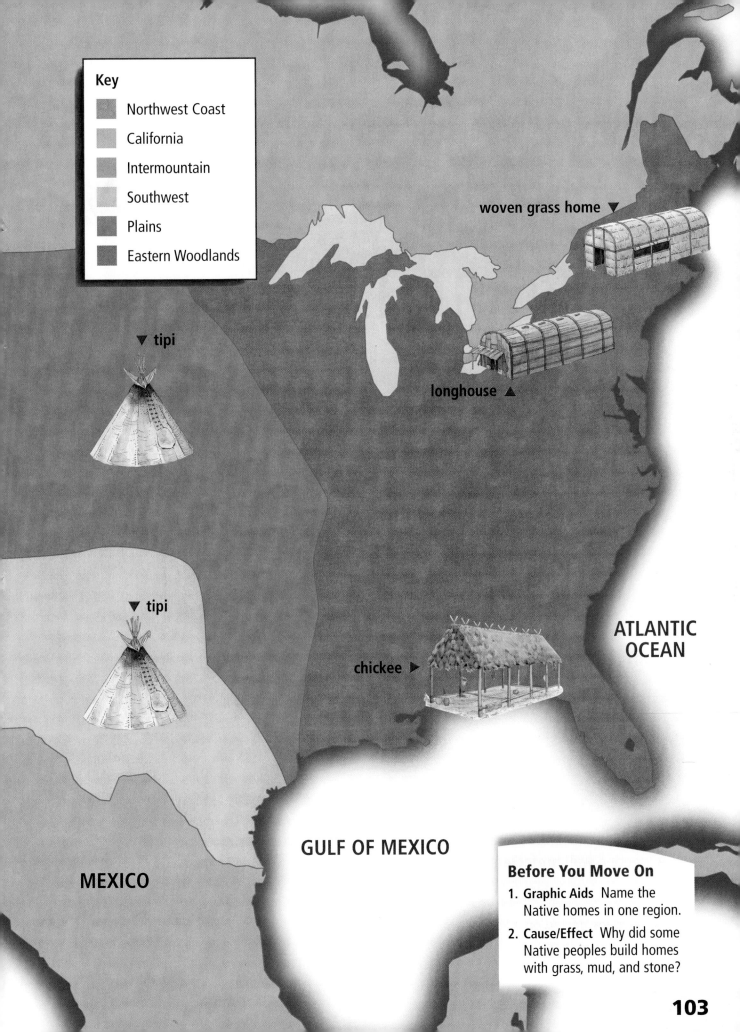

Key

- Northwest Coast
- California
- Intermountain
- Southwest
- Plains
- Eastern Woodlands

woven grass home ▼

▼ tipi

longhouse ▲

▼ tipi

chickee ▶

ATLANTIC
OCEAN

GULF OF MEXICO

MEXICO

Before You Move On

1. **Graphic Aids** Name the Native homes in one region.

2. **Cause/Effect** Why did some Native peoples build homes with grass, mud, and stone?

Longhouses: Homes of Wood and Bark

In the northeastern woodlands, most of the people stayed in one place. They lived in permanent homes called longhouses. A longhouse is a large rectangular building with a framework of wooden poles covered with bark. Villages were made up of several longhouses **surrounded** by a wooden wall. They were built in **clearings** in the woods and on the banks of rivers and streams. Many were located high on hilltops for extra protection.

▲ **A wooden wall protected the longhouse village.**

---

surrounded protected on all sides
clearings open spaces

1. First, the men went to the woods to peel bark off young trees and find long, thin tree trunks. They laid the bark flat to dry and cut it into large sheets.

sheets of bark

bark

2. They used the trunks to make poles. On a flat area of ground, they marked the outline of the house, dug holes along it, and set the poles into the holes. The poles were the framework for the outer walls. For the roof, they tied poles to the tops of the walls, **slanted** them toward the center, and tied them together.

tree trunk

3. The frame was covered with sheets of bark turned **rough-side** out and tied with bark strips. The **overlapping sheets** of bark kept out the wind and rain.

overlapping sheets of bark

frame

bark strips

slanted leaned
rough-side bumpy side
overlapping sheets layers

Before You Move On
1. **Details** Where did people build longhouse villages? Why?
2. **Graphic Aids** Look at the diagram, and tell a partner how a longhouse was made.

105

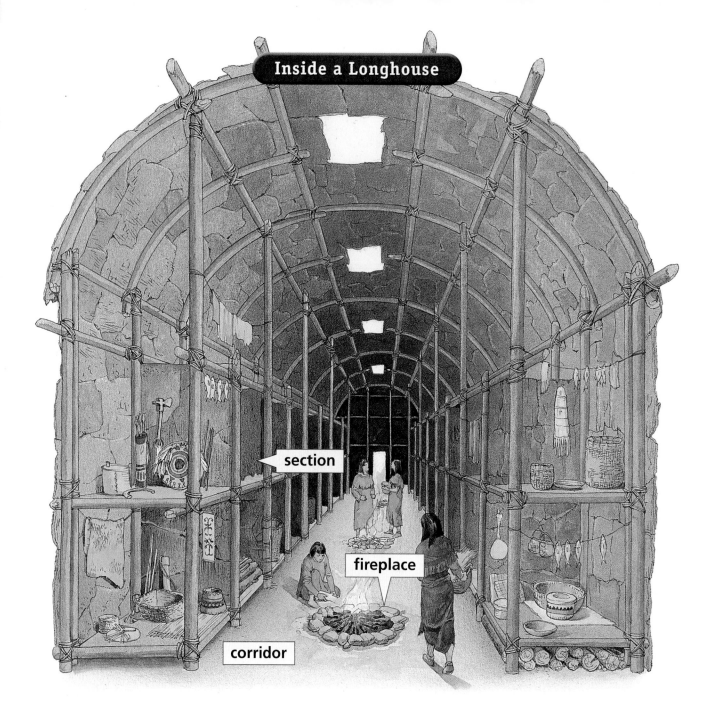

Inside a Longhouse

section

fireplace

corridor

The longhouse was divided in half by a wide corridor that **stretched** from one end to the other. On either side of the corridor were sections, which were used by individual families. Fireplaces were dug into the ground along the corridor. Families who lived across from one another shared a fireplace.

---

stretched went all the way

Woven Grass Homes

The people who lived in areas with **a mild climate** built villages that looked like longhouse villages, but the building materials they used were different. Winters were not as cold as those of the northern woodlands, and the summers were quite hot.

Instead of bark, these curved-roof homes were covered with woven grass mats. The mats could be pulled down in cold weather and rolled up in warm weather to allow breezes to blow through.

---

a mild climate weather that usually wasn't too cold

▼ **Woven grass homes were warm in the mild winter and cool in the summer.**

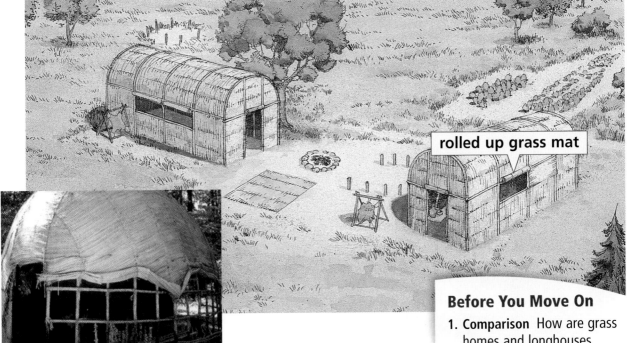

rolled up grass mat

▲ **Mats could be rolled up to let in fresh air.**

Before You Move On

1. **Comparison** How are grass homes and longhouses alike? Different?

2. **Details** What keeps grass homes warm in the winter and cool in the summer?

107

Wickiups, Chickees, and Lean-tos: Thatched Homes

In warm areas of North America, many Native **nations** built homes with thatched roofs. Thatch is a covering made up of layers of leaves, grasses, **reeds**, or straw. Thatch helps keep out rain and wind, but it allows air to **circulate** inside the dwelling. Thatched homes include the wickiup, chickee, and lean-to. These dwellings were most commonly used in the Southeast and the area that is now California.

---

reeds stems of tall grasses
circulate move around

▼ **These wickiups were covered with straw.**

Wickiup A wickiup had a dome-shaped frame. It was thatched with **brush**, grass, or **tule**. When the thatch wore out, the wickiup was burned and a new one was built.

▲ Some wickiups were thatched with brush.

Chickee The frame of a chickee was made of **cypress logs** and the roof was thatched with woven **palmetto leaves** or other plants. The side walls were left open to allow breezes to circulate freely.

▲ Open walls in a chickee let fresh air move through.

Lean-to A lean-to frame was made of wooden poles that were covered in thatch. In some areas, these shelters were covered with bark, mats of woven leaves, or hides instead of thatch.

▲ Some lean-tos were covered with animal hides.

brush cut bushes

tule thick, strong grass

cypress logs wood from a tree that grows along the coast

palmetto leaves leaves shaped like large fans

Before You Move On

1. **Details** Why is thatch a good material for homes in warm areas?

2. **Comparison** How are a wickiup and a chickee alike? How are they different?

Tipis: Cone-shaped Homes

Many nomadic nations lived in large **portable tipis**. A tipi often belonged to the woman of the family, and it was her job to set it up and take it down at each campsite. When not set up, tipis were **compact** and lightweight, making it easy to move them from place to place. People covered their tipis with **buffalo hides** or bark.

Families stayed comfortable inside their tipis through every kind of weather. In summer, women left a wide **gap** between the ground and the cover, which allowed fresh breezes to blow through the tipi. In winter, they added another layer of hide to the cover and stuffed moss or grass between the layers **for extra insulation**. They pulled the lining snug against the ground to block the wind.

---

portable tipis homes that were easy to move
compact small
buffalo hides skins of buffalo or bison
gap space
for extra insulation to keep the tipi warm

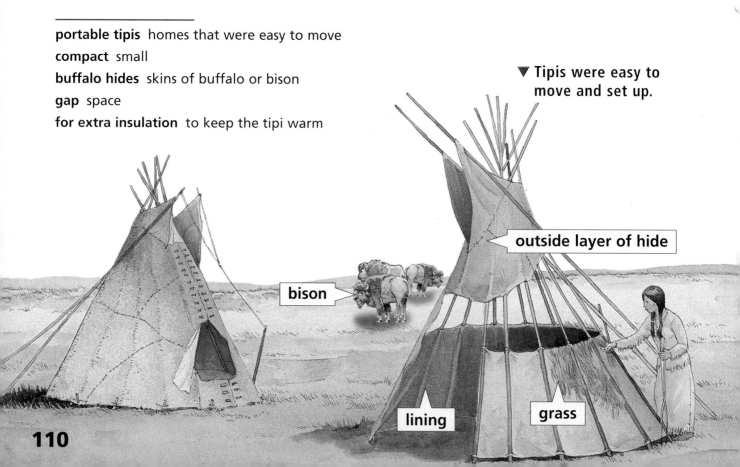

▼ Tipis were easy to move and set up.

outside layer of hide

bison

lining

grass

Everyone and everything had a certain spot within the tipi. Beds were arranged around the fire, and clothing and tools were placed among them. An opening at the top of the tipi allowed smoke to escape. An open doorflap signaled that visitors were welcome.

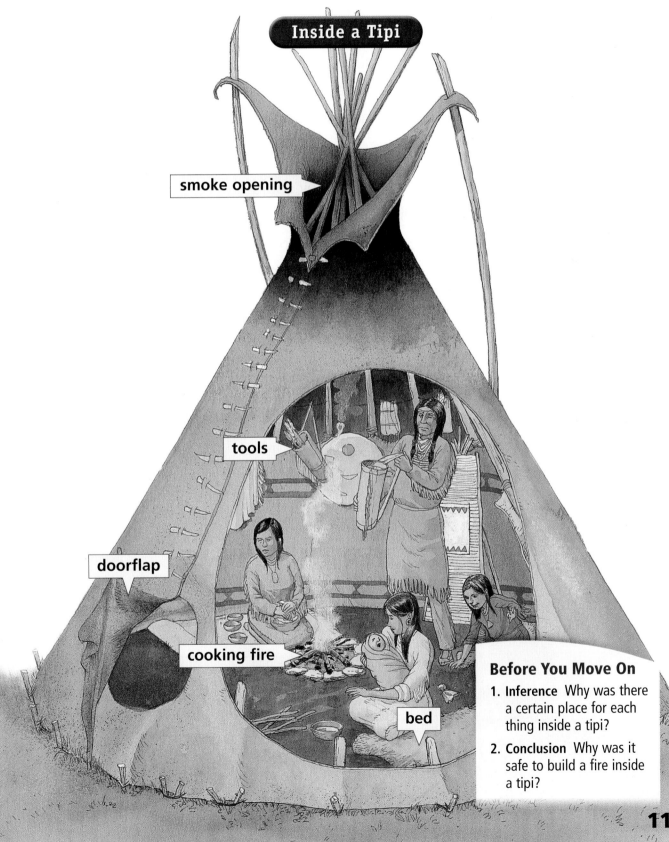

Inside a Tipi

smoke opening

tools

doorflap

cooking fire

bed

Before You Move On

1. **Inference** Why was there a certain place for each thing inside a tipi?

2. **Conclusion** Why was it safe to build a fire inside a tipi?

Pueblos: Homes of Bricks and Mud

People have been living in the Southwest for at least ten thousand years. Long ago, these people were mainly nomadic hunters who followed animal herds. More than two thousand years ago, however, people learned to farm corn. With **a reliable food source**, they **no longer had** to follow the buffalo herds.

They began building permanent homes so they could grow corn **year round**. Many families lived in pueblos, which resembled apartment buildings. Some of the rooms in the pueblo were living rooms, and others were used as work or storage areas. As families grew, rooms were added.

---

a reliable food source food always available
no longer had did not need
year round every month of the year

▼ **Pueblos looked like apartment buildings.**

storage room

work area

kitchen

112

1. Workers mixed mud, grasses, and ashes. Then they put the mixture in forms to make bricks.

2. Warm sun dried the adobe bricks. Then workers stacked the bricks in layers.

3. Then they packed mud into the spaces between the bricks to hold them together.

4. Finally, they covered the walls with a thin layer of mud.

Before You Move On

1. **Cause/Effect** Why did some Native peoples build permanent homes?

2. **Sequence** When did workers stack the adobe bricks?

Plankhouses: Homes of Cedar

For thousands of years, many nations in the northern area of the West Coast built large rectangular wooden homes that were richly decorated with beautiful paintings and **carvings**. These homes were known as plankhouses. They were built of red cedar. Cedar is an ideal building material. It splits naturally and easily in straight lines to make planks, and it does not **rot** in the **damp** climate of the Pacific Coast.

---

carvings pictures cut into wood
rot go bad
damp wet

▼ **This plankhouse village was the winter home for a Pacific Coast nation.**

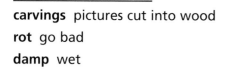

▲ Villagers raise a totem pole to decorate their village.

Totem poles are the **most distinctive feature** of the homes of Northwest Coast nations. Totem poles are tall cedar trunks carved and painted to resemble a series of totems stacked one upon the other.

Totems are the spirits of animals and other beings, which are considered to be **ancestors** or special protectors of individuals and families. Totem poles tell about a family's history or **accomplishments**. They decorated both the insides and outsides of plankhouses.

---

most distinctive feature most noticed part
ancestors family members who died long ago
accomplishments important things they have done

Before You Move On

1. **Conclusion** Why is cedar a good building material? Give two reasons.

2. **Inference** Why were totem poles important to people of the Northwest?

In the past, **extended families** lived together in a single plankhouse. Some houses had large central fire pits, and others had individual fireplaces for cooking meals. People hung food and animal hides from rafters and racks above the fires. The smoke would dry the food and hides and **preserve them**. People also stored food inside large wooden boxes. They often sat on mats of woven cedar bark.

---

extended families groups of children, parents, grandparents, aunts, and uncles

preserve them keep them from rotting

Inside a Plank House

rafter

animal hide

drying fish

planks

cedar bark mat

People, Homes, and Nature

Each home you have read about was built from materials that were naturally found in the region. Yet each home was **uniquely suited to** the needs of the people who used it.

Permanent homes were best for people who stayed in one place all year long. Temporary homes were best for those who moved around a lot.

Homes made of wood were perfect for the northern woods. Adobe homes with thick mud walls kept people cool in the hot summers and warm in the cold winters of the western plains. Grass and leaves let the air move in and out of homes in the south.

What kind of home would be best for where you live?

---

uniquely suited to perfect for

wood and bark

mud

grass and leaves

animal hides

Before You Move On

1. **Paraphrase** How did people cook and store food in a plankhouse?

2. **Conclusion** Why were adobe homes perfect for their region?

Cloud Brothers

Four directions
cloud brothers
share one sky.

Each has its own path.
Each has its own mood.
Each has its own face.
The cloud brothers are many
But they are one family.

The cloud brothers are scattered
but they **are one in spirit**.

They **mingle**
within themselves
changing with every moment.

They tell us
that we too
are brothers
on this land.

---

are one in spirit still belong together
mingle mix and move

And

like our cloud brothers

we are all yellow
    as are the sunrise clouds
we are all white
    as are the **noonday clouds**
we are all black
    as are the thunder clouds
we are all red
    as are the sunset clouds.
So let us look out to our cloud brothers
as one family
and one spirit.

For we are truly different
and yet
    we are truly the same.
        —*Ramson Lomatewama*

---

noonday clouds clouds in the
middle of the day

Meet the Poet

Ramson Lomatewama
belongs to a Native
American culture called
the Hopi. For the
author, the clouds in
his poem are like the
people on the Earth.
We are all different,
yet in some ways we
are all the same.

Before You Move On
Details Name two ways
clouds can be different.

Think and Respond

Strategy: Make Comparisons

Make a comparison chart. Show how Native homes are alike and different.

Native Homes

Kind of Home	Permanent or Temporary	Location	Materials
Longhouse	permanent	Northeast woods	wood bark
Woven Grass Home			
Thatched Home			
Tipi			
Pueblo			
Plankhouse			

Share and Compare

Study one row in the chart. With a partner, take turns telling about the details of the home in your row. Then talk with a group to compare all of the homes.

Talk It Over

 1 Personal Response Which kind of Native home do you think is the most interesting? Explain.

 2 Summary Tell why different tribes built different kinds of houses.

 3 Text Structure Both pages 104 and 105 of "Native Homes" tell about longhouses. How are the two pages different?

4 Author's Purpose Why did the author write this article? Did the author do a good job? Why or why not?

Compare Genres

Compare "Cloud Brothers" and "Native Homes." How are they different? How are they alike?

Both tell about many different kinds of people.

Content Connections

Interview an Expert

Learn all about one Native American nation. Then talk about what makes the tribe special. Interview another group about its tribe. Talk about what you learned.

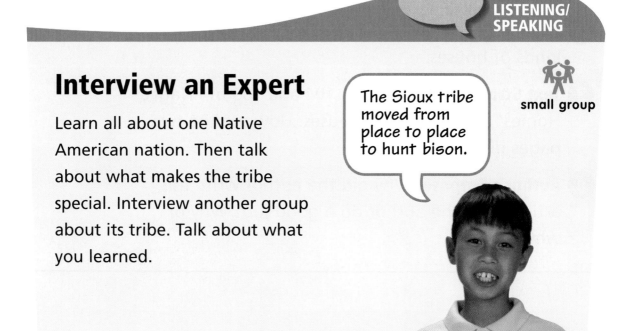

The Sioux tribe moved from place to place to hunt bison.

small group

Build a Scale Model

partners

Choose one kind of Native home. On graph paper, draw a floor plan of the home. Then build a scale model. Use natural materials such as twigs, leaves, and grass. Compare your model to others.

SOCIAL STUDIES

partners

Make a Map
Internet

In the U.S., many place names come from Native American words. Choose an area of the U.S. from page 73. Use books or the Internet to find names that might have come from Native American languages. Make a map.

WRITING

on your own

Write a Message

What do you want people in the future to know about how you lived? Choose objects or pictures. Write a message that tells why each object is important. Put all this in a time capsule.

On the time capsule box:

My Music

Dear people of the future, I chose a baseball because I play a lot of baseball with my family.

Plural Nouns

Listen and sing.

Song

HOMES

Families gather stones and wood,
Stones and wood,
Stones and wood.
Families gather stones and wood
To build their houses.

Families gather branches and leaves,
Branches and leaves,
Branches and leaves.
Families gather branches and leaves
To build their houses.

—Jane Zion Brauer

Tune: "London Bridge"

How Language Works

A **singular noun** shows "one."
A **plural noun** shows "more than one."

How to Make a Noun Plural	Examples:	
1. To make most nouns plural, add **-s**.	home	home**s**
2. If the noun ends in **x**, **ch**, **sh**, **s**, or **z**, add **-es**.	grass	grass**es**
3. For most nouns that end in **y**, change the **y** to **i** and add **-es**.	sky	sk**ies**
4. Some nouns cannot be counted. They have only one form for "one" and "more than one."	fun rain	wind water

Practice with a Partner

Make each red noun plural. Then say the sentence.

star   1. The _____ came out in the night sky.

family   2. Many _____ gathered around the fire.

story   3. They listened to several exciting _____ .

fox   4. The best story was about some _____ and bears.

fun   5. The families had a lot of _____ .

Put It in Writing

Pretend that you go camping with your family. You sleep under the stars and cook food over a fire. Write about your trip.

The wind blows in the trees.

Show What You Know

Talk About Native Peoples

In this unit, you read a play and a social studies article about Native America. Look back at this unit. What was most interesting to you? Tell your group why you found this interesting.

Make a Mind Map

Work with a partner. Make a web to show what you learned about Native America.

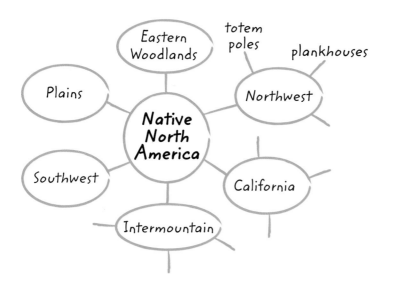

Think and Write

What questions do you still have about Native America? Make a list. Add the list to your portfolio. Also include work that shows what you learned.

Read and Learn More

Leveled Books

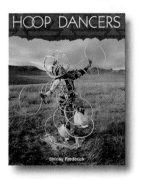

Hoop Dancers
by Shirley Frederick

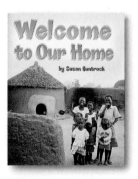

Welcome to Our Home
by Susan Buntrock

Theme Library

Beardream
by Will Hobbs

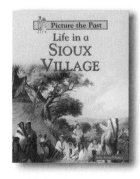

Life in a Sioux Village
by Sally Isaacs

Internet

Go to: www.hbavenues.com

Native American Cultures

U.S. Place Names

Native American Shelters

Once Upon a Storm

Make a Storm Story

1. Work with a group to choose a kind of storm.
2. Make a story strip. Draw pictures to show what happened before, during, and after the storm.
3. Use your story strip to tell a storm story.

Weather

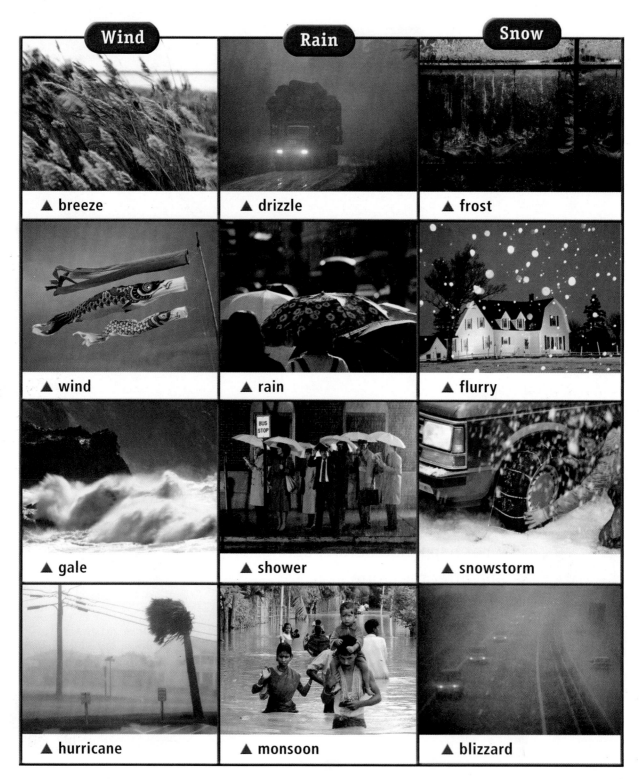

Wind	**Rain**	**Snow**
▲ breeze	▲ drizzle	▲ frost
▲ wind	▲ rain	▲ flurry
▲ gale	▲ shower	▲ snowstorm
▲ hurricane	▲ monsoon	▲ blizzard

Weather Map

Friday, January 24

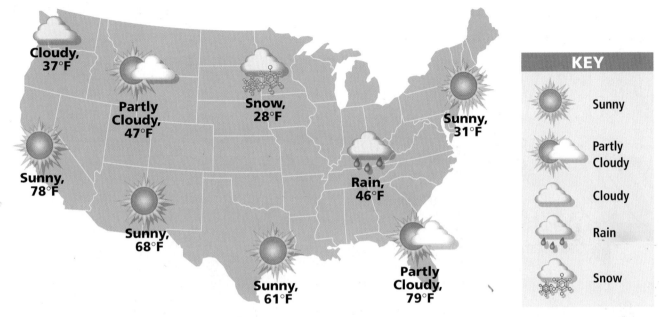

KEY

- ☀ Sunny
- ⛅ Partly Cloudy
- ☁ Cloudy
- 🌧 Rain
- 🌨 Snow

Cloudy, 37°F

Partly Cloudy, 47°F

Snow, 28°F

Sunny, 31°F

Sunny, 78°F

Sunny, 68°F

Rain, 46°F

Sunny, 61°F

Partly Cloudy, 79°F

Climate Map

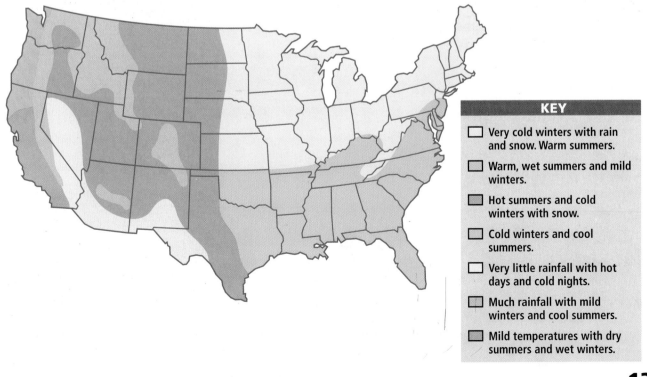

KEY

- ☐ Very cold winters with rain and snow. Warm summers.
- ☐ Warm, wet summers and mild winters.
- ☐ Hot summers and cold winters with snow.
- ☐ Cold winters and cool summers.
- ☐ Very little rainfall with hot days and cold nights.
- ☐ Much rainfall with mild winters and cool summers.
- ☐ Mild temperatures with dry summers and wet winters.

Vocabulary

Chant

I AM

A Chant for Two Voices

Voice 1: I am **Twister**.
Voice 2: Hear me **howling**
as I come.

Voice 1: I am Twister!
Voice 2: **Hail** and **lightning**
go before me.

Voices 1 and 2: Run to your
cellar! Run!

Voice 1: I am Twister!
Voice 2: Hear the **thunder**
as I come!

Voice 1: I am Twister!
Voice 2: A path of **damage**
follows me!

Voices 1 and 2: Now all is **silent**. I'm gone!

—Evelyn Stone

Key Words

twister

howling

hail

lightning

cellar

thunder

damage

silent

133

TWISTER

by Darleen Bailey Beard

illustrated by Nancy Carpenter

Read a Story

Genre

An **adventure story** tells about events that are dangerous and exciting. This story tells what happens to a girl and her younger brother during a tornado.

Characters

Lucille

Natt

Mama

Mr. Lyle

Setting

This story takes place in the U.S. where a lot of tornadoes happen.

Tornado Alley

🔘 Selection Reading

135

Lucille and Natt play outside. Find out why they have to run inside.

136

Screeeek scraaaawk. Screeeek scraaaawk. Our porch swing hangs by two chains. Its **slats** are warm with sunshine. The paint is peeling. **Specks** of green stick to the backs of our legs. But we don't mind. Our porch swing can be anything we want it to be. **Today it is our throne**.

I'm Queen Lucille. My brother is King Natt. We're licking orange frozen fruit bars, because that's what kings and queens do.

---

slats thin wooden boards

Specks Small pieces

Today it is our throne Today we pretend it is a special chair for a king or queen

I give Natt his royal wheelbarrow ride, all over our yard. Under Mama's clothesline, between sheets and towels, and along the fence that **separates our grass from Mr. Lyle's.**

"Say hey!" shouts Mr. Lyle, the way he always does. He **hobbles** through his daffodils to the barbed-wire fence.

"Say hey!" we **holler** back. We give him our royal handshake—up, down, touch elbows, high-five.

---

separates our grass from Mr. Lyle's
is between our yard and Mr. Lyle's yard

hobbles walks slowly

holler shout

We **barrel on** over tickly grass and sandy molehills that sink when I step on them. After a while, I **dump Natt out**. "It's my turn," I say.

I lie back in the wheelbarrow. Far away, the sky looks green, like Mama's guacamole. **Sprinkles dot** my face. The air feels so thick I can almost poke my finger through it.

Natt pushes me fast. I jiggle along, tasting raindrops as we go.

---

barrel on continue the ride in the wheelbarrow
dump Natt out let Natt fall out of the wheelbarrow
Sprinkles dot Raindrops fall on

Lightning crackles. Natt **spills me out**.
Thunder chases us inside.

"There you are," Mama says as she opens
the screen door. "Looks like we're **in for a
gully washer**."

Thunder shakes the windows. Rain **splinks**
onto the tin roof of our trailer.

---

spills me out lets me fall onto the ground

in for a gully washer going to have a big storm
with a lot of rain

splinks splashes

We look out the kitchen window. Bird feeders twirl on their strings, spilling seed and knocking into branches. Mr. Lyle's daffodils droop, their petals full of water.

The rain stops. **Hail** cracks onto the roof and bounces in the grass like popcorn popping. The porch swing bangs and clangs. The rabbit who lives under the snowball bush **zips out, dashing** across our yard. "Hurry, little rabbit," I whisper. It **skitters** under an old pile of brush and tires.

---

zips out, dashing jumps out, running
skitters runs quickly

Our lights **blink off**. So do Mr. Lyle's.
I hold my breath. Mama pulls us close.
"Will Mr. Lyle be okay?" I ask.
"Sure," Mama says, but her eyebrows look **scrunched** and worried.

Mama lights a candle. We move to her bedroom and turn on the radio, watching **clouds dark and furious**. Far away, one looks like a lion. Its tail reaches down.

---

blink off go off
scrunched squeezed together
clouds dark and furious clouds that look dark and angry

"**Twister**!" shouts Mama. "Head for the **cellar**!"

Out we run, like the little rabbit. Wind **shoves** us forward, knocking us into each other.

Mama pulls up the door. "You two go in!" she shouts. "Don't open this door until I come back with Mr. Lyle!"

———————————

shoves pushes

Before You Move On

1. **Details** What do Lucille and Natt see and hear after it starts to rain?

2. **Inference** Why does Mama say that Mr. Lyle will be okay?

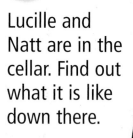
2

Lucille and Natt are in the cellar. Find out what it is like down there.

e **scramble** down the steep steps, **batting cobwebs**. My shoulder touches a **clammy** wall.

Mama slams the door.

Hail **pounds**, trying to get in. Or has Mama changed her mind?

"Mama!" I shout. "Is that you?"

I feel along the shelves, searching for the flashlight. I shine it up the steps, but all I see is a chain dangling from the door and Natt's face as white as the rabbit's tail.

"Sit down," I tell him. We sit on folding chairs in the dark spidery room, which smells of old rain and earthy potatoes.

"I want Mama," Natt says, his voice tiny and **quivery**.

"Me, too," I say. "She'll be here any minute with Mr. Lyle."

---

scramble move quickly
batting cobwebs hitting spiderwebs away from us
clammy cold and wet
pounds hits against the door
quivery shaky

We tap our toes in puddles. We count to a hundred and three.

"What about the rabbit?" Natt asks.

"He's probably found a **hiding spot**, just like us," I say. But I'm worried, too.

I **zigzag the flashlight** over empty jars and potatoes spread out on newspapers. "Let's make wall shadows."

Natt makes a crown on his head. I make a dog **yapping and snapping**.

Then I stop to listen for Mama.

"Mama!" I shout. "Are you there?" But all I hear is the roaring wind and our banging, clanging porch swing.

We tap our toes in puddles We move our toes up and down in the water

hiding spot place to hide

zigzag the flashlight move the flashlight back and forth

yapping and snapping barking and biting

"Where's Daddy?" Natt asks.

"Daddy's at work," I tell him. "We'll be okay."

Natt's eyes look big and round and full of tears.

"Let's compare scars," I say, **yanking** off my flip-flop.
"See? This was done by a **posthole digger**. But you're too
little to remember."

Natt shows me **his fence-hopping scar**, the scab on
his right knee, and a freckle on his **pinky**.

Suddenly it's silent. So silent I can hear Natt breathe.

---

yanking taking

posthole digger tool used to make holes in
the ground

his fence-hopping scar the place where he hurt
himself as he jumped over a fence

pinky smallest finger

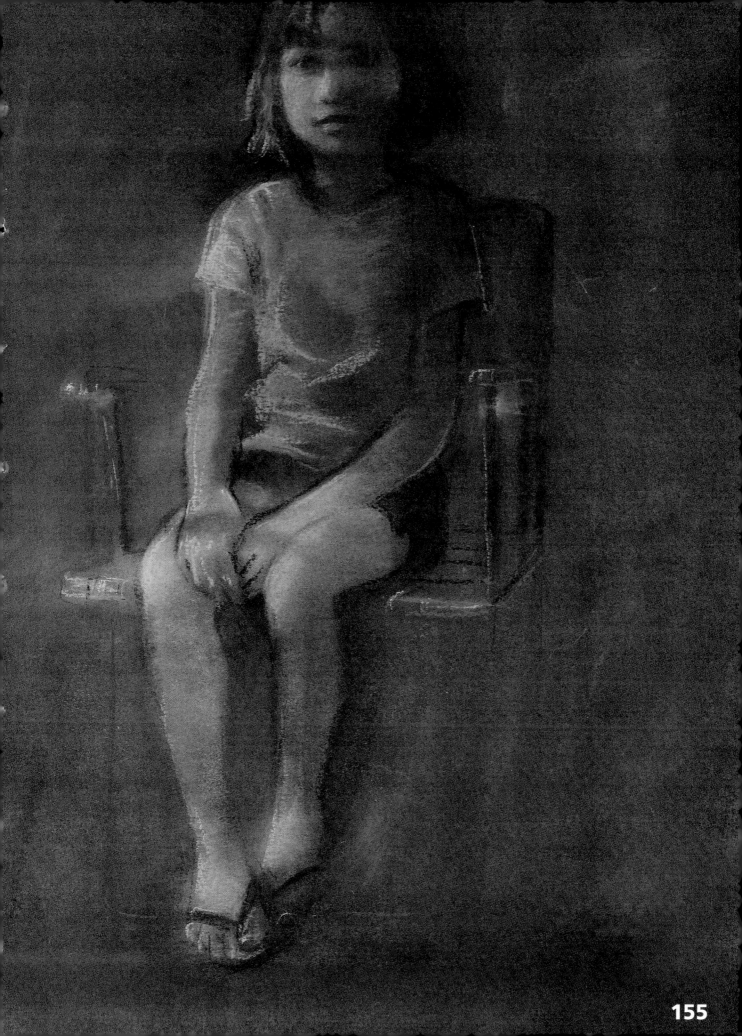

Then, with a **ferocious roar**, the twister **strikes**.
It claws and chomps and pulls at our cellar door.

I rush to grab the chain. "Hold on!"

"What if it's Mama? Or Mr. Lyle?" Natt shouts.

"It's <u>not</u>! Hold on!"

The **monstrous howling** shakes my chest and makes my insides shiver. Then, once again, it's silent.

We collapse on the steps, shaking and crying, holding each other tight.

"Should we open the door now?" Natt whispers. "It's safe."

"Mama said not to."

"But Mama might need us."

"You're right," I say.

---

ferocious roar loud and angry sound
strikes comes
monstrous howling big and scary noise

Before You Move On

1. **Character** How does Natt feel during the storm? How do you know?

2. **Plot** Why do Lucille and Natt decide to leave the cellar?

3

The storm is over. Will Lucille and Natt find Mama and Mr. Lyle?

We push open the door. **New air hits our faces**, and we **squint** in the bright sunshine.

"Mama!" we call. "Mama!"

I turn toward Mr. Lyle's, but the sight of our porch swing stops me. An arm is broken, a slat is missing, it's **sloping** on one chain.

New air hits our faces We feel the fresh air outside

squint close our eyes a little

sloping hanging with one end lower than the other

"Mama! Mr. Lyle!"

"There they are!" Natt says. "Under the porch!"
He grabs my hand and runs.

"Say hey!" shouts Mr. Lyle.

"Say hey!" we holler back.

Mama reaches out to us, and we hug and cry until
there are no tears left. Holding hands, we walk through
our yards, shaking our heads at the **damage**.

Hailstones sparkle like **glittering** diamonds and **crunch** under our shoes. I put one on top of my finger and pretend it's a ring. Natt lifts the hem of his T-shirt and **stuffs it belly-full**.

"Look!" he says. "We're rich!"

Mama looks at us, with our king and queen faces. Then a tear rolls down her cheek.

---

glittering bright, shiny
crunch make a breaking sound
stuffs it belly-full fills it with hailstones

162

Quickly, I lift the porch swing. I hook it back on its chain and **prop up** its arm. "Here," I tell Mama. "Sit down."

Mama and Mr. Lyle sit. We squeeze in between them.

Screeeekity scraaaawk. Screeeekity scraaaawk. Our porch swing makes a <u>new</u> sound, even better than before.

An arm is broken, a slat is missing, and now it **swerves** to the left. But we don't mind. Our porch swing can be anything we want it to be.

Today it is our throne.

---

prop up fix
swerves turns

Before You Move On

1. **Viewing** What does the twister do to the houses and yards?

2. **Inference** Why do you think Mama cries when Natt says, "We're rich!"?

Meet the Author

When **Darleen Bailey Beard** was in fifth grade, her teacher said, "If you work hard, Darleen, you might publish a book someday." Darleen did work hard, and she published her first book in 1995.

Ms. Beard wrote *Twister* because she remembered a tornado when she was a teenager. She and her dog, Brutus, ran to the cellar of her home. The tornado blew right over the house! Like Natt and Lucille, she was happy when it was over.

AWARD WINNER

Wind Song

When the wind blows
The quiet things speak.
Some whisper, some clang,
Some creak.

Grasses swish.
Treetops sigh.
Flags slap
and snap at the sky.
Wires on poles
whistle and hum.
Ashcans roll.
Windows drum.

When the wind goes—
suddenly
then,
the quiet things
are quiet again.

—Lilian Moore

Ashcans Trash cans

Puddle

is a rain word,
like squish,
and slosh,
splash
and **galosh**.

—*Audrey B. Baird*

___

galosh rain boot

Meet the Poets

Lilian Moore says, "To me a poem is like a balloon on a string. What you get out of it depends on how tall you are and how long the string is."

Audrey B. Baird likes interesting weather and has written two books of weather poems: *Stormy Weather!* and *A Cold Snap*.

Before You Move On
1. **Comparison** How are these poems alike? How are they different?

Think and Respond

Strategy: Analyze Plot

The order of events in a story is called the plot. Make a story map for "Twister" to show the plot.

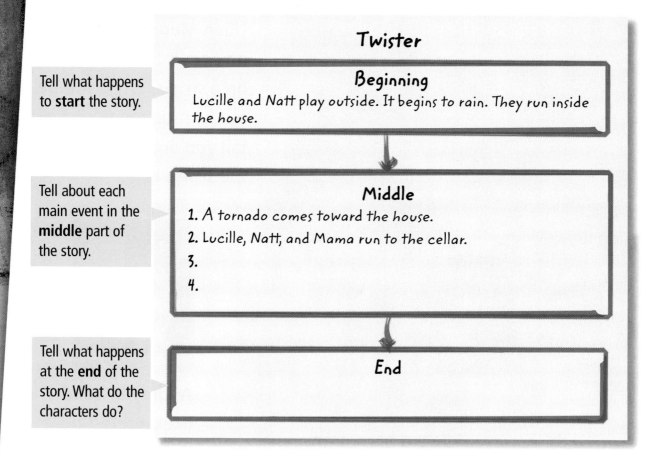

Tell what happens to **start** the story.

Twister

Beginning
Lucille and Natt play outside. It begins to rain. They run inside the house.

Tell about each main event in the **middle** part of the story.

Middle
1. A tornado comes toward the house.
2. Lucille, Natt, and Mama run to the cellar.
3.
4.

Tell what happens at the **end** of the story. What do the characters do?

End

Retell the Story

Pretend you are Lucille or Natt and your partner is Dad. Dad comes home from work. Use your story map to tell Dad about the twister.

Talk It Over

 Personal Response How are you like Lucille? How are you different?

 Judgment Was Mama right to leave Lucille and Natt alone in the cellar? Why or why not?

3 **Personal Experience** Tell a partner about a time you were scared by a storm.

4 **Comparison** Compare tornadoes to other storms you know about.

Compare Issues

In "Pushing Up the Sky," the People did what the chiefs said. In "Twister," the kids left the cellar before they were supposed to. Compare how people decide what to do.

Content Connections

Make a Phone Call

partners

Pretend you see a storm coming. Make a "phone call" to a friend to tell about it. Try it different ways:

- Speak calmly. Just tell the facts.
- Speak with feeling. Show excitement or fear.

Then talk about the differences.

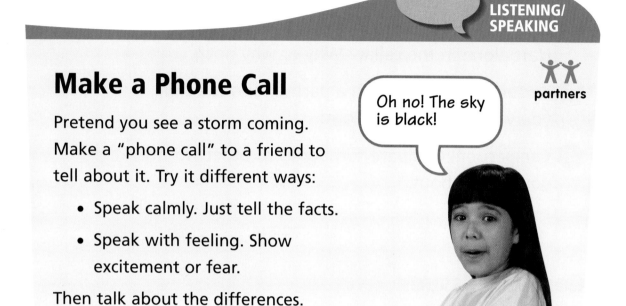

Oh no! The sky is black!

Research a Tornado

Internet

small group

What is a real twister like?

1. Use an almanac and the Internet to find out about a real tornado.
2. Take notes on notecards.
3. Use your notes to describe the tornado to the class.

The Storm of 1999

Web site: www.weather.com

On May 3, 1999, tornadoes in Oklahoma caused about $1.2 billion in damage.

170

large group

Make a Safety Plan

Do you know how to stay safe during a storm or other emergency? Listen to a guest speaker. Take notes. Use your notes to make a plan for safety at home.

Earthquake Safety Plan

1. Duck and cover until the earthquake stops.
2. Meet at family meeting place.
3. Call other family members.

WRITING

on your own

Write a Poem

Write a poem that describes a storm. Name the storm. Tell what it looks, sounds, and feels like. Share your poem with the class.

Thunderstorm
Thunder
Booming, popping
Cracking like a rocket
Bright bolts streaking across the sky
Lightning

Summarize

A **summary** tells the most important information in what you read. To summarize:

✔ Tell the key events.
✔ Don't repeat any information.
✔ Keep your summary short.

Try the strategy. First make a list of the key events in Part ❶ of "Twister." Then summarize them.

TWISTER

"Twister!" shouts Mama. "Head for the cellar!"

Out we run, like the little rabbit. Wind shoves us forward, knocking us into each other.

Mama pulls up the door. "You two go in!" she shouts. "Don't open this door until I come back with Mr. Lyle!"

Natt and Lucille see a storm coming. Mama gets them into the cellar. She goes to get the neighbor.

Practice

Take this test and **summarize** "Twister."

Read each item. Choose the best answer.•••

Test Strategy

Read the directions carefully. Make sure you understand what to do.

1 Read Part **2** on pages 150–157 again. Which of these sentences belongs in a summary of Part **2** ?

   A   Natt and Lucille compare scars.

   B   The cellar smells of old rain and earthy potatoes.

   C   Natt and Lucille play hide and seek.

   D   Natt and Lucille play games while they wait in the cellar.

2 Which of the following completes this summary of the whole story?

> Natt and Lucille see a storm coming. Mama gets them into the cellar. She goes to get the neighbor. They play games and tell stories. They are scared.
>
> _____

   A   They leave the cellar. They pick up hail. They find out that the swing makes a new sound.

   B   The twister comes. They leave the cellar. Mr. Lyle shouts, "Say hey!" They sit on the swing and look at the damage.

   C   The twister comes. They leave the cellar to find Mama and Mr. Lyle. Everyone looks at the damage and sits on the swing together.

   D   They compare scars. The twister comes. They leave the cellar to find Mama. Natt fills his shirt with hail. Then they sit on the swing together.

Vocabulary

Will It Rain?

Act out each scene.

A **mass** of cold air is coming into the Midwest. **Temperatures** will be very cold.

Be ready for a heavy snowstorm, a real **blizzard**.

COLD AIR

weather forecaster

The cold air will meet warm air to form a **cold front**. Then there will be **thunderstorms** with heavy rain.

Key Words

mass

temperature

blizzard

forecaster

cold front

thunderstorm

tornado

dangerous

Watch out for **tornadoes**, too. These **dangerous** storms can cause a lot of damage.

COLD AIR

COLD FRONT

WARM AIR

Read a News Article

A **news article** is nonfiction. It tells about events that really happened.

✔ Look for **locator maps**. They tell you where events happened.

locator map

Track The Storm

Rocky Mountains

April 1 | **Rain and Snow**

The storm moved swiftly over the Rocky Mountains. It spread blizzards from Montana to Arizona. In Colorado, fierce winds gusted to 141 miles per hour and overturned

✔ Look for **maps** and **photos**. They help you see what an event is like and how it happened.

Selection Reading

THE BIG STORM

by Bruce Hiscock

Set Your Purpose

Find out what the big storm brings to each part of the United States.

The Big Storm
Crosses the United States, 1982

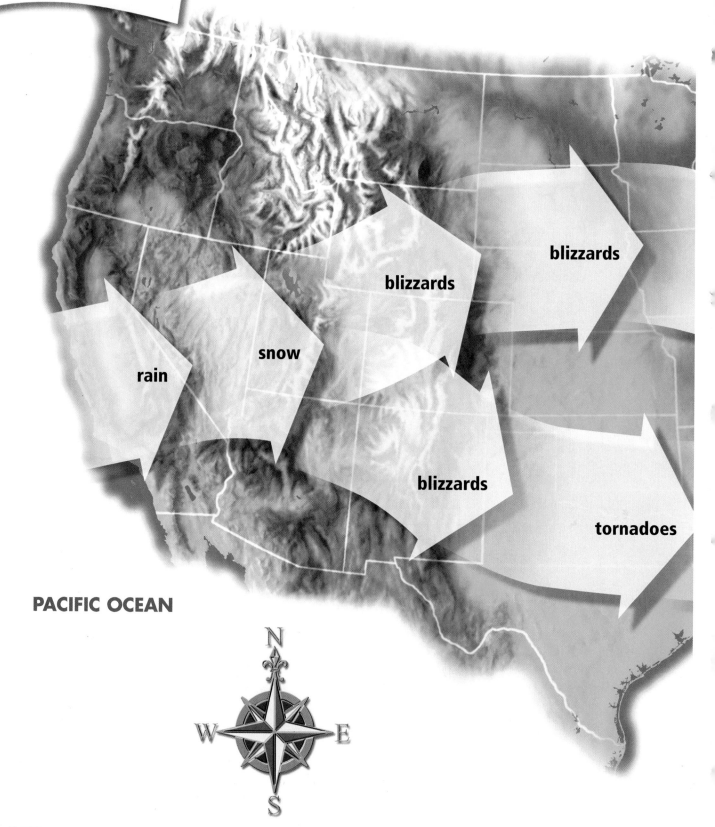

blizzards

blizzards

snow

rain

blizzards

tornadoes

PACIFIC OCEAN

N
W   E
S

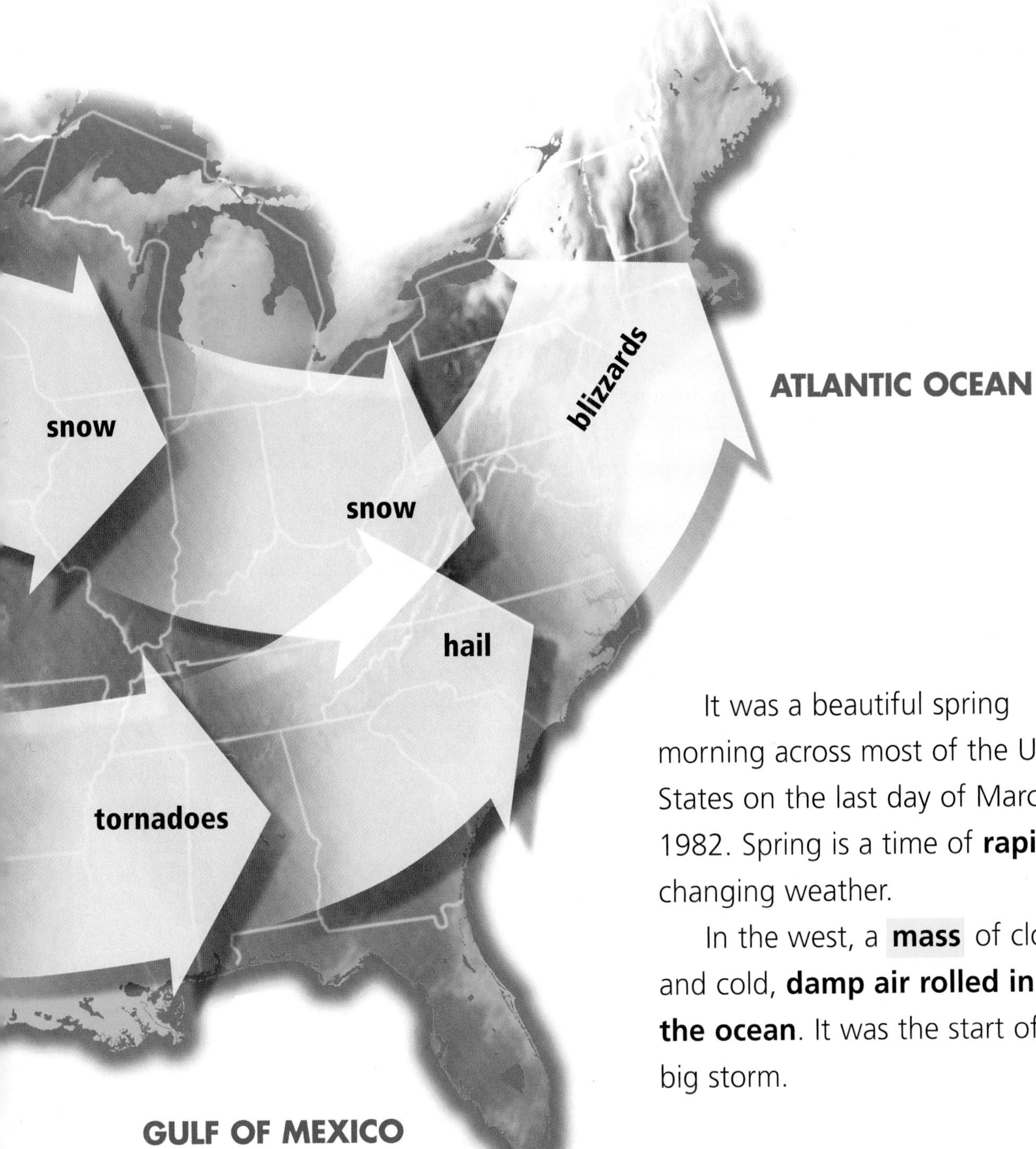

snow

snow

blizzards

hail

tornadoes

ATLANTIC OCEAN

GULF OF MEXICO

It was a beautiful spring morning across most of the United States on the last day of March in 1982. Spring is a time of **rapidly** changing weather.

In the west, a **mass** of clouds and cold, **damp air rolled in off the ocean**. It was the start of the big storm.

---

rapidly quickly

damp air rolled in off the ocean wet air came from the ocean toward the land

The clouds brought heavy rain to the Pacific Coast as the storm moved **inland**. It was carried along by the winds that nearly always blow from west to east across the **continent**.

Soon the storm ran up against the **mountains of the Sierra Nevada range** in California. The wind pushed the clouds up the **steep slopes**. In the cold mountain air, the rain changed to snow.

---

inland from the ocean toward the land

continent area that includes Canada, the U.S., and Mexico

mountains of the Sierra Nevada range row of mountains called the Sierra Nevada

steep slopes tall sides of the high mountains

▼ A storm moves into the mountains.

It snowed hard all day in the Sierras. The flakes **clung** to the tall pines, **coating them in heavy layers of white**.

Any storm can be **dangerous** as well as beautiful, but this one was a **real powerhouse**. And it was just getting started.

---

clung stuck tightly

coating them in heavy layers of white covering the trees with snow

real powerhouse very strong storm

▼ **Heavy snow covers pine trees in the Sierras.**

Before You Move On

1. **Details** What happened as the storm moved into the Sierras?

2. **Prediction** Where will the storm go next? How do you know?

181

The storm moved swiftly over the Rocky Mountains. It spread **blizzards** from Montana to Arizona. In Colorado, **fierce winds gusted to** 141 miles per hour and overturned vans and campers.

---

fierce winds gusted to strong winds blew as fast as

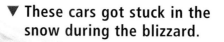

▼ **These cars got stuck in the snow during the blizzard.**

The Big Storm grew worse as it **swept out** over the Great Plains. Across South Dakota, Illinois, and Wisconsin, weather **forecasters** watched their barometers as the **readings fell to record low levels**.

---

swept out moved along quickly

readings fell to record low levels marks showed very low air pressure levels

Barometer

A barometer measures the pressure of the air, or how much the air pushes down on things.

High pressure brings fair weather with a lot of sunshine.

When the pressure is low, a storm may be coming. Scientists know that very low pressure means the storm will be a very big one.

▼ The storm moves across the plains.

▲ **National Meteorological Center**

As the blizzard **raged on**, weather stations reported **the conditions** to the National Meteorological Center near Washington, D.C. Forecasters used computers to predict what the storm would do next. They sent these predictions back to each weather station. There, a detailed forecast was made for the local area. This work goes on every day, but with a killer storm **on the loose**, the forecasts were especially important.

---

raged on went on and on
the conditions what the weather was like
on the loose happening

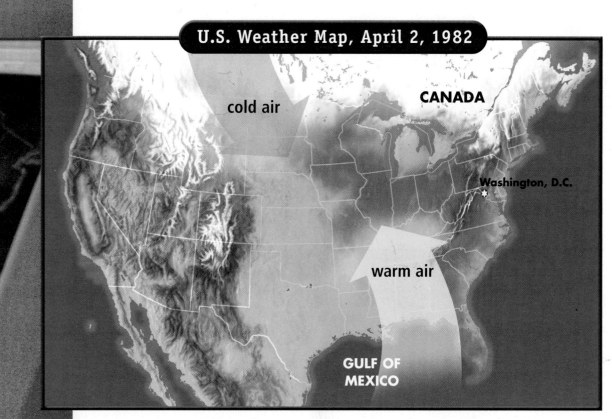

cold air

CANADA

Washington, D.C.

warm air

GULF OF MEXICO

▲ Two air masses move toward each other.

Forecasters studied changes in air pressure and **temperatures** all across the United States. They found that a mass of cold air was pushing down from Canada in the north. Warm air flowed from the Gulf of Mexico in the south.

Where would the two air masses meet? Their meeting could cause a powerful **cold front** and produce violent **thunderstorms** and **tornadoes** in the area. Forecasters checked their radar screens constantly, looking for signs of the front. Everyone waited.

Before You Move On

1. **Graphic Aids** What is the weather like when air pressure is high? Low?

2. **Cause/Effect** What can happen when a warm air mass meets cold air?

185

Track The Storm

Texas
April 3 | Tornadoes

The afternoon was warm and **humid** when a line of tall clouds appeared across the Texas plains. Lightning flashed in the distance. Soon the rumble of thunder was heard.

Dogs whined and hid under beds. The clouds moved in, and **an eerie darkness fell**. Then slashing winds hit. Rain and hail poured down. The cold front raced through. Temperatures dropped sharply. All along the front, police and other people watched for tornadoes.

---

humid wet
an eerie darkness fell the sky got dark and scary

▼ **Clouds grow in the Texas sky.**

Tornadoes are violent whirlwinds, funnel-shaped clouds that may spiral down from thunderstorms. They are extremely dangerous.

Suddenly a tornado was sighted **heading for** Paris, Texas. Sirens blew. A tornado warning was broadcast. Families rushed for the nearest bathroom, closet, or basement shelter.

The tornado hit with **the roar of** a freight train. Houses and churches were torn apart. Trees **shattered**. Cars were tossed around. The funnel cloud stayed down for twenty minutes, ripping a path through the city two blocks wide and five miles long.

---

heading for moving toward
the roar of a loud sound like
shattered broke apart completely

▼ **The tornado caused great damage in Paris, Texas.**

▲ **A funnel-shaped cloud moves toward a town.**

More than eighty tornadoes **touched down** that afternoon and night in Texas, Oklahoma, Arkansas, Missouri, and other states as far east as Ohio.

_____

touched down hit the ground

Tornadoes, April 2–3, 1982

Iowa

Illinois

Indiana

Ohio

Kansas

Missouri

Kentucky

Tennessee

Arkansas

Oklahoma

Alabama

Georgia

Texas

Mississippi

Louisiana

Key:
■ tornado areas

Before You Move On

1. **Conclusion** How did people know that a tornado was coming?

2. **Graphic Aids** Name the states where the tornadoes happened.

Track The Storm

The Southeast and Midwest Thunderstorms, Rain, Hail, and Snow

When the front passed, the tornadoes stopped, but thunderstorms continued throughout the Southeast. Heavy rain drenched Alabama and Georgia. Hail the size of golf balls dented cars and broke windows in Kentucky.

For the next three days, the huge mass of Arctic air behind the cold front brought more snow and high winds to the Midwest. Driving became very dangerous. Five hundred travelers **were stranded** in Michigan and had to spend the night in school gyms. Rush-hour traffic in Chicago **was a tangle of accidents**.

---

were stranded had to stay

was a tangle of accidents moved slowly because there were many car crashes

▲ Hail the size of golf balls fell during the storm.

◀ People could not drive through the deep snow.

189

The great swirl of clouds around the low, or area with low air pressure, **was clearly visible** from space. As the swirl moved east, clear skies and **intense cold** followed it. **Low temperature records were set** from Idaho to the **Appalachians**. And still the storm was not through!

---

was clearly visible could easily be seen

intense cold very cold weather

Low temperature records were set Temperatures were colder than anyone had ever known

Appalachians mountain range near the East Coast

Before You Move On

1. **Details** Name three kinds of weather caused by the storm in the Southeast.

2. **Prediction** Where do you think the storm will go next? Why?

Tuesday, April 6, was opening day for the baseball season, and the New York Yankees were scheduled to play at home. The main storm center was now out at sea, but still the forecast was not good. Cold air continued to **pour in**, forming new lows over Pennsylvania and the New Jersey coast.

Around three in the morning, snow began to fall softly on New York City. Soon the wind picked up. By noon it was a howling blizzard. Traffic **snarled**. Trains were delayed. The pace of the great city slowed to a **sloppy** walk.

---

pour in move quickly into the area
snarled stopped or moved slowly
sloppy wet, messy

▼ **Life in New York City
slows to a walk.**

Over a foot of snow fell in New York before the storm moved on to Boston. It was the first blizzard ever to hit New York City in April. The Yankee game was delayed for four days. Many adults said bad things about the weather, but few kids **complained**. They all had a day off from school.

The big storm finally ended. Snow turned to slush and melted away. People cleaned up their towns. Spring returned. Birds began traveling north again, and the evenings **lost their chill**.

The storm is just a memory now, but every spring the cycle repeats itself. Warm air from the south meets with cold Arctic air, **triggering** storms of all sizes and giving the United States one of the most varied and exciting **climates** on Earth.

---

complained said they didn't like it
lost their chill got warmer
triggering causing
climates kinds of weather

▼ **Spring returned to New York City after the big storm.**

Before You Move On

1. **Sequence** What happened in New York City on April 6, 1982?

2. **Conclusion** Could a big storm like this happen again? Why or why not?

Meet the Author

Bruce Hiscock

AWARD WINNER

Bruce Hiscock worked as a scientist for many years after college. What he really wanted to do, though, was to write children's books. He taught himself how to paint and write. Now he uses his knowledge of science to write books.

"I have always loved storms," Mr. Hiscock says. "As a kid, I lived in Alaska. There, the wind can rip the doors off of cars, and snowdrifts can bury your house." Mr. Hiscock now lives in the woods of New York in a house he built himself.

Think and Respond

Strategy: Sequence

Make a time line. Show the order of events in "The Big Storm." Tell when, where, and what happened.

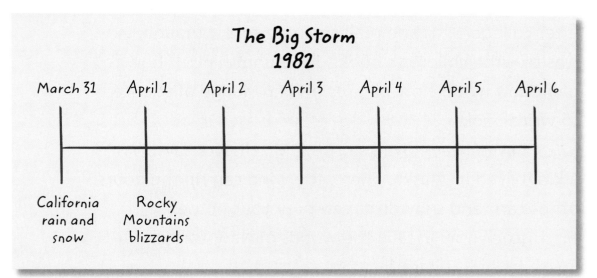

Summarize

Use your time line to summarize what happened during "The Big Storm." Include only the most important details about the storm, and keep your summary short. Tell your summary to a partner. Are your summaries alike? How?

Talk It Over

 Personal Response What day of the storm is the most exciting to you? Explain.

 Comparison How was the storm in California different from the storm in Texas? How was it the same?

3 **Conclusion** Why are some parts of the United States not talked about in the story?

4 **Opinion** Do you think forecasters have important jobs? Why or why not?

Compare Genres

Compare what you learned about storms in "Twister" with what you learned in "The Big Storm."

In "Twister," I learned how scary a tornado is. In "The Big Storm," I learned what causes tornadoes.

Content Connections

LISTENING/
SPEAKING

Give a Weather Forecast

small group

1. Watch a television weather forecast or find a forecast in a newspaper.

2. With a group, make a map that shows what kind of weather you will have tomorrow.

3. Tell your class about tomorrow's weather.

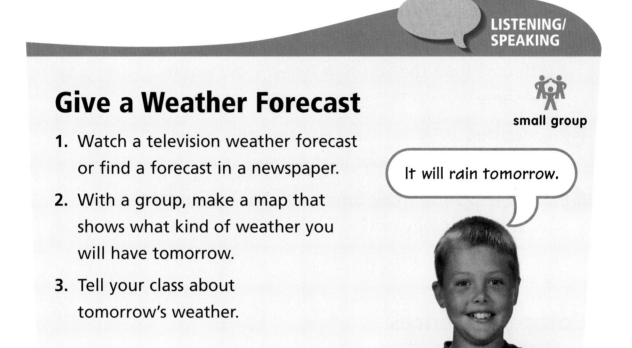

It will rain tomorrow.

2×5   MATH

Make a Storm Graph

large group

What is the storm most people have seen? Ask five people outside your class. Add your numbers to a class graph. Study the graph. Which kind of storm have the most people seen?

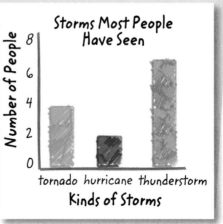

Storms Most People Have Seen

Number of People

Kinds of Storms
tornado hurricane thunderstorm

SCIENCE

Research Climates

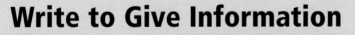

Internet

small group

Study one area of the U.S. Use books and the Internet to find out what the climate is like there. Tell the class about it.

The Arizona Desert Region
I. Landforms
  A. Plateaus and canyons
  B. Mountain ranges
  C. Desert basins
II. Temperature extremes
  A. High temperatures
    1.
    2.
  B. Low temperatures

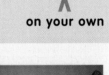

WRITING

Write to Give Information

on your own

Find information about a vacation place. Record what the weather is like there. Choose the best form to give information:

- a report
- instructions for what to pack for a visit
- a review

Be sure your writing is organized well.

A Week in Buenos Aires

Buenos Aires had sunny, beautiful blue skies last week. Temperatures were between 65°F and 85°F.

197

Subject-Verb Agreement

Listen and sing.

Song 🔘

My friend Wanda Jane
Likes to walk in the rain.
She is never upset
Even though she gets wet.

Her friends are inside.
How they moan and complain.
But not Wanda Jane
Because she loves the rain.

—*Jane Zion Brauer*

Tune: "Five Hungry Mice"

How Language Works

The **verb** always goes with the **subject** of the sentence.

Action Verb	Is, Are
■ Some action verbs tell what one other person does. Use -**s** at the end of these verbs.	■ Use **is** for one other person. Use **are** for more than one other person.
Examples: Mai see**s** her brother in the rain. She run**s** outside.	**Examples:** He **is** with his friends. They **are** wet.

Practice with a Partner

Choose the correct verb. Then say the sentence.

hold / holds	**1.** Mai _____ a big umbrella.
bring / brings	**2.** She _____ a jacket for her brother.
is / are	**3.** Sometimes he _____ so silly!
is / are	**4.** The two kids _____ happy to see Mai.
put / puts	**5.** She _____ the umbrella over them.

Put It in Writing

Pretend that it's a stormy day. Draw a picture. Write a sentence to tell what someone does. When you edit your work, make sure each verb goes with its subject.

Sonia hides under the chair. She is scared.

Show What You Know

Talk About the Weather

In this unit, you read a story and a news article about weather. Look back at this unit. Tell your group an interesting fact and why it is interesting.

Make a Mind Map

Work with a partner. Make a chart to show what you learned about different kinds of weather.

	Looks Like	Sounds Like	Feels Like
Tornado	tall clouds funnel-shaped clouds	loud	warm very windy
Blizzard			
Thunderstorm			
Hailstorm			

Think and Write

What is the most important thing you learned about staying safe in a storm? Add this writing to your portfolio. Also add other work that shows what you learned about weather.

Read and Learn More

Leveled Books

**A Year
Without Rain**
by Evelyn Stone

Weather Words
by Gail Gibbons

Theme Library

**Sergio and the
Hurricane**
by Alexandra Wallner

**The Best Book
of Weather**
by Simon Adams

Internet

Go to: www.hbavenues.com

Wild Weather Facts

Make A Weather Station

U.S. Weather

Watery World

Hide a Fish

1. Draw a fish and cut it out.
2. Choose a place in your classroom.
3. Color the fish so it can "hide" in that place.
   Can your classmates find it?

What Animals Need to Survive

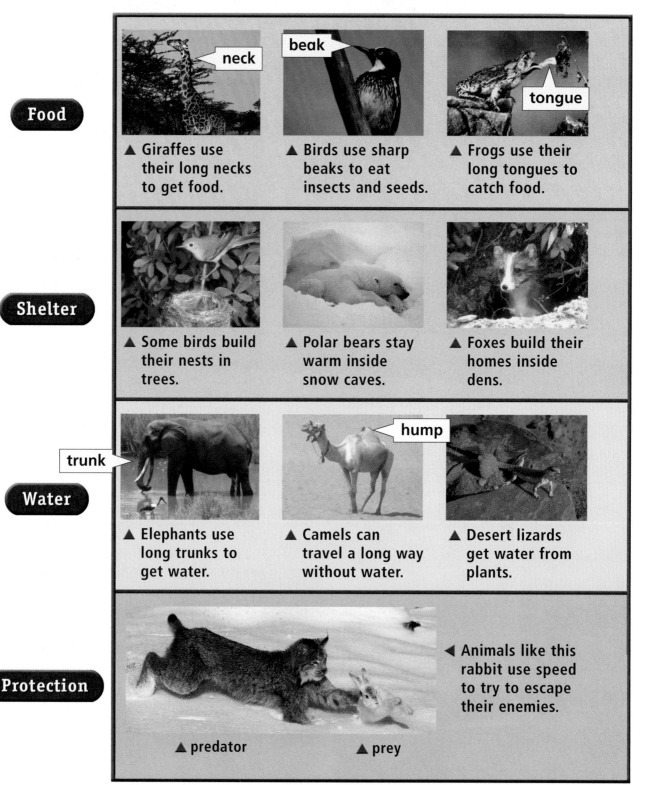

Food

neck
beak
tongue

▲ Giraffes use their long necks to get food.

▲ Birds use sharp beaks to eat insects and seeds.

▲ Frogs use their long tongues to catch food.

Shelter

▲ Some birds build their nests in trees.

▲ Polar bears stay warm inside snow caves.

▲ Foxes build their homes inside dens.

Water

trunk
hump

▲ Elephants use long trunks to get water.

▲ Camels can travel a long way without water.

▲ Desert lizards get water from plants.

Protection

◄ Animals like this rabbit use speed to try to escape their enemies.

▲ predator   ▲ prey

How Animals Adapt

All animals have special features to help them survive.

tail to help make quick turns

lean body to run fast

long, strong legs

claws to catch prey

sharp teeth to tear apart meat

▲ The cheetah uses many adaptations to hunt prey.

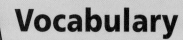

Vocabulary

From the Beach

Les writes postcards to his friend.

Dear Terry,

I **promised** to write, so I am!
My family and I are staying at a little house on an empty beach. Only a few people know about this house. It feels so **mysterious** to stay in a **secret** place.

I'll write again when something interesting happens!

Your friend,
Les

Terry Sanchez
356 Green Street
Small Town, CA
90000

Key Words

- promise
- mysterious
- secret
- boldness
- discover
- backward
- capture
- curious

Dear Terry,

My **boldness** almost got me in trouble today! I **discovered** something on the beach. It can move fast in two directions: forward and **backward**. I tried to **capture** it, but it tried to pinch me!

Are you **curious** about what it was? It was a crab!

Your pal,
Les

Terry Sanchez
356 Green Street
Small Town, CA
90000

The Secret Footprints

by Julia Alvarez
illustrated by Fabian Negrin

Read a Legend

Genre

A **legend** is a story that has been told for many years. Legends often tell about events that could not happen in real life. This one tells about a special tribe that lives underwater.

Characters

Guapa, a ciguapa

a human boy

Setting

This legend happens on an island in the Dominican Republic.

Dominican Republic

▲ island

💿 Selection Reading

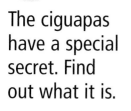

1 The ciguapas have a special secret. Find out what it is.

On an island not too far away and in a time not so long ago lived a **secret** tribe called the ciguapas. They made their homes underwater in cool, blue **caves hung with** seashells and seaweed. They came out on land to hunt for food only at night because they were so fearful of humans. Some ciguapas said they would rather die than be **discovered**.

Luckily, the ciguapas had a special secret that kept them safe from people. Their feet were on **backward**! When they walked on land, they left footprints going **in the opposite direction**.

That is how the ciguapas had **kept their whereabouts unknown** for so long. But once, their secret was almost discovered.

---

caves hung with homes decorated with
Luckily Happily
in the opposite direction the wrong way
kept their whereabouts unknown kept people from knowing where they lived

In the tribe lived a young ciguapa who was very beautiful. She had bright eyes and golden skin and black hair that **flowed** all the way down her back. Unlike the other ciguapas, she was not fearful of humans. That is why her name was Guapa, which means **brave and bold**, and also beautiful, in Spanish.

Sometimes Guapa **set out** hunting at night before it was really dark enough.

---

flowed fell, hung
brave and bold not afraid and not shy
set out went

One night, she **wandered** too close to a house where the family was still awake. When she saw their laundry hung out to dry, Guapa tried their clothes on. "This one fits me!" she cried out in a loud voice, and lights came on in the dark house.

A boy opened the window. "*¡Hola!*" he called in a friendly way.

Guapa was **curious** about him. "What is it like to be a human child?" she **wondered**. But she hurried away.

---

wandered walked
¡Hola! Hello! (in Spanish)
wondered thought

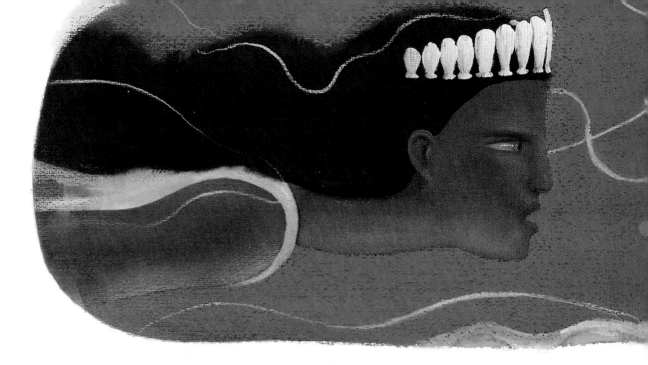

The tribe worried that Guapa's **boldness** might **reveal their secret**. They asked the queen to speak to her.

"Stop **being such a mischief**!" the queen ciguapa **scolded her**.

"But I'm bold and brave and curious about everything," Guapa said, defending herself. "That's why you named me Guapa, remember?"

"You must protect our secret," the queen said **sternly**.

"But why?" Guapa asked.

No ciguapa had ever dared ask the queen <u>that</u> question before.

The queen said, "If people find out where we live, they will **capture** us because we are so beautiful. Doctors will want to put us in cages and study us. We will **be forced to** live on land."

---

reveal their secret let people know about them
being such a mischief acting so badly
scolded her told her in anger
sternly very seriously
be forced to have to

Guapa's mouth fell open. "*¡Ay, no!* I love living underwater, with fish **tickling** my neck and **currents flowing** through my hair so I never have to comb it. I don't want to live on land. I just like to visit!"

"Then you must stop **taking chances**," the queen warned. "Humans are **unkind**. They will force you to take baths and do laundry and wash your hands before meals."

That's when Guapa **promised** with all her heart that she would be very, very careful.

¡Ay, no! Oh, no! (in Spanish)
tickling softly touching
currents flowing water moving
taking chances going to places where humans can see you
unkind not nice

Before You Move On
1. **Character** Who is Guapa? What is she like?
2. **Plot** Why is the queen angry with Guapa?

2

Guapa wants to keep her promise to the queen. Do you think she will?

Guapa did work hard to keep her promise. She stayed underwater until it was dark, which was not always exciting. She followed behind everyone else in their food hunts, which was **certainly frustrating**. When she passed the clothesline at the boy's house, Guapa did not try the clothes on, which was no fun. She walked on **tiptoes**, which was not that easy for a ciguapa.

---

certainly frustrating very upsetting
tiptoes the ends of her toes

One afternoon, Guapa forgot her promise. She was looking up through the water at the sun **sparkling like a thousand starfish** in the sky. She came up to the surface to take a closer look. It was that time of day when the island is most beautiful. The air seemed splashed with gold. Birds with feathers the colors of rainbows were practicing their favorite songs. Palm trees were **swaying**, as if they were listening to a **catchy tune in the breeze**. From the woods came the sweet smell of flowers.

"Maybe the boy is out playing," she almost said out loud.

Guapa could not help herself. She climbed out of the water and started walking in the woods.

---

sparkling like a thousand starfish shining like many bright star-shaped fish

swaying moving slowly back and forth

catchy tune in the breeze good song in the wind

She **came upon** the family having a picnic under a shade tree by the river: the mother, the father, the boy, and his two little sisters.

Guapa hid behind some bushes and watched them eating fried ***pastelitos*** and mangoes on a large piece of cloth laid out on the grass. The sight made her hungry, so hungry. She had not eaten anything since the night before.

Soon the family **got up for a walk**. Guapa ran from her hiding place and **snatched** a snack from the leftovers in the basket.

---

came upon saw

pastelitos small cakes filled with fruit (in Spanish)

got up for a walk went walking

snatched quickly took

The sound of the breeze **stirring** the leaves **startled** her. She turned to **run off**, but she was not used to running on cloth. She came down with a loud thump!

Hearing the noise, the family turned around. "Are you all right?" they asked as they ran to her side.

For once in her life, Guapa could not **get a word out**. The secret of the ciguapas was going to be discovered! They would have to leave their cool, blue caves at the bottom of the river and live on dry land forever. Doctors would put them in cages and stare at them. All because Guapa could not **contain** her curiosity.

---

stirring blowing
startled scared
run off run away
get a word out speak
contain stop, control

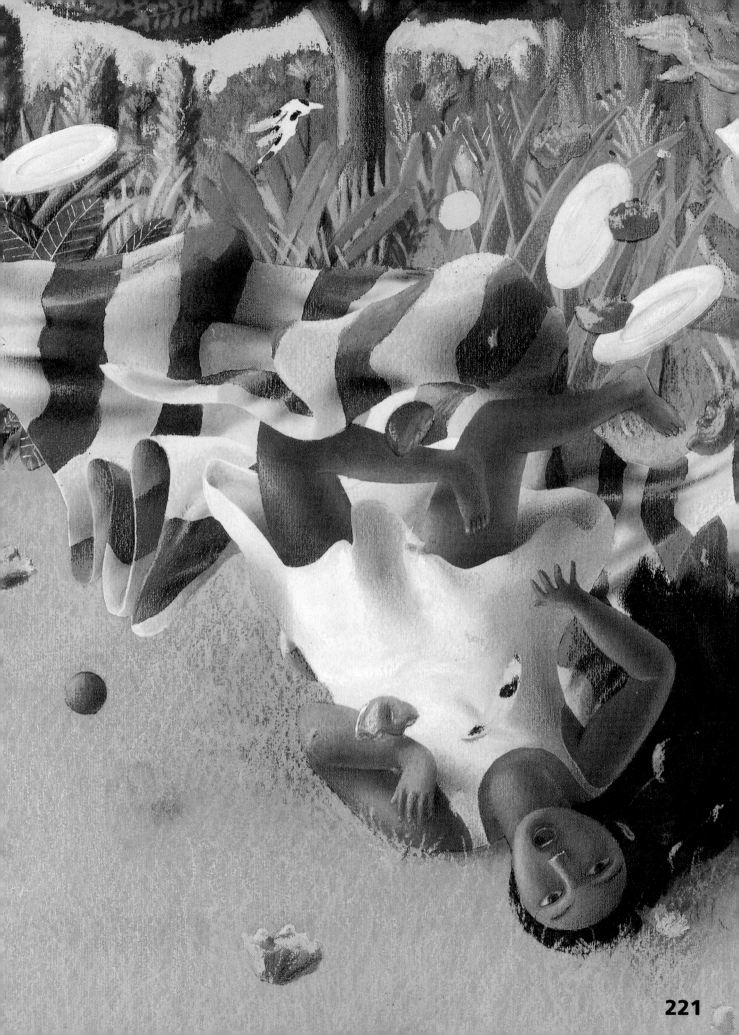

"*¡Ay, ay, ay!*" she cried at the thought of such
a disaster.

"She's really hurt," the boy said. "She can't walk."

"I'm afraid you're right, **mi'jo**," the father said,
unwinding the cloth from around Guapa's feet. "She's
twisted both her ankles badly."

"Does it hurt?" one of the two little girls asked. The
other little girl was too little to think up her own question,
so she also asked, "Does it hurt a lot?"

Guapa nodded. She would pretend that her ankles were
twisted. No matter what, she would keep the secret of the
ciguapas safe.

¡Ay, ay, ay! Oh, no! (in Spanish)
mi'jo my son (in Spanish)
twisted bent, hurt

Then she heard the **dreaded words**. "We'd better take her to the doctor," said the mother. "He'll want to **examine her**."

"¡Ay, ay, ay!" Guapa cried when they tried to pick her up.

"We should not move her," the father said. "We should get the doctor and bring him here."

"We can't leave her alone," the mother said. By now it was dark in the **grove** beside the river.

"I'll stay with her," the boy said, **puffing** his chest out proudly.

---

dreaded words words she did not want to hear
examine her look at her to see what's wrong
grove group of trees
puffing pushing

Before You Move On

1. **Inference** Why does Guapa forget her promise?
2. **Plot** What happens to Guapa?
3. **Motive** Why does Guapa pretend she is hurt?

223

3

Find out if the humans discover the ciguapas' secret.

The mother took the two little girls home to bed while the father went for the doctor. "**Buenas noches**," said the bigger little girl as they left. "Buenas noches," sang the littler little girl.

Guapa could hear **whisperings, hoots, and soft whistles**. She knew her tribe of ciguapas was all around, hiding in the woods. The tribe was waiting to see what would happen and was frightened that its secret had been given away.

Buenas noches Good night (in Spanish)

whisperings, hoots, and soft whistles soft, low voices and noises

The young boy was thoughtful. He **stood guard beside** Guapa. He offered her another *pastelito* from the basket, and she **gobbled it right up**. "Have more," he **urged**.

He put soft leaves under her head so she would be comfortable.

"How nice of him," Guapa thought, smiling to herself.

"Is there anything else I can get you?" the boy asked her.

This was the chance she had been waiting for. "I could use some water," Guapa said. She was telling the truth. She needed something to **wash down** the *pastelitos* that had gotten her into all this trouble.

---

stood guard beside stayed near
gobbled it right up ate it quickly
urged begged
wash down help her swallow

"I'll bring you a coconut shell of water from the river," the boy said. "Will you be all right by yourself?"

Guapa could not believe her good luck. "Oh, yes," she said. "**Sí, sí, sí**." Around the grove a breeze ran through the trees. All the little leaves seemed to be whispering, "*Sí, sí, sí*."

Sí, sí, sí Yes, yes, yes (in Spanish)

The minute the boy was out of sight, the ciguapas
rushed out to carry Guapa away. "*Sh, sh, sh,*" the ciguapas
said when Guapa tried to explain that she could walk on
her own. She **scooped up** some *pastelitos* to show her
ciguapa friends how kind the human boy had been. Then
she left a seashell as a **thank-you in their place**.

When the boy came back, the beautiful young girl was
gone. The strangest thing was that all the footprints in the
sand led back to the picnic spot. "These must be my
family's **tracks**," he said, scratching his head.

---

scooped up picked up

thank-you in their place gift for the
family where the *pastelitos* used to be

tracks footprints

When the tribe returned with Guapa and her **delicious**
snacks, the queen ciguapa did not know what to say.
"I suppose some human beings can be kind," she **admitted**.

Guapa would have answered, but her mouth was full.

Now, when the tribe wanders near the family's house,
Guapa is allowed to go right up to the windows and **peek in**.

Sometimes the boy goes walking in the woods, looking
for Guapa. He carries his seashell in his pocket to remind
him of his **mysterious** friend.

---

delicious tasty
admitted said
peek in look inside

Guapa has asked the ciguapas not to take any eggs from this family. When the laundry is left out, Guapa helps fold the clothes on the line for the kind boy and his two little sisters.

She always finds *pastelitos* waiting in the boy's pockets.

Before You Move On

1. **Details** Why can't the boy use the footprints to find Guapa?

2. **Conclusion** How do the tribe's feelings about humans change? Explain.

Meet the Author
Julia Alvarez

Julia Alvarez was born among storytellers in the Dominican Republic. She loved to listen to their tales about life near the ocean. "I first heard about the ciguapas when I was a little girl," Ms. Alvarez says. "My mother and aunts told me all about these beautiful creatures who live in caves."

Julia didn't read much, though, until her family came to the United States. "I found in books a place to go," she says. Books helped her learn the language of her new home, too. By the end of high school, Ms. Alvarez knew she wanted to be a writer. She has been writing ever since.

Think and Respond

Strategy: Analyze Character Motives

You can understand characters better if you think about their motives, or why they do things. Look for:

✔ what the character does
✔ what the character thinks or feels.

	Guapa's Actions	Guapa's Motives
Actions are what the character does.	*The Secret Footprints*	**Motives** are why the character does things.
pages 210-212	1. Guapa goes out before it is dark.	She is bold.
page 213	2. Guapa goes too close to the house.	
pages 214-215	3.	
pages 216-217	4.	
pages 218-219	5.	

Make a chart for "The Secret Footprints."

Retell the Story

Use the chart to retell the story with a partner. One person tells what Guapa does. The other person tells why she does it. Do you and your partner agree? Talk about it.

Talk It Over

1 **Personal Response** Do you like, or admire, Guapa? Tell why or why not.

2 **Judgment** Was it right for Guapa to break her promise? Tell why or why not.

3 **Character Traits** Guapa is bold, brave, and curious. Are those traits helpful or harmful? Explain.

4 **Comparison** What other legends have you heard or read? How are they like "The Secret Footprints"?

Compare Characters

Compare Guapa from "The Secret Footprints" with Rigo from "If the Shoe Fits."

Content Connections

Research Legends

small group

Find a legend about a water creature in a book or on the Internet. Put the name and a picture of the creature on a card. Put the card on a map to show where people first told the legend. Describe the creature to your group.

Scotland's Loch Ness Monster

Design an Adaptation

partners

Backward feet helped the ciguapas hide. With a partner, design a new creature with a special feature. Explain how the feature helps the creature.

Be a News Reporter

The ciguapas are discovered by humans! Talk with your group about what happens to them. Do doctors put them in cages? Do they have to live on land? Pretend you are a news reporter. Tell the class what happens to the ciguapas.

Our top story tonight: a secret tribe of sea creatures was found!

Write a Letter

Pretend you and a partner are Guapa and the boy. Write a letter to your partner. Describe the place you live and the people you live with. Read your partner's letter. Ask your partner for more details.

Dear Boy,
    My name is Guapa. I live under the water in a beautiful, blue cave. My cave is by a small island. There are many seashells around the cave.

Read Long Words

Some long words have a root word and a suffix. A **suffix** is a word part that is added to the end of a word. When you read a long word:

✔ Find word parts you know.
✔ Use the meaning of the word part to help you figure out what the whole word means.

Try the strategy.

Suffix	Example	Meanings
-able	washable comfortable	can be washed can have comfort
-ful	thankful	full of thanks; with a lot of thanks
-less	fearless	without fear

from The Secret Footprints

The young boy was thoughtful. He stood guard beside Guapa. He offered her another *pastelito* from the basket, and she gobbled it right up. "Have more," he urged.

He put soft leaves under her head so she would be comfortable.

> I know what *comfort* means. I also know that -*able* means "can have." I can figure out that *comfortable* means "can have comfort."

Practice

Take this test and **read long words**.

Read each item. Choose the best answer.

1 Read this sentence: "The ciguapas were <u>fearful</u> of humans." What does the word <u>fearful</u> mean?

A brave

B not afraid

C full of fear

D without fear

✔ **Test Strategy**

Skip an item if you're not sure of the answer. Come back to it later. Make your best guess.

2 Read this sentence: "Guapa was <u>thoughtless</u> and let the humans catch her." The word <u>thoughtless</u> means —

A without care

B thinking a lot

C with great thought

D with very little thought

3 Read this sentence: "Guapa promised that she would be very, very <u>careful</u>." If Guapa is <u>careful</u>, she —

A acts with a lot of care

B acts as if she cares again

C acts as if she doesn't care

D acts like a person who has no cares

Vocabulary

Song

OCEAN CREATURES

Many **creatures** in the ocean

Have a lot of common sense.

Camouflage can help them **blend** in.

Hiding is a great **defense**!

Deadly predators cannot find them.

They find **safety**. Never fear.

When in **shelter** or in the open,

Clever creatures DISAPPEAR!

—Joyce McGreevy

backbone

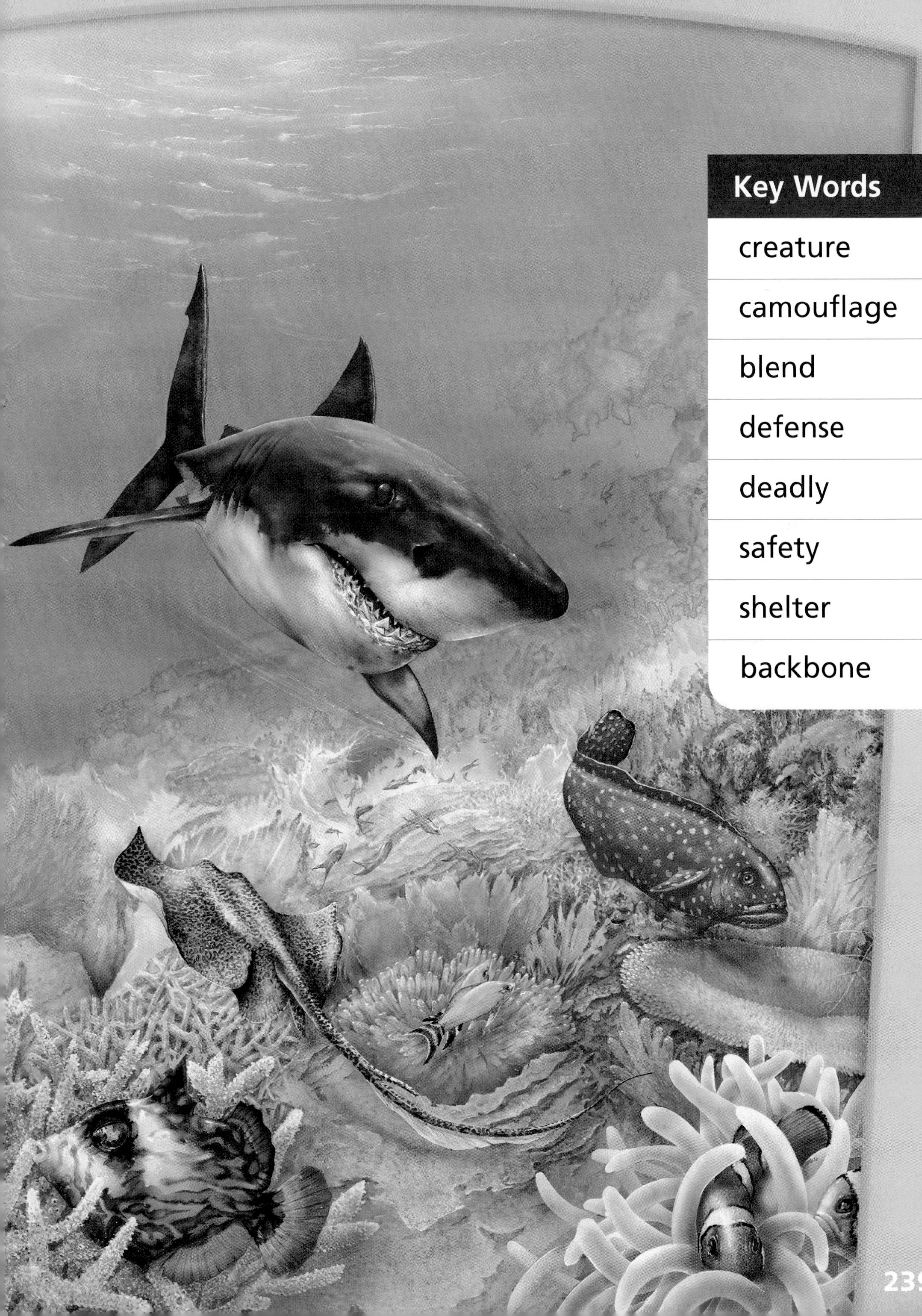

Key Words

- creature
- camouflage
- blend
- defense
- deadly
- safety
- shelter
- backbone

Read a Photo-Essay

A **photo-essay** is nonfiction. It uses a lot of photographs to tell about a topic.

✔ Look at the **photographs** to see what things are like.

✔ Read the **captions** to find out more facts about the topic.

photograph

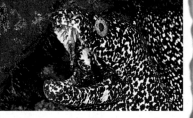

caption

▲ A moray eel's long, sharp teeth help it hold on to its slippery meals.

Selection Reading

Hello, Fish!

by Sylvia A. Earle

with photographs by Wolcott Henry

Set Your Purpose

Find out how fish in coral reefs protect themselves from danger.

The Coral Reef

Of all the kinds of **creatures** that have **backbones** (people, frogs, snakes, and birds to name a few), fish are the most numerous. They have gills to help them breathe, scales to **protect** their skin, and fins for swimming through the waters of the world.

---

protect take care of

Queen Angelfish

fin

scales

gill

coral

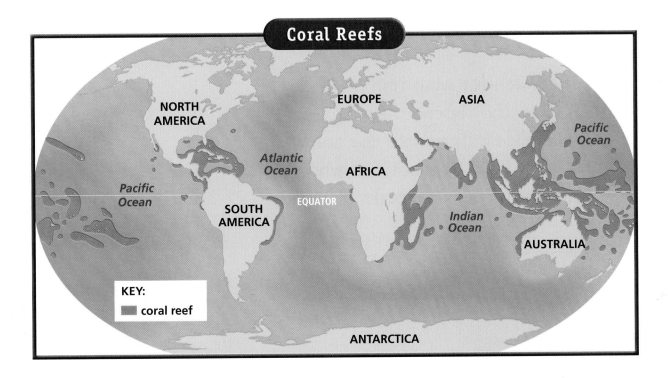

All of the fish on these pages live in and around coral reefs. These rock-like structures take thousands of years to form. They are made up of billions of **skeletons** from tiny animals called corals. These reefs, shown in orange on the map, **flourish in shallow areas of** warm ocean waters. You will discover that reef fish come in a variety of shapes, colors, and sizes. Each has its own special place in the wondrous world of the coral reef.

---

skeletons old bones
flourish in shallow areas of grow well in places that are not very deep in

Before You Move On

1. **Details** How are fish like people, frogs, snakes, and birds?

2. **Graphic Aids** Look at the map. Name the oceans that have coral reefs.

If you wonder what fish do all day
And how they spend their nights,
Come **glide** with me into the sea.
We'll say hello to creatures who
Make their home in **a realm** of blue.

---

glide slide smoothly
a realm an area

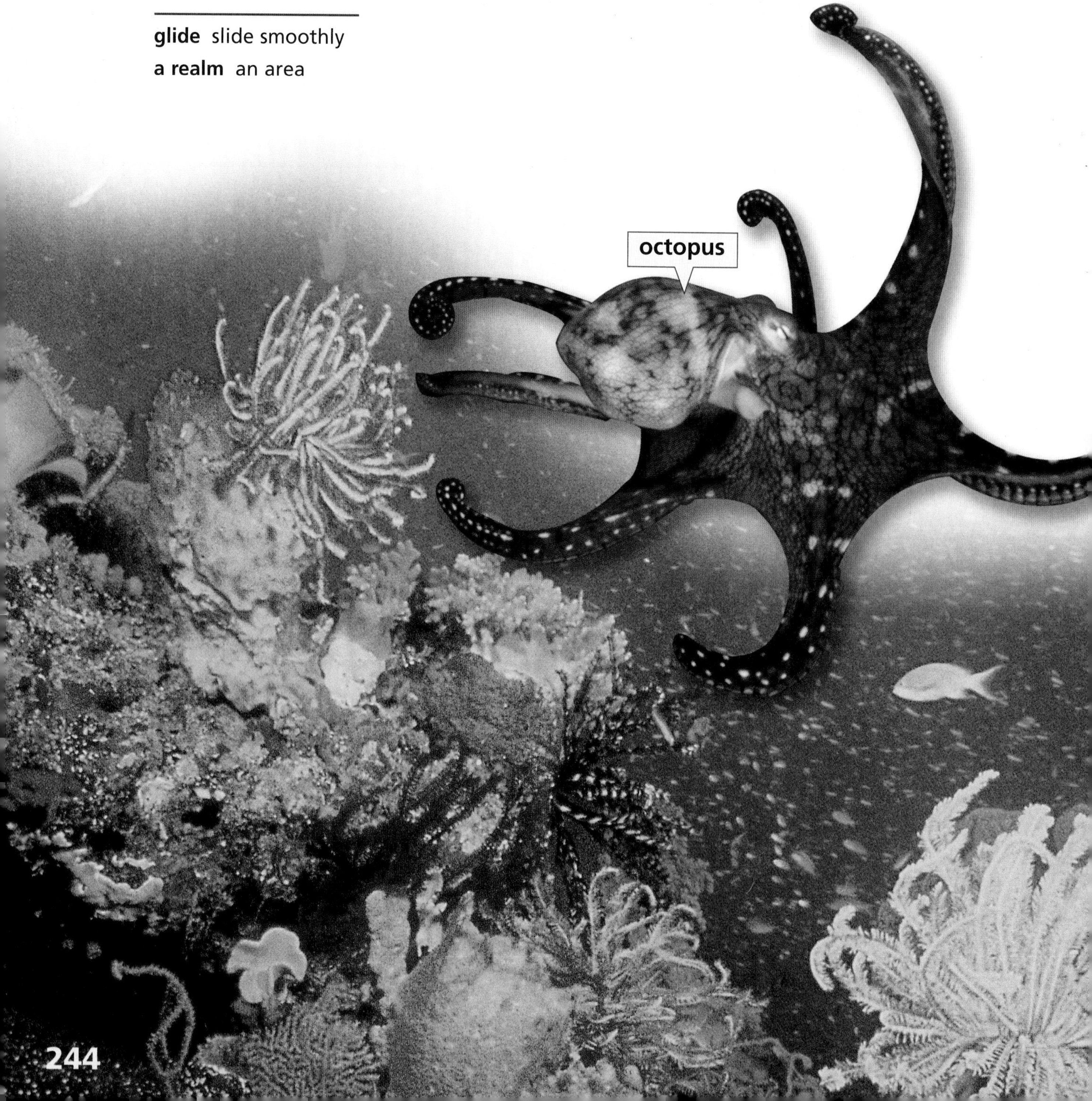

octopus

Spotted Moray

I often stop and play with morays.
I've even hugged a few!

Moray eels can be dangerous, though, if you happen to be a small fish or octopus. Watch out! You could become an eel meal!

People aren't on their menu, though. In fact, these gentle and curious fish remind me of kittens. It's easy to see why this one is called a spotted moray, a fine name for a totally freckled fish.

Moray Eel

▲ A moray eel's long, sharp teeth help it hold on to its slippery meals.

Before You Move On

1. **Paraphrase** What does "You could become an eel meal!" mean?

2. **Details** Describe the moray eel to a partner.

Damselfish

This jewel-like creature with
Blue-and-gold eyes is a damselfish.

It is one in a family of hundreds of creatures most commonly found in **tropical seas** around coral reefs. Most are no bigger than your hand, but inside that **sheath of sleek scales** is a very tough fish. When **provoked**, damselfish will chase away creatures many times their size, even me!

---

tropical seas warm ocean waters

sheath of sleek scales covering of smooth and shiny scales

provoked bothered

◄ A damselfish may bite larger fish to scare them away.

Clownfish

In an anemone's soft, slippery arms
A clownfish hides as large fish pass by.

It looks as though this fish might be in trouble among the **stinging tentacles of a sea anemone**. But no! This is a clownfish, one of dozens of kinds of small fish that actually makes its home and raises its family in places that are **deadly** to other creatures. Clownfish **coat** their fins and scales with a wonderful kind of **slimy goo** that keeps them from being stung.

---

stinging tentacles of a sea anemone parts of a sea anemone that are covered with poison

coat cover

slimy goo slippery, wet covering

a predator an enemy

Clownfish

tentacle

sea anemone

◄ **If a predator is nearby, the clownfish can hide in the tentacles of a sea anemone.**

Before You Move On

1. **Conclusion** Why does the author call the damselfish a jewel-like creature?

2. **Details** Name two ways a clownfish protects itself.

247

Rainbow Scorpionfish

Hovering still against the reef,
A scorpionfish hides.

You might think that a red fish would be easy to find in a blue ocean, but is it really? Against colorful sponges and corals, this scorpionfish **blends** right in so he is hard to see. His spiny fins are a good **defense**, but if you don't hurt him, he won't hurt you. His large, beautiful eyes help him find his way around in the sea. While I watch him, he watches me.

Hovering still Floating without moving

Rainbow Scorpionfish

spiny fins

It is hard to see a rainbow scorpionfish in all the bright colors of the coral reef.

sponge

Stargazer

Now you see it, now you don't.
Is it a pile of pebbles and sand, or a fish?

With **clever camouflage**, stargazers fool big fish that might want to eat them. They also trick the little fish they want to eat. When something tasty swims by, that big, toothy mouth quickly opens and **gulps down** a meal.

With eyes that always look up, it's easy to see why these fish are called stargazers. Since they live in the sea, maybe they should be called **starfish** gazers!

---

clever camouflage a smart way to hide

gulps down eats, swallows

starfish sea star

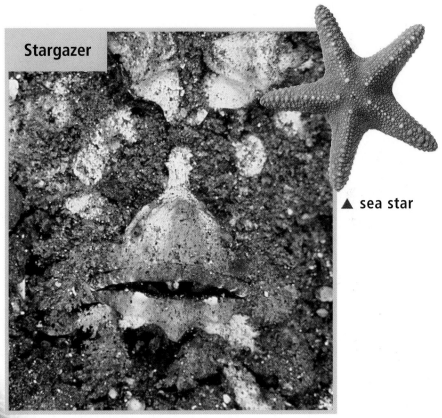

Stargazer

▲ sea star

▲ Sand is good camouflage for a stargazer.

Before You Move On

1. **Details** How did the stargazer get its name?
2. **Comparison** How are the rainbow scorpionfish and the stargazer alike?

Spotted Stingray

Graceful, gentle creatures, rays glide
Through the sea like giant butterflies.

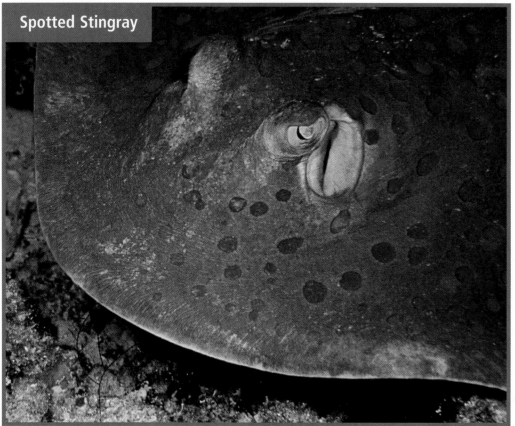

Spotted Stingray

▲ The blue spots and gray skin of the spotted stingray
blend in with the water and pebbles of the ocean floor.

▼ clam

Spotted stingrays pause now and then to **dine on**
clams, snails, and other small animals that live in soft
sand or mud on the **seafloor**. Many kinds of rays
and their toothy relatives, the sharks, live in the
oceans of the world. Millions of years ago rays and
sharks were swimming in the deep sea. They still are!

▲ snail

---

dine on eat
seafloor bottom of the ocean

Brown Goby

Look closely to find little gobies,
Like this one peeking out at you.

This brown goby may **venture out** a short distance from his **adopted home**, an empty worm tube. At the first hint of danger, he'll dive back into **shelter** for **safety**.

Like most gobies, this one **props** himself up on the small fins under his chin when he wants to look out at the world.

---

venture out travel

adopted home home that used to belong to another creature

props holds

▼ A brown goby stays safe near his home.

Brown Goby

worm tube

worm tube

Before You Move On

1. **Viewing** Tell how the stingray blends into its environment.
2. **Details** What does a brown goby do to see outside his worm tube?

251

Frogfish

With bulbous eyes and slippery skin,
This must be the well-named frogfish!

Actually, all frogs, fish, birds, mammals, turtles, lizards, and snakes have something in common. We all have backbones, called vertebrae, unlike most of the rest of life on Earth. Beetles don't, crabs don't, starfish don't, octopuses don't, nor do jellyfish, of course! Those who have backbones are frogs and fish and people everywhere, including you!

---

bulbous eyes large, round eyes that stick out of its head

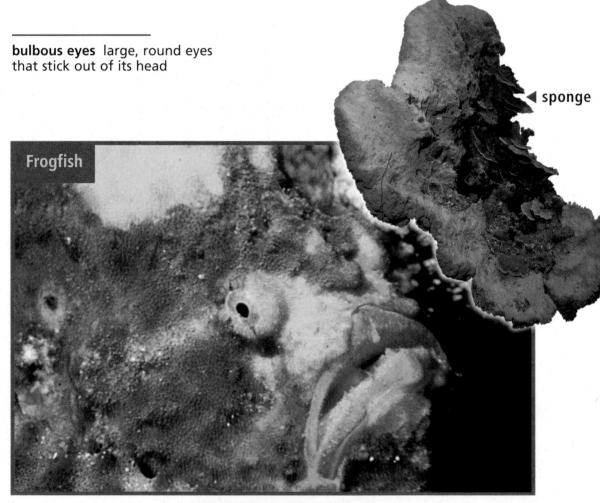

sponge ◀

Frogfish

▲ This frogfish sits very still and looks a lot like a sea sponge. Its predators find it hard to see.

Seahorse

This curvy fish, what could it be?
A seahorse, with room to **roam** the sea.

Seahorses are small fish with large eyes. **They have a big appetite for tiny crustaceans**. Like people, they choose partners for life. They usually stay together, even during stormy weather.

Seahorse mothers lay their eggs in special **pouches** that seahorse fathers have in their bellies. Weeks later, fully formed little fish swim out of the pouches into the sea. They are ready to grow up and find partners of their own.

---

roam move around in

They have a big appetite for tiny crustaceans They are always hungry for small animals like shrimp

pouches bags

Seahorse

shrimp

▲ A seahorse hangs onto a piece of coral with its special tail. A predator might think it's just a plant.

Before You Move On

1. **Details** Tell what the frogfish does to hide from predators.
2. **Details** Where do seahorse eggs live until they become fish?

Silvertip Shark

A silver swimmer in the reef, this shark
Is one of the **ancient ocean dwellers**.

If you could go back in time 300 million years, you would find
no whales, no dolphins, no seals, no elephants, no birds, or
trees or flowers or grass. There would be sharks in the sea,
however.

Many people are afraid of sharks, but of
the more than 350 kinds now
known, very few ever even
nibble on us. People kill
so many sharks,
though, that some
kinds may soon be
gone forever. Let's
take care so the sea
can always be home
to sharks.

ancient ocean dwellers animals that have
lived in the ocean for a long time
nibble on bite

▼ A silvertip shark's colors blend in with the water so it can sneak up on **prey**.

prey animals it wants to eat

Now that you've met
A few of my friends,
I hope you'll learn more
About the sea where they live.

Before You Move On

1. **Inference** How long have sharks been living in the sea?

2. **Opinion** Is it important to take care of the sea? Why or why not?

Meet the Author

Sylvia Earle

When **Sylvia Earle** was three years old, an ocean wave knocked her over. "I have loved the sea ever since!" she says. She has spent more than 6,000 hours diving deep to explore the oceans of the world. "The strange and wonderful forms of life, like the ones in *Hello, Fish!*, can only be found under water," she says.

Dr. Earle has written more than 125 books and articles. She talks to thousands of people every year about how people can help keep the ocean healthy.

Think and Respond

Strategy: Main Idea and Details

Make a cluster to show the main idea and supporting details in "Hello, Fish!"

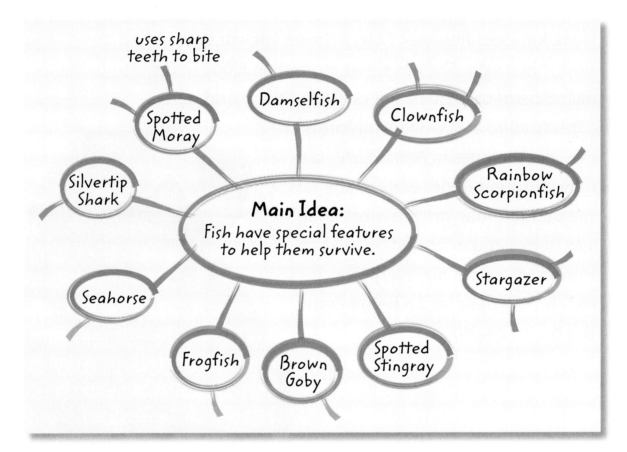

Summarize

Summarize what you learned about the stargazer and the spotted moray. Use the main idea as your first sentence. Then give supporting details to tell about each fish.

Talk It Over

 Personal Response Which fish would you like to learn more about? What would you like to know?

 Generalization What are three things all the fish in this essay have in common?

3 Opinion Which fish do you think has the best protection? Explain.

4 Author's Style Why do you think the author uses poetry to tell about each fish?

Compare Nonfiction

Compare this photo-essay to another nonfiction article. How are they alike? How are they different?

"Hello, Fish!" tells about one fish at a time. "The Big Storm" is like a story. It has a sequence of events.

Content Connections

Play a Fishy Game

small group

With your group, choose one fish from the selection. The first person gives one clue, or detail, about the fish. The next person repeats that clue and adds one more. Keep going until someone guesses the fish's name.

I am a red fish. I am a red fish with spiny fins.

Make a Food Chain

partners

Make a food chain about your lunch.

1. Draw a picture of yourself.

2. Draw a picture of what you eat.

3. Draw a picture of where each food comes from. If it comes from an animal, show what the animal eats.

Food Chain

bread

cheese

potato

cow

wheat plant

grass

Give an Aquarium Tour

Internet

large group

Find the Web site of a public aquarium. Learn all you can about it. Then give your class a tour of the aquarium. Show and tell about what a visitor can see there.

Write to Inform

on your own

Many animals are vertebrates. Find out about one. Choose the best way to tell about it:

- a poem
- a paragraph
- a story

Remember to use adjectives in your writing.

The Giraffe
The giraffe is the tallest animal on Earth. Its enormous neck is sometimes longer than its legs. It has a butter yellow coat with dark brown patches.

Adjectives That Compare

Listen and sing.

Song

Goldfish

Pretty goldfish,
You're smaller than white fish,
Larger than striped fish.
But you're the most
Beautiful fish of all.

—Jane Zion Brauer

Tune: "Red Leaves, Gold Leaves"

How Language Works

Adjectives can help you make a comparison.

	small smaller smallest
-er, -est	▪ Add **-er** to the adjective to compare two things. Example: The green fish is **smaller** than the red fish. ▪ Add **-est** to compare three or more things. Example: The blue fish is the **smallest** of all.
more, most, less, least	▪ If the adjective is a long word, use **more** or **most**. Examples: This fish is **less dangerous** than the red fish. It is the **most colorful** of all, too.

Practice with a Partner

Choose the correct adjective. Then say the sentence.

1. The yellow fish is <u>brighter / brightest</u> than the green fish.

2. It is <u>more colorful / most colorful</u> than the striped fish.

3. It is the <u>more beautiful / most beautiful</u> fish I have.

4. This is the <u>cuter / cutest</u> fish in my tank.

5. It is the <u>less expensive / least expensive</u> fish of all.

Put It in Writing

Draw a fish tank. Write about some of the fish. Tell how they are different and alike. When you edit your work, check that your adjectives are correct.

The small fish is more colorful than the big one.

263

Show What You Know

Talk About Animal Adaptations

In this unit, you read a legend and a photo-essay about sea creatures. Look back at this unit. Find a picture of your favorite creature. Use the picture to tell your group how the animal survives.

Make a Mind Map

Work with a partner. Make a chart to show what you learned about how adaptations help animals survive.

Animal Adaptations

Food	Shelter	Water	Protection
sharp teeth			speed

Think and Write

What else would you like to learn about ocean creatures? Make a list of questions. Add this writing to your portfolio. Also add other work that shows what you learned about animal adaptations.

Read and Learn More

Leveled Books

Hide and Seek
by Evelyn Stone

Sharks
by Gail Gibbons

Theme Library

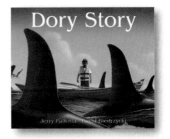

Dory Story
by Jerry Pallotta

Ocean Tide Pool
by Arthur L'Hommedieu

Internet

Go to: www.hbavenues.com

Fun Fish Facts

Shark Cam

Aquariums and Museums

Cultural Ties

Make a Quilt of Cultures

1. Make a square for a class quilt. Draw a picture or pattern that tells something about you, your family, or your culture.
2. Put the quilt together.
3. Tell about your square.

Some Reasons People Immigrate

▲ to escape war

▲ to find jobs

▲ to join families

The Bill of Rights

Amendment I
...stablishment of religion, or prohibiting the fre...
...ople peaceably to assemble, and to petition the ...

Amendment II
...e security of a free State, the right of the people...

Amendment III
...ed in any house, without the consent of the Ow...

Amendment IV
...persons, houses, papers, and effects, against u...
...probable cause, supported by Oath or affirmat...
...ed.

Amendment V
...all, or otherwise infamous crime, unless on a ...
...s, or in the Militia, when in actual service in t...
...ice put in jeopardy of life or limb; nor shall...
...liberty...

▲ to be free

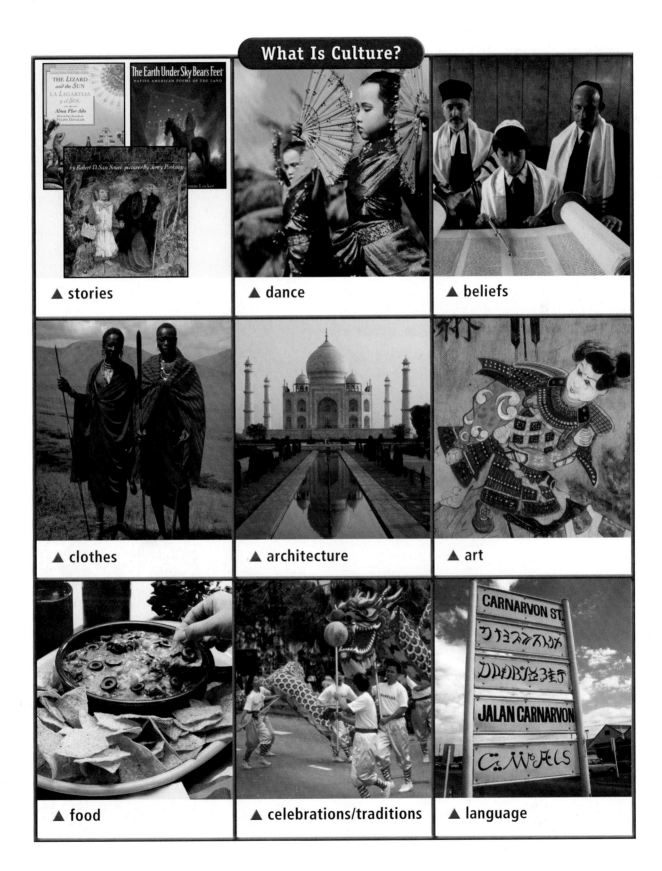

What Is Culture?

▲ stories

▲ dance

▲ beliefs

▲ clothes

▲ architecture

▲ art

▲ food

▲ celebrations/traditions

▲ language

The Lotus Seed

Vocabulary

A TRIP TO VIETNAM

My parents left Vietnam many years ago, but they never **forgot** it. Last year, my family took a **special** trip there.

When we **arrived**, we went to a museum. One picture showed an **emperor** who ruled the country for many years. He was sitting on a golden **throne**.

Key Words

forgot

special

arrive

emperor

throne

lotus

bloom

remember

The plants in Vietnam were beautiful! The pink and white **lotus** flowers were my favorites. I saw their **blooms** all over Vietnam. I will always **remember** their sweet smell.

The Lotus Seed

by Sherry Garland

illustrated by Tatsuro Kiuchi

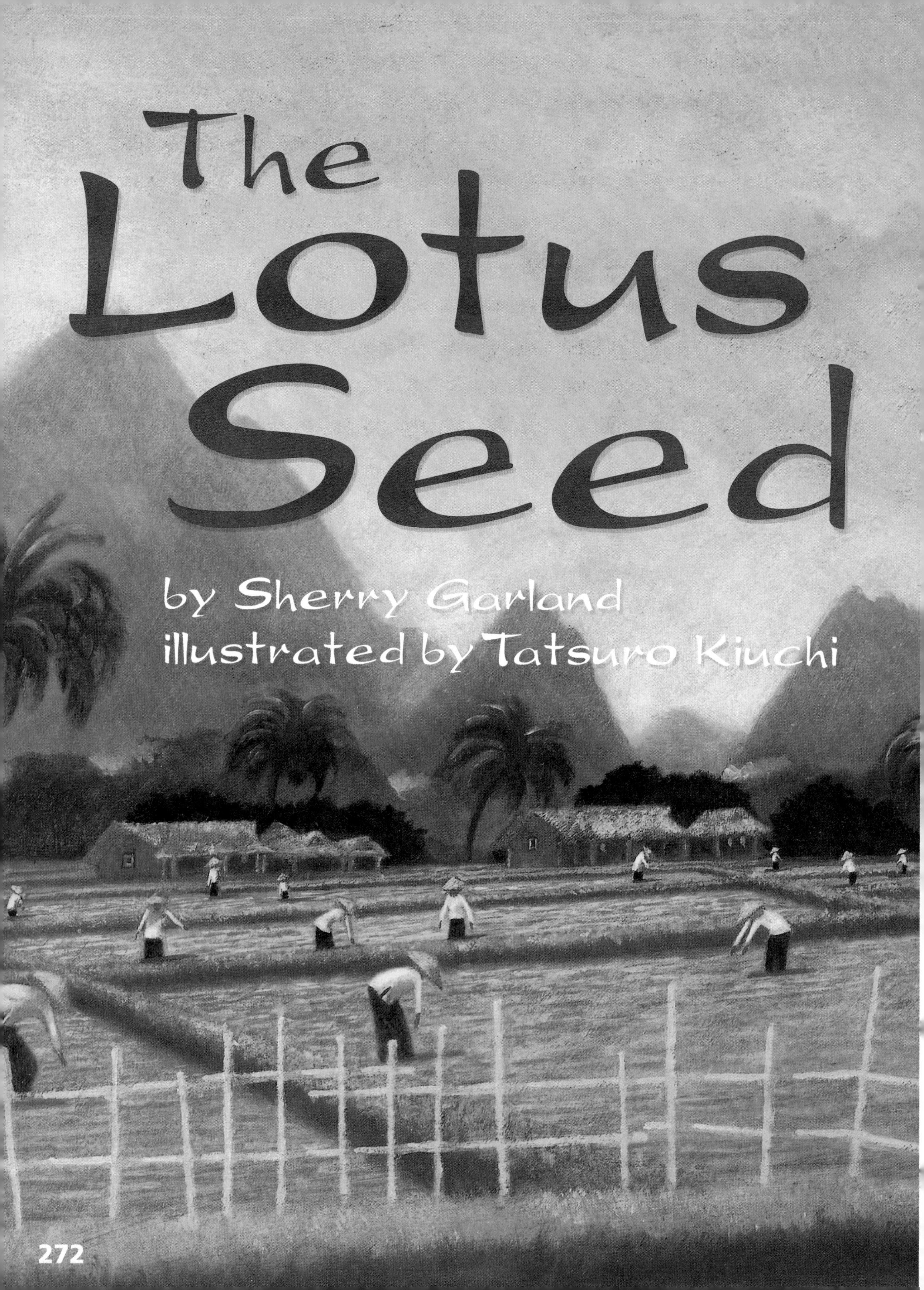

Read a Story

Genre

A **realistic fiction** story tells about events that could really happen. In this story, a young girl tells why a lotus seed is so important to her grandmother.

Characters

Bà, the grandmother

Bà's granddaughter

Bà's grandson

Setting

This story begins in Vietnam. It ends in the United States.

U.S.   Vietnam

Selection Reading

1

Bà has to leave her country. Find out what she takes with her.

My grandmother Bà saw the **emperor** cry the day he lost his golden dragon **throne**.

She wanted something to **remember** him by. She **sneaked** down to the silent palace, near the River of Perfumes. She plucked a seed from a **lotus** pod that rattled in the **Imperial garden**.

▲ lotus pod

---

sneaked went quietly
Imperial garden garden of the emperor

274

She hid the seed in a **special** place under **the family altar**, wrapped in a piece of silk from the *ao dai* she wore that day. Whenever she felt sad or lonely, she took out the seed and thought of the brave young emperor.

When she married a young man chosen by her parents, she carried the seed inside her pocket for good luck, long life, and many children. When her husband marched off to war, she **raised** her children alone.

---

the family altar a table that had important meaning for the family

ao dai dress (in Vietnamese)

raised took care of

One day bombs fell all around, and soldiers **clamored door to door**. She took the time to grab the seed, but left her **mother-of-pearl hair combs** lying on the floor.

One terrible day her family scrambled into a crowded boat and set out on a stormy sea. Bà watched the mountains and the **waving palms** slowly fade away. She held the seed in her shaking fingers and silently said good-bye.

---

clamored door to door went noisily from house to house

mother-of-pearl hair combs valuable hair clips

waving palms gently moving trees

276

She **arrived** in a strange new land. There were blinking lights, speeding cars, and **towering buildings that scraped the sky**. People spoke a language she didn't understand.

She worked many years, day and night. Her children, her sisters, and her cousins worked hard, too. They all lived together in one big house.

---

towering buildings that scraped the sky very tall buildings

Before You Move On

1. **Cause/Effect** Why does Bà take a lotus seed from the Imperial garden?

2. **Conclusion** Why does Bà leave the hair combs behind?

277

2

Bà's grandson takes the lotus seed. What do you think will happen now?

ast summer my little brother found the special seed and asked questions again and again. He'd never seen a lotus **bloom** or an emperor on a golden dragon throne.

So, one night he **stole** the seed from beneath the family altar. He planted it in a pool of mud somewhere near Bà's onion patch.

Bà cried and cried when she found out that the seed was gone. She didn't eat, and she didn't sleep. My silly brother **forgot what spot of earth held** the seed.

---

stole took

forgot what spot of earth held didn't remember where he planted

Then one day in spring, my grandmother shouted, and we all ran to the garden. There we saw a beautiful pink lotus **unfurling its petals**, so creamy and soft.

"It is the flower of life and hope," my grandmother said. "No matter how ugly the mud or how long the seed **lies dormant**, the bloom will be beautiful. It is the flower of my country."

When the lotus **blossom faded** and turned into a pod, Bà gave each of her grandchildren a seed to remember her by. She kept one for herself to remember the emperor by.

---

unfurling its petals opening its flower, blooming
lies dormant stays in the ground without growing
blossom faded flower lost its color

I wrapped my seed in a piece of silk and hid it in a secret place. Someday I will plant it and give the seeds to my own children. I will tell them about the day my grandmother saw the emperor cry.

Before You Move On

1. **Sequence** How does Bà find the lotus seed?

2. **Details** What does Bà do with the seeds from the lotus pod? Why?

Meet the Illustrator

Tatsuro Kiuchi

AWARD WINNER

The Lotus Seed was the first children's book **Tatsuro Kiuchi** ever illustrated. The book taught him about another country. "I have never been to Vietnam," he says. "Finding information for the paintings was hard. I used books of photographs to help me create the scenes from Vietnam's history."

Mr. Kiuchi lives in Japan. He loves working in his studio in Tokyo, creating beautiful illustrations for books and stories.

Think and Respond

Strategy: Sequence of Events

The order of events in a story is called the sequence of events. Look for sequence words like *then*, *last*, and *one day* to follow the events.

Make a sequence chain for "The Lotus Seed."

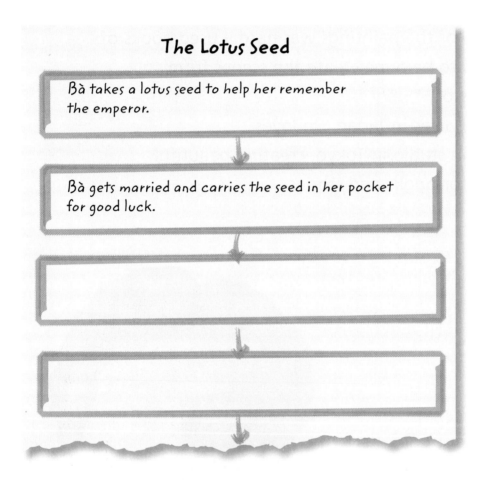

The Lotus Seed

Bà takes a lotus seed to help her remember the emperor.

Bà gets married and carries the seed in her pocket for good luck.

Retell the Story

Pretend you are Bà. Use your sequence chain to retell the story to a partner. Use sequence words to tell the order of the events.

Talk It Over

 Personal Response How did this story make you feel? Why?

 Inference Why do you think it was so important for Bà to have something to remember the emperor by?

3 **Cause/Effect** Name three changes in Bà's life. What caused each change?

4 **Conclusion** Bà gave each grandchild a lotus seed. Was the seed important to her granddaughter? Tell how you know.

Compare Illustrations

Look at the illustrations in "The Lotus Seed" and "Twister." How do the illustrations in each story make you feel?

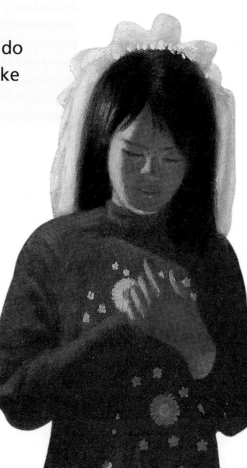

Content Connections

Role-Play the Future

partners

Pretend you are a grandparent and your partner is your grandchild. Give a special object to your grandchild. Tell why it is important to you. How does the grandchild feel about the gift? Perform the scene for the class.

> My great-grandmother brought me this ring from India.

Make a Family Time Line

on your own

Make a time line to show important events in your family's history. Describe each event. Add pictures. Use the time line to tell the class about your family.

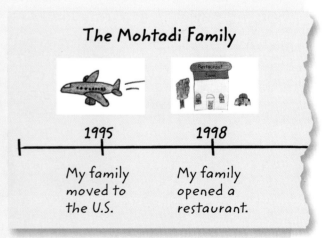

The Mohtadi Family

1995 — My family moved to the U.S.

1998 — My family opened a restaurant.

Make a Seed Packet
Internet

Lotus seeds need a lot of water to grow. What do other kinds of seeds need? Find out about another kind of plant. Then make a seed packet. Use it to tell about the plant.

Violas
Light: needs full sun
Water: keep soil wet
Temperature: keep cool
Season: plant in late summer

WRITING

Write to Express Your Feelings

on your own

What changes have happened in your life? Write about those changes. Choose the best form to express your feelings:

- a journal entry

- a story

- a poem

Does your writing sound like you?

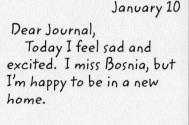

January 10
Dear Journal,
    Today I feel sad and excited. I miss Bosnia, but I'm happy to be in a new home.

▲ journal entry

Draw Conclusions

When you read and **draw conclusions**, you figure out things on your own. To draw a conclusion:

✔ Read carefully.
✔ Think about the details the author gives you.
✔ Combine the details with what you already know.

Try the strategy.

New Ways

In China, students do not call their teachers by name. They use *laoshi*, the word for "teacher." When Tsang Ying first went to school in the United States, he said, "Good morning, teacher," every morning. Then Tsang Ying discovered that everyone else in his class called his teacher "Ms. Morris." Soon he fit in with the rest of his classmates.

> Other students called the teacher by her name. Soon Tsang Ying fit in with his classmates, so I can guess that he started to call her "Ms. Morris," too.

Practice

Take this test and **draw conclusions** about "The Lotus Seed."

> **Read each item. Choose the best answer.**

1 Which detail helps you draw this •••••••
   conclusion: Bà liked the emperor.

   Test Strategy

   Read parts of the
   story again. Then
   choose your
   answer.

   A She saw the emperor cry.

   B She went into the Imperial garden.

   C She sneaked down to the silent palace.

   D She wanted something to remember him by.

2 What conclusion can you draw about the girl who
   tells the story?

   A She has her own children.

   B She likes to plant flowers.

   C She thinks the seed is very special.

   D Lotus flowers have always been important to her.

3 Look at this diagram.

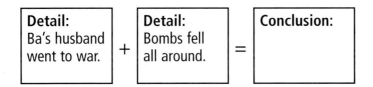

   | Detail:
Ba's husband
went to war. | + | Detail:
Bombs fell
all around. | = | Conclusion: |

   What is the best conclusion you can draw?

   A Bà wanted to stay in Vietnam.

   B Bà's husband was a good soldier.

   C Bà had to leave Vietnam to be safe.

   D Bà had always wanted to see the United States.

Song

HELLO, AMERICA!

We **come from** so far.
We pass through the gate,
Where **opportunity**
And a **better future** await.

"Hello, America. Hello to you."
"Hello, America. Hello to you."

We bring to your shores
Our **culture** and **pride**.
We **adjust** to your ways
With hope as our guide.

—*Maria Del Rey*

Key Words

come from

opportunity

better future

culture

pride

adjust

Read a Magazine

A **magazine** is a collection of articles. The articles can be all about one topic.

✔ Look at the **cover** and the **table of contents** on page 293. These tell you what articles you will find in the magazine.

✔ Look for article **titles.**

title — **I Are You Hungry?**

Immigrants bring many different food recipes from their home countries to the United States. Here are just a few recipes for

Selection Reading

Where We Come From

ISSUE 5   JANUARY

Where I Come From!
Song about immigrants

In Their Own Words
Interviews with young immigrants

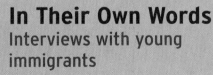

PLUS!

Are You Hungry?
Recipes from three immigrant groups

Where I Come From!

by Victor Cockburn and Judith Steinbergh

Where I **come from**, we eat **moussaka**.
Where I come from, we eat no meat.
Where I come from, we eat **sushi**.
Where I come from, papaya's sweet.

Where I come from, it's "Buenas noches."
Where I come from, we say "Good night."
Where I come from, we say "Bonsoir."
However you say it, it sounds just right.

Chorus

Where we come from,
We bring you stories.
They are deep inside.
All these stories that we carry
*Help us feel a special **pride**.*

_____

moussaka meat or eggplant in sauce
sushi a cold rice dish

Where I come from, we wear **pajamas**.
Where I come from, we wear wool shirts.
Where I come from, we just wear jeans.
Not me! I wear **embroidered skirts**!

Where I come from, our skin is dark.
Where I come from, our eyes are blue.
Where I come from, our hair is curly.
Tell me something about you.

Chorus

Where I come from, we had some mountains.
Where I come from, they planted oats.
And I come from a noisy city.
Where I come from, we live on boats.

Where I come from, we sing in Russian,
Mandarin, Vietnamese.
Where I come from, we speak in Farsi,
Spanish, Hebrew, Portuguese.

Chorus

---

pajamas loose shirts and pants
embroidered skirts skirts with designs
sewn onto them

Before You Move On

1. **Inference** Why do stories make people feel a special pride?

2. **Generalization** What is the important idea in this song? Explain.

In Their Own Words

What do kids say about their experiences as immigrants to the United States? *Where We Come From* talked to kids from Seaside, California.

Rogelio Lorenzo III, 8 years old PHILIPPINES

1 When and why did you immigrate to the United States?	I came last year when I was seven years old. My dad had already been living here for seven years, and he was lonely. Mom and I came here to be with him.
2 What was the hardest thing about moving to the United States?	The hardest thing for me was to understand English. I miss my friends in the Philippines, but I can **handle** it because I got to meet my father.
3 Tell about the people you remember in your native country.	My grandparents, aunt, and cousins still live there. I have a lot of cousins, but one really cares about me. We call each other and speak in **Tagalog**.
4 What surprised you most about life in the United States?	Halloween was new for me. In the Philippine **culture**, we celebrate the Day of the Dead. On that day we visit my granddad's grave.

---

handle get used to it
Tagalog a language spoken in the Philippines

**Jasmine Aviles,
8 years old
EL SALVADOR**

**Namita Nardan,
12 years old
FIJI**

We came here four years ago to be with my grandparents and uncles.	We came 10 years ago for the jobs in America. My dad is **an accountant**. He can get better pay in the United States.
I didn't want to come because I didn't know what was going to happen. I had to leave my family and friends.	Finding a job was hard. Dad had to work as a waiter before he found a job in accounting.
I have an aunt with curly hair and one who looks like me. I talk with them on the telephone about once a month.	We often call our family in Fiji. I don't remember Fiji too well because I was young when we left. My parents keep asking me what our house looked like so I won't forget.
All the cars surprised me! In El Salvador, animals, like dogs and cows, walk in the streets. Most people can't own a car. They have to **rent one**.	I think the best thing about living here is the education system and that there are more opportunities to succeed.

---

rent one pay money to use one for a while

an accountant someone who helps people keep records of money

> **Before You Move On**
> 1. **Details** What was hard for each student when they moved to the U.S.?
> 2. **Opinion** Which answer is the most surprising? Why?

297

José Villegas,
8 years old
EL SALVADOR

1 When and why did you immigrate to the United States?

We moved to the United States to have a **better future** .

2 What was the hardest thing about moving to the United States?

I was afraid. I didn't know what it was going to be like. I had to leave my grandparents, aunts, uncles, and three cousins. That made me sad.

3 Tell about the people you remember in your native country.

When I was in El Salvador, my oldest cousin would take me for rides in his car. Now he sends me cards. We talk on the phone and send letters.

4 What surprised you most about life in the United States?

In the United States, cars can go over 100 **m.p.h.**! The ocean is colder here, too. In El Salvador, the water is always warm and great for swimming.

---

m.p.h. miles per hour

Charlotte Fale, 9 years old TONGA	Gabriel Balesteros, 8 years old MEXICO
I was only two years old when my family immigrated to this country. I don't know why we left Tonga.	We came here four years ago. One of my dad's friends said there were more **opportunities** for work in California.
For me, it was not hard. It was easy to **adjust** because I was so young.	Getting out of Mexico was the hardest thing. My dad had to get a **work permit**.
I have aunts and uncles in Tonga. They **spoil me** when I visit. We visit every year and stay several months. We have a pink house there.	I remember my uncle. He told stories to my brothers and me. Once, we visited our family when I was in the second grade. I still write to them and send notes on the fax machine.
The food is different here. I like sandwiches. They don't have sandwiches in Tonga. They don't have freeways, either. The money is different, too.	I was surprised to see so many houses and big towers.

Before You Move On

1. **Comparison** How are the answers to question 1 alike? Different?

2. **Generalization** Why do most immigrants seem to come to the U.S.?

---

spoil me are very nice to me

work permit piece of paper from the government that lets a person work in the United States

299

Are You Hungry?

Immigrants bring many different food recipes from their home countries to the United States. Here are just a few recipes for rice dishes.

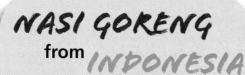

NASI GORENG from INDONESIA

Ingredients:

2 cups water

1 cup uncooked rice

2 tablespoons oil

1 onion, sliced

1 clove garlic, chopped

2 red Indonesian chilies, chopped

1 tablespoon **soy sauce**

1/2 teaspoon brown sugar

Directions:

1. Heat water and uncooked rice until **it boils**.
2. Turn down the heat and cook the rice over low heat for 20 minutes.
3. In another pan, heat the oil.
4. **Stir-fry** the onion, garlic, and chilies for 1 minute.
5. Add the soy sauce and brown sugar.
6. Mix the vegetables with the rice.

---

soy sauce salty flavoring made from soybeans

it boils the water bubbles

Stir-fry Mix while frying

Risi e Bisi
from Italy

Ingredients:

1 3/4 cups chicken broth

1 cup uncooked rice

1 cup canned or cooked
   tomatoes in juice

3 cloves garlic, chopped

1 cup peas

1/2 cup chopped green onions

1 teaspoon Italian **seasoning**

salt

Directions:

1. Heat broth until it boils.
2. Add the uncooked rice.
   Cook over low heat for
   20 minutes.
3. Add the tomatoes, garlic, peas,
   and green onions.
4. Stir in the seasoning.
5. Add salt to taste.

Green Pulao
from India

Ingredients:

2 cups water

1 cup uncooked rice

1/2 cup **grated** coconut

1 tablespoon chopped
   coriander leaves

2 cloves of garlic, chopped

1 tablespoon chopped ginger

6 tablespoons chopped green
   bell pepper

3 tablespoons oil

3/4 cup peas

salt

Directions:

1. Heat water and rice until it boils.
2. Turn down the heat and cook over
   low heat for 20 minutes.
3. Grind coconut with coriander,
   garlic, ginger, and green peppers
   until it looks like a smooth paste.
4. In another pan, heat the oil. Add
   the coconut mixture and cook for
   1 minute.
5. Add the peas and cook for 5
   minutes. Add salt to taste.
6. Spread the rice on a flat dish.
   Spread the coconut mixture over
   the rice.

Before You Move On

1. **Steps in a Process** Are the
   first two steps in each
   recipe the same? Explain.

2. **Opinion** Which recipe do
   you think will taste the
   best? Why?

---

seasoning spices
grated shredded; finely chopped

Think and Respond

Strategy: Fact and Opinion

Make a fact-and-opinion chart. Look back at the interview on pages 296–299.

✔ A statement is a fact if you can check whether it's true. Statements about dates, times, how many, or places give facts.

✔ A statement is an opinion if it tells what a person thinks or feels. Words like *surprised*, *best*, *hardest*, *like*, and *don't like* signal that the statement is an opinion.

In Their Own Words

Person	Facts	Opinions	Opinion Signal Words
Rogelio Lorenzo III, page 296	I came when I was seven years old. My grandparents still live there.	I miss my friends.	miss

Draw Conclusions

Form a group of six. Choose one person in the chart. When it is your turn, talk about the person's opinions. What conclusion can you draw?

Talk It Over

 Personal Response Did you enjoy reading this magazine? Why or why not?

2 **Comparison** How are the articles alike? How are they different?

3 **Personal Experience** What idea from your culture would you add to each verse of "Where I Come From!"?

4 **Generalization** Do foods and languages connect people to their home cultures? How are immigrants connected to American culture?

Compare Themes

Why do you think "The Lotus Seed" and this magazine article are in the same unit? What theme do they share?

I think that both are about how important it is for immigrants to remember where they come from.

Content Connections

MATH

Make an Immigration Graph

Internet

large group

Find out how many immigrants from one country have come to the U.S. Make a line graph to show the number of people who came during a certain time period. Talk about the results with the class.

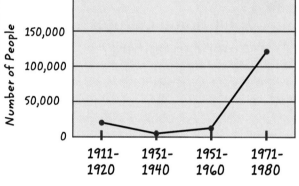

Chinese Immigrants to the U.S.

Number of People

150,000
100,000
50,000
0

1911–1920 1931–1940 1951–1960 1971–1980

MUSIC

Create a New Verse

small group

With a group, create a new verse for "Where I Come From." Make the second and fourth lines rhyme. Sing your new verse for the class.

Where I come from, we say Hello.
Where I come from, we say Bonjour.
Where I come from, it's Hola.
Come to my country, let's take a tour!

Interview a Classmate

partners

Interview a partner. Ask the questions on page 296 or other questions you want to ask. Take notes as you listen to your partner's answers. Then introduce your partner to the class.

Nadia is from Somalia. She moved here two years ago.

Write to Inform

on your own

What are your family's special traditions? Write about one. You could choose to write:

- instructions (a recipe)
- a report
- a review

Try to use correct spelling, capitalization, punctuation, and grammar.

Chicken Tacos

Ingredients:

1 pound cooked
   chicken, chopped
1/4 cup onion
1 cup salsa
12 taco shells
1 cup sour cream
grated cheese
chopped lettuce

Directions:

1. Mix the chicken, onions, and salsa.
2. Put some mixture in each shell.
3. Add some cheese.
4. Top with lettuce and sour cream.

Pronouns

Listen and sing.

Song

Risi e Bisi

Risi e bisi, chicken broth and rice,
Risi e bisi, it tastes so very nice.
My mama stirs the chicken broth.
She adds the onions, peas, and spice.
Papa licks his lips,
So Mama lets him taste it twice.

—*Jane Zion Brauer*

Tune: "Funiculi, Funicula" (chorus only)

How Language Works

A **pronoun** can take the place of a noun.

■ Use these **pronouns** in the subject of a sentence.

One	More than One
I	we
you	you
he, she, it	they

Example: **Lupe** likes to cook.

↓

She likes to cook.

■ Use these **pronouns** after the verb or a small word like **to** or **from**.

One	More than One
me	us
you	you
him, her, it	them

Example: We have a recipe for **Lupe**.

↓

We have a recipe for **her**.

Practice with a Partner

Choose the correct pronoun. Then say the sentence.

us / we   **1.** Mom shows _____ how to cook beans.

she / her   **2.** First _____ puts the beans in a bowl.

they / them **3.** She pours cold water over _____ .

They / Them **4.** The beans soak for a long time. _____ get soft.

we / us   **5.** Then _____ watch Mom boil the beans.

Put It in Writing

Think about a special family recipe. Tell what your family does to prepare it. When you edit your work, make sure your pronouns are correct.

Dad cuts the onions. He will add them to the soup.

Show What You Know

Talk About Culture

In this unit, you read a story and a magazine about culture. Look back at this unit. What idea was new to you? Why? Tell your group about it.

Make a Mind Map

What are "cultural ties"? Make a chart to show some cultural ties. First list ideas from the unit. Then add your own ideas.

Cultural Ties

Parts of Cultures	Examples
languages	Japanese Spanish
foods	moussaka sushi
gifts	lotus seed
clothes	

Think and Write

Write a sentence about each cultural tie in your life. Add this writing to your portfolio. Also add other work that shows what you learned about culture.

Read and Learn More

Leveled Books

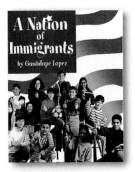

A Nation of Immigrants
by Guadalupe Lopez

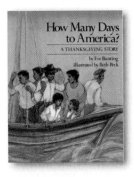

How Many Days to America?
by Eve Bunting

Theme Library

Journey Home
by Lawrence McKay, Jr.

Mama and Papa Have a Store
by Amelia Lau Carling

Internet
Go to: www.hbavenues.com
Immigrant Stories
The Immigrant Experience
Immigrant Cookbook

Make a State Model

Every state is special. What is your state like?
1. Use clay, cardboard, or paper to make a model that shows something about your state.
2. Make a class exhibit.
3. Talk about what the models show about your state.

Regions of the United States

	States		**Landforms**
Northeast	• Connecticut • Delaware • Maine • Maryland • Massachusetts • New Hampshire	• New Jersey • New York • Pennsylvania • Rhode Island • Vermont	▲ forests, lakes, and mountains
Southeast	• Alabama • Arkansas • Florida • Georgia • Kentucky • Louisiana	• Mississippi • North Carolina • South Carolina • Tennessee • Virginia • West Virginia	▲ lakes, rivers, and bays
Midwest	• Illinois • Indiana • Iowa • Kansas • Michigan • Minnesota	• Missouri • Nebraska • North Dakota • Ohio • South Dakota • Wisconsin	▲ farmland and grassy plains
Southwest	• Arizona • New Mexico	• Oklahoma • Texas	▲ canyons and deserts
West	• Alaska • California • Colorado • Hawaii • Idaho • Montana	• Nevada • Oregon • Utah • Washington • Wyoming	▲ mountains, forests, and lakes

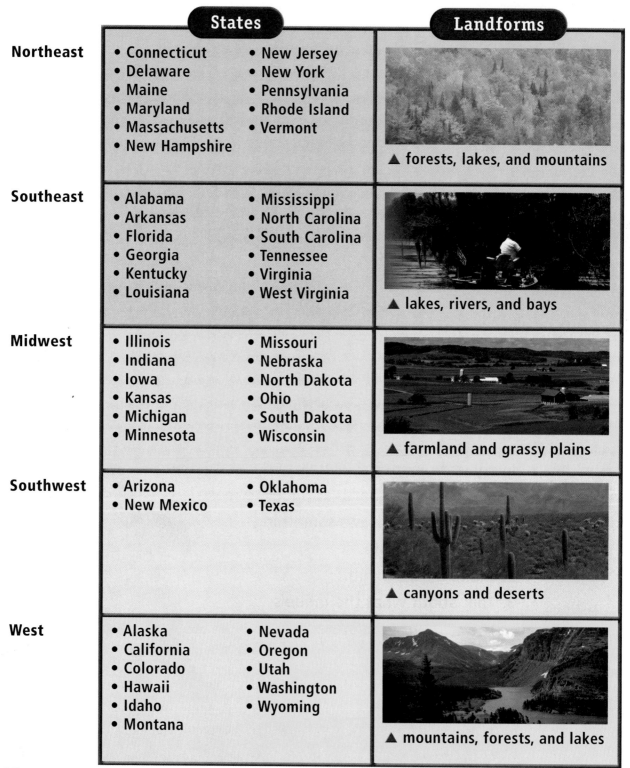

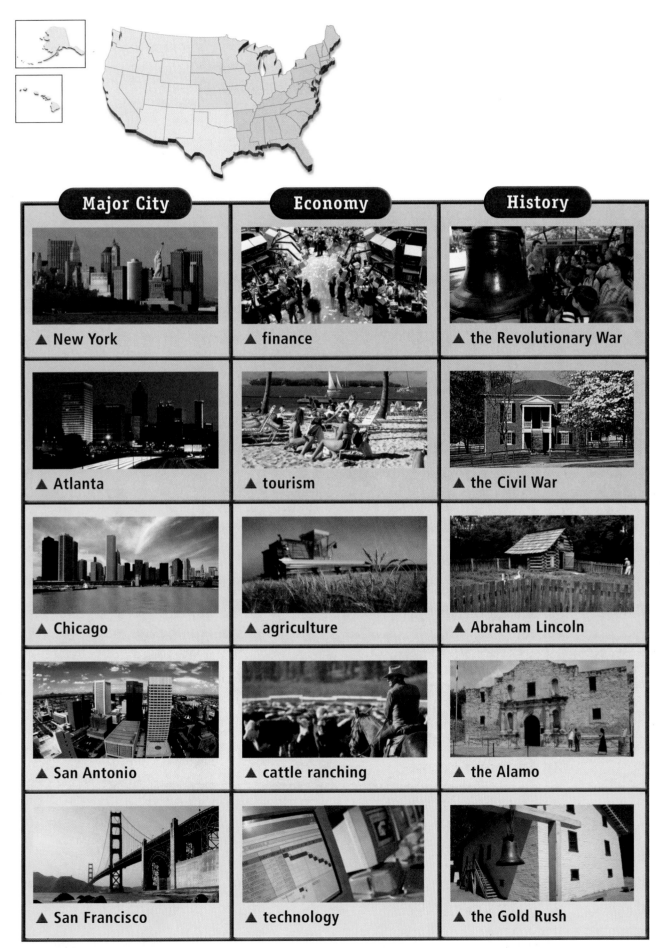

Major City	Economy	History
▲ New York	▲ finance	▲ the Revolutionary War
▲ Atlanta	▲ tourism	▲ the Civil War
▲ Chicago	▲ agriculture	▲ Abraham Lincoln
▲ San Antonio	▲ cattle ranching	▲ the Alamo
▲ San Francisco	▲ technology	▲ the Gold Rush

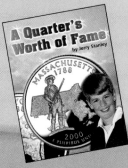

Vocabulary

Song

The Contest

I entered a **contest**.
I wanted to win.
My ideas were good,
But I couldn't begin.

I had to come up with
A winning **design**.
But I have no **talent**.
I can't draw a line.

My mom tried to help me.
My dad also tried.
I drew and erased
And erased till I cried.

At last I was **honored**
To win second place.
No, not for my **sketch**,
But for what I erased.

— *Evelyn Stone*

Tune: "Sweet Betsy from Pike"

314

Key Words

contest

design

talent

honor

sketch

315

Read an Interview

In an **interview**, one person asks another person questions to get information.

✔ When you read an interview, read each **question** and its **answer** carefully.

question

answer

Mr. Stanley: Do you think of yoursel
an artist?

Xander: No, not really. **I'm more int
things**. I'm interested in theater.
musical instruments like the clarin
and piano. I can't draw well, but
some computer graphics and
photography.

✔ Look for each speaker's name.

Selection Reading

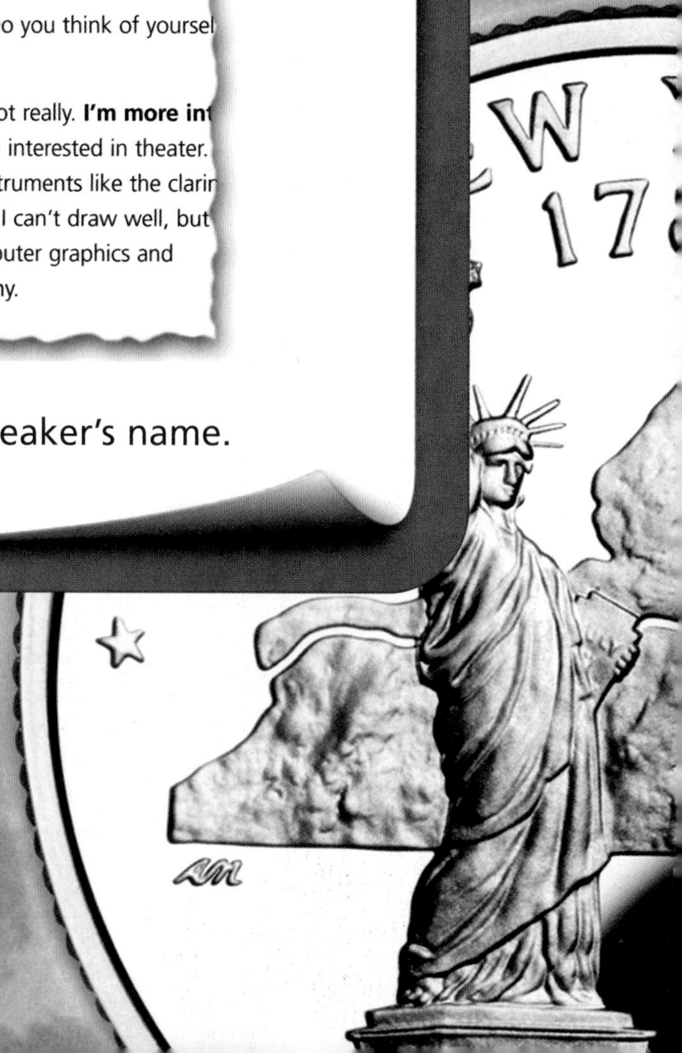

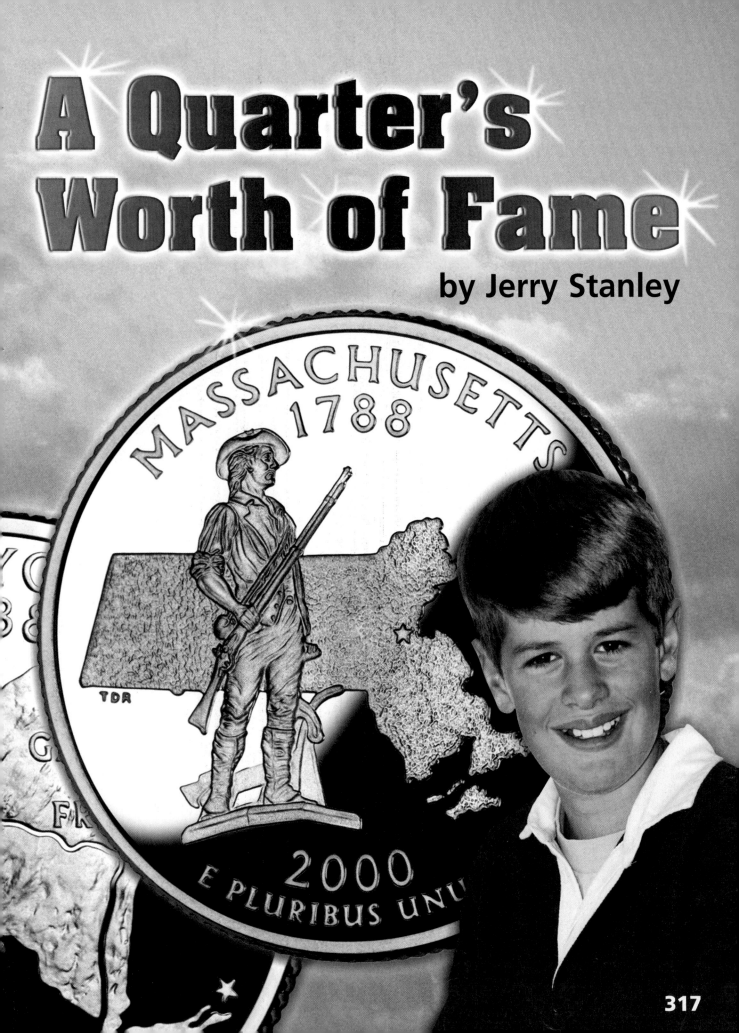

A Quarter's Worth of Fame

by Jerry Stanley

Set Your Purpose

Xander Kotsatos enters a contest at school. Find out what happens.

Xander with his dog, Cally

Xander with his brother, Niko

One day in 1998, 10-year-old Xander Kotsatos sat **squirming** at his desk at Belmont Day School in Belmont, Massachusetts. He was supposed to be drawing a **design** for a new state quarter, but he couldn't **come up with** a good design. His first idea didn't seem quite right. When his second idea finally came to him, he didn't think it was very great either. He never dreamed that his ideas might make him famous some day.

Xander is now 15 years old, and he still remembers that day. Xander and I talked about it on the phone.

---

squirming moving around
come up with think of

318

◀ The bald eagle was on the back of United States quarters before the 50 State Quarters® program began.

Mr. Stanley: Xander, before we **get into your story**, tell me about the 50 State Quarters® program. What is that program all about?

Xander: The **United States Mint** started the 50 State Quarters® program. The Mint wanted to create fifty new quarter designs to **honor** the fifty states. Most states had **professional** artists design their quarters. The Massachusetts governor thought it would be a good idea to have a student do the design. So, he started a school **contest** for the best design.

---

get into your story start to talk about what you did

United States Mint part of the government that makes coins

professional paid

Before You Move On

1. **Details** Who is Xander? Why do you think Mr. Stanley called him?

2. **Paraphrase** Use your own words to tell about the 50 State Quarters® program.

319

Mr. Stanley: Do you think of yourself as an artist?

Xander: No, not really. **I'm more into other things**. I'm interested in theater. I play musical instruments like the clarinet, sax, and piano. I can't draw well, but I do some computer graphics and photography.

Mr. Stanley: Why were you interested in the quarter contest?

Xander: I wasn't <u>that</u> interested, but it was a class assignment, so I did it. I did think it was a good idea that the states would have their own quarters. My big problem was what to draw!

Xander, at fifteen, plays his sax, or saxophone. ▶

I'm more into other things I enjoy other activities more

Mr. Stanley: What was your first idea?

Xander: It was brilliant! I'd show the Boston Red Sox baseball team! But the contest rules said the design couldn't be a group of people or people who were still living.

Mr. Stanley: So you **were stumped**?

Xander: Well, I was stumped for a while. Then **it hit me**, a minuteman soldier! The minutemen fought for Massachusetts during the American Revolution. They were called minutemen because they could be ready to fight in a minute.

Minuteman Statue in Concord, Massachusetts ▶

were stumped didn't know what to do

it hit me I thought of something

Before You Move On

1. **Cause/Effect** Why wasn't Xander very interested in the contest at first?

2. **Details** Why did Xander think a minuteman soldier was a good idea?

321

Mr. Stanley: So you drew a minuteman soldier.

Xander: Not at first. I started with the easiest part of my idea. I drew the **outline** of the state. Then, on the right side, I drew the *Mayflower*. That's the ship that people used to get from England to Massachusetts in 1620.

Mr. Stanley: That sounds like a pretty **complicated sketch**. It must have been difficult to draw.

Xander: It was terrible. I erased it and drew it again. On the left side, I drew a smiling minuteman.

Mr. Stanley: Let me guess. It was terrible, and you drew it again.

---

outline shape
complicated detailed

Model of the *Mayflower* in Plymouth, Massachusetts ▶

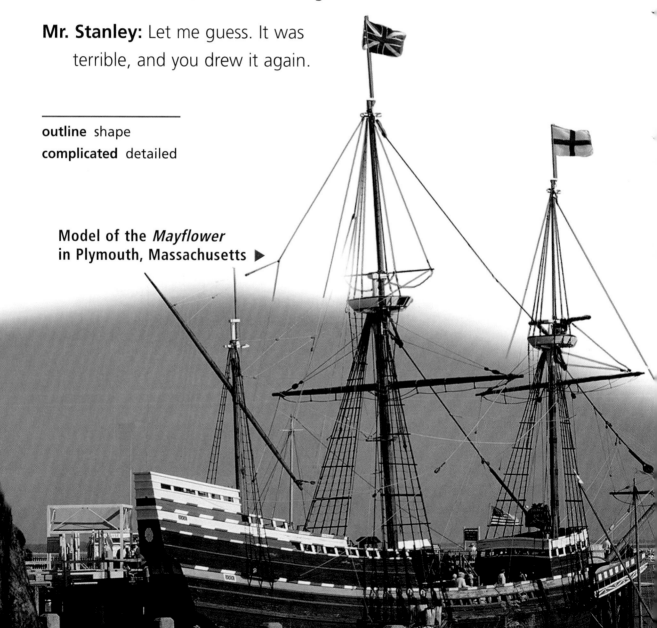

Xander: I had to. The hat and coat were all wrong, and a minuteman soldier wouldn't be smiling. Anyway, it must have looked pretty good when I finished because the next day my teacher, Mr. Jordan, **pulled me aside** after class. He said he wanted to **submit** my sketch for the contest. "I can only submit one design," Mr. Jordan said. "Yours is it." That came as a total surprise to me.

Mr. Stanley: Wow! And then what?

———————————

pulled me aside asked to talk to me
submit send

Xander in 5th grade with Mr. Jordan

Before You Move On

1. **Inference** Why did Mr. Stanley guess that Xander's sketch was terrible?

2. **Conclusion** Was Xander's last design the best in his class? How do you know?

Xander and his family

Xander: I had to draw it again. I added some detail to the *Mayflower*, and **sharpened the lines of** the soldier's coat. I turned in my sketch and then, nothing. I forgot about the contest.

Mr. Stanley: So, when did you hear about the contest again?

Xander: It was almost a year later. I was in the sixth grade then. When my mother **picked me up at** school one day, she was yelling, "Your drawing is **in the final 24**!" I said, "What?" It took me a minute to understand what she was saying.

---

sharpened the lines of made the lines darker and clearer in

picked me up at came to take me home from

in the final 24 among the 24 best drawings

Mr. Stanley: No wonder. A lot of time had passed.

Xander: Yeah! But then I started following the Mint Web
site to see how the contest was going. Finally, in June
we got the news. "You've won!" Mom told me.
"You've won the Massachusetts quarter contest!"

No wonder I'm not surprised

Before You Move On

1. **Sequence** What did
   Xander do to improve his
   minuteman sketch?

2. **Cause/Effect** Why did
   Xander look at the U.S.
   Mint Web site?

325

Mr. Stanley: Had you ever won a contest before?

Xander: Only once when I was in the third grade. I was in a seed-spitting contest at the fair. I spit a watermelon seed 8 feet and 2 inches.

Mr. Stanley: You are a person of many **talents**. What was it like after you won the quarter contest?

Xander gives his acceptance speech at the strike ceremony.

Xander: It was fun. The big event was the strike ceremony. That was when the Mint produced the first coins based on my design. We all watched a big-screen TV showing the United States Mint in Philadelphia. The printing machine **rattled and clanked** and the first quarters **came popping out**.

Mr. Stanley: How did the coin look?

---

rattled and clanked shook and made loud noises
came popping out suddenly came out of the machine

Xander talks to reporters about the contest. ▶

Xander: It **was pretty cool**. They changed my design, but just a little. They replaced the *Mayflower* ship with the words "The Bay State." That's **a nickname** for Massachusetts because Massachusetts Bay is so big. I think it was a good change. It made the design less complicated. In fact, the design looked better than I thought it would. Seeing it on a quarter was pretty amazing!

Mr. Stanley: How did you celebrate?

Xander: I had a quarter party! I gave everyone a new quarter with my design, even though **the quarters weren't officially out** yet.

---

was pretty cool looked very good

a nickname another name

the quarters weren't officially out the Mint had not given the new quarters to other people

Mr. Stanley: That's a great story, Xander. What did you learn from the experience?

Xander: It taught me to believe in myself. I learned that getting it right the first time isn't so important. Sticking with it, doing it again is more important.

Today, Xander usually carries a few new quarters in his pocket to **hand out on the right occasion**. The state quarters will **circulate** for about 30 years. Some people are collecting the special coins, however. They plan to give the coins to their children. Imagine! Xander's design could show up in coin collections for hundreds of years!

Xander admires a Massachusetts State Quarter. ▶

hand out on the right occasion
give people for special events

circulate be used as money

Before You Move On

1. **Conclusion** What lesson did Xander learn from his experience?

2. **Inference** How do you think Xander feels about his quarter today?

Meet the Author
Jerry Stanley

AWARD WINNER

Jerry Stanley is a teacher, a historian, and a writer. As a teacher, he reminds kids to read. He says, "Good writing takes good thinking. Good thinking takes good reading."

As a historian and writer, Mr. Stanley likes to describe people who leave their marks on history. That's why he wrote "A Quarter's Worth of Fame." Mr. Stanley says, "What I liked about Xander was that he was an ordinary kid, but then an opportunity came along, and he grabbed it. It is a good lesson and a great story."

Real Kids News

Quarter Kids

March 20, 2000
Boston, Massachusetts

Massachusetts is **flipping over** its new state quarter, thanks to Kathleen Raughtigan, 12, and Xander Kotsatos, 13.

Kathleen's and Xander's design for the new coin **took top honors in** a contest for kids across the state. Although the two kids had never met, they **drafted almost identical designs**, a minuteman standing in front of a drawing of the state of Massachusetts. So, when their design won the competition, Xander and Kathleen shared the honors.

▲ Kathleen Raughtigan and Xander Kotsatos at the Massachusetts quarter design ceremony

After first thinking about the state bird and the state flower, Kathleen decided the brave soldiers best represented Massachusetts' **unique** history.

continued on next page

---

flipping over very excited about

took top honors in won

drafted almost identical designs drew designs that were almost exactly alike

unique special

"They fought for our freedom," Kathleen said. "Massachusetts would not be what it is today without them."

The Massachusetts coin was the sixth quarter issued as part of the United States Mint's State Quarters® program. The Mint will produce five new state quarters each year. The quarters will be made in the order in which the states **joined the Union**.

In all, more than 1 billion Massachusetts quarters will **find their way into cash registers** across America.

▲ **These shiny new quarters represent four states.**

joined the Union became part of the United States

find their way into cash registers be used in stores

Before You Move On

1. **Comparsion** How are Kathleen's ideas like Xander's? Different?

2. **Viewing** Name something special about each state shown on this page.

Think and Respond

Strategy: Steps in a Process

Make a flow chart. Show all of the steps Xander went through to win the Massachusetts State Quarter contest.

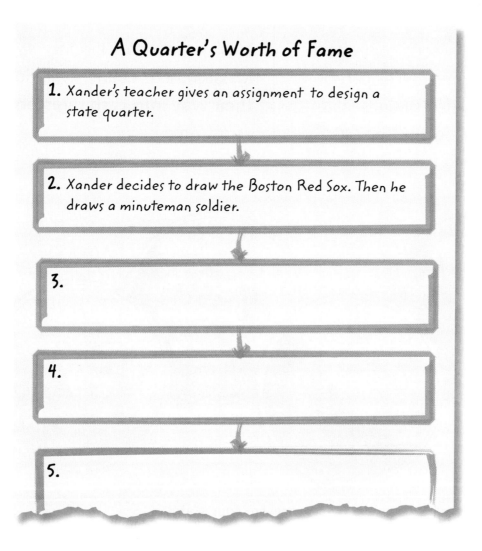

A Quarter's Worth of Fame

1. Xander's teacher gives an assignment to design a state quarter.

2. Xander decides to draw the Boston Red Sox. Then he draws a minuteman soldier.

3.

4.

5.

Make Judgments

Was it fair that the Mint changed Xander's design? Should he still have won the contest? Talk to a partner about it.

Talk It Over

1 **Personal Response** What additional questions would you ask Xander?

2 **Inference** Why did Xander's teacher have all his students draw designs for the contest?

3 **Conclusion** What most helped Xander to win the contest: his talent or how hard he tried? Explain.

4 **Opinion** Was it a good idea to have a student design the Massachusetts state quarter? Why or why not?

Compare Genres

Compare the interview with Xander to the news article. How are they alike? How are they different?

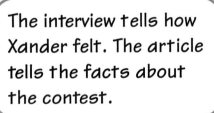

The interview tells how Xander felt. The article tells the facts about the contest.

Content Connections

Report the News

Internet

What important events are happening in your state? Listen to state and local news on the television, radio, or the Internet. Take notes. Report the news to the class.

> Chinese Dragon Dance! A great parade will take place this weekend...

MATH

Quarter Experiment

on your own

1. Keep track of the quarters you see in one week.

2. Record how many of them are state quarters and how many are not.

3. What percentage are state quarters?

Compare your results with the class.

	Tally	Total	%
State Quarters	⫲⫲⫲ ⫲⫲⫲ ⫲⫲⫲	15	75%
Other Quarters	⫲⫲⫲	5	25%
Grand Total	20	20	100%

334

ART

Have a Coin Contest

large group

1. Design a coin for your state. Research your state's history to get ideas.

2. Explain your design to the class.

3. Talk about what you like about each design.

4. Vote for the design you like best.

New Mexico

WRITING

Write a Personal Narrative

on your own

Xander won a contest with his coin design. Write a story about something you have done in your life. Tell how you got started and how you finished.

Now I Can Play!
When I was 8, I heard beautiful piano music. I just had to learn to play! Soon I started my lessons.

Identify Fact and Opinion

A **fact** is a statement you can check to be sure it's true. An **opinion** is a statement that tells what someone thinks, feels, or believes. To tell a fact from an opinion:

✔ Look to see if you can prove the statement. If you can, it is probably a **fact**.

✔ If you can't prove it, the statement is probably an **opinion**. *Think*, *should*, *agree*, and *must* are some clues that the writer is giving an opinion.

Try the strategy.

Help Save Old Pond Park

Yesterday the newspaper had an article about Old Pond Park. The article said that some people want to close the park!

Builders think that building more houses is better than having a park. I don't agree. We should keep the park open.

I believe that Old Pond Park is important to our town. Some trees are hundreds of years old. Every year thousands of children swim in the pond. The high school band plays there every summer. We must save the park!

> I know the second sentence is a fact because I can check the newspaper. The writer says we must save the park. That is an opinion because it tells what the writer thinks.

Practice

Take this test and **identify facts and opinions**.

Read the letter on page 336 again. Then read
each item. Choose the best answer.

1 **Which sentence is an opinion?**

   A   We should keep the park open.

   B   The high school band plays there
       every summer.

   C   Some trees are hundreds of years old.

   D   Yesterday the newspaper had an article
       about Old Pond Park.

> ✔ **Test Strategy**
>
> Check your answers if you have time. Reread the questions and the answers you marked.

2 **Which sentence is a fact?**

   A   We must save the park.

   B   Building more houses is more important than having
       a park.

   C   Every year thousands of children swim in the pond.

   D   I believe that Old Pond Park is important to our town.

3 **Complete this sentence with an opinion. The park —**

   A   has a pond.

   B   has trees in it.

   C   is called "Old Pond Park."

   D   is a fun place for children.

Vocabulary

ILLINOIS TALK

Mr. News: Hello, Illinois, your name is French, isn't it?

Illinois: Yes. In the 1600s, French people built **settlements** here. English people were interested in my land, too. The French and English fought over me for years. In 1763, though, the two countries signed a **treaty** to end the war. I could live in **peace**.

Mr. News: When did you join the United States?

Illinois: In 1818. The Mississippi River is the western **boundary** between me and Iowa and Missouri.

In 1839, Springfield became my **capital**. Most state **government** offices are there.

Mr. News: Thank you! Tomorrow we'll talk to Ohio.

Key Words

settlement

treaty

peace

boundary

capital

government

Springfield

THE
TREE
That Would Not Die

by **Ellen Levine**

illustrated by **Ted Rand**

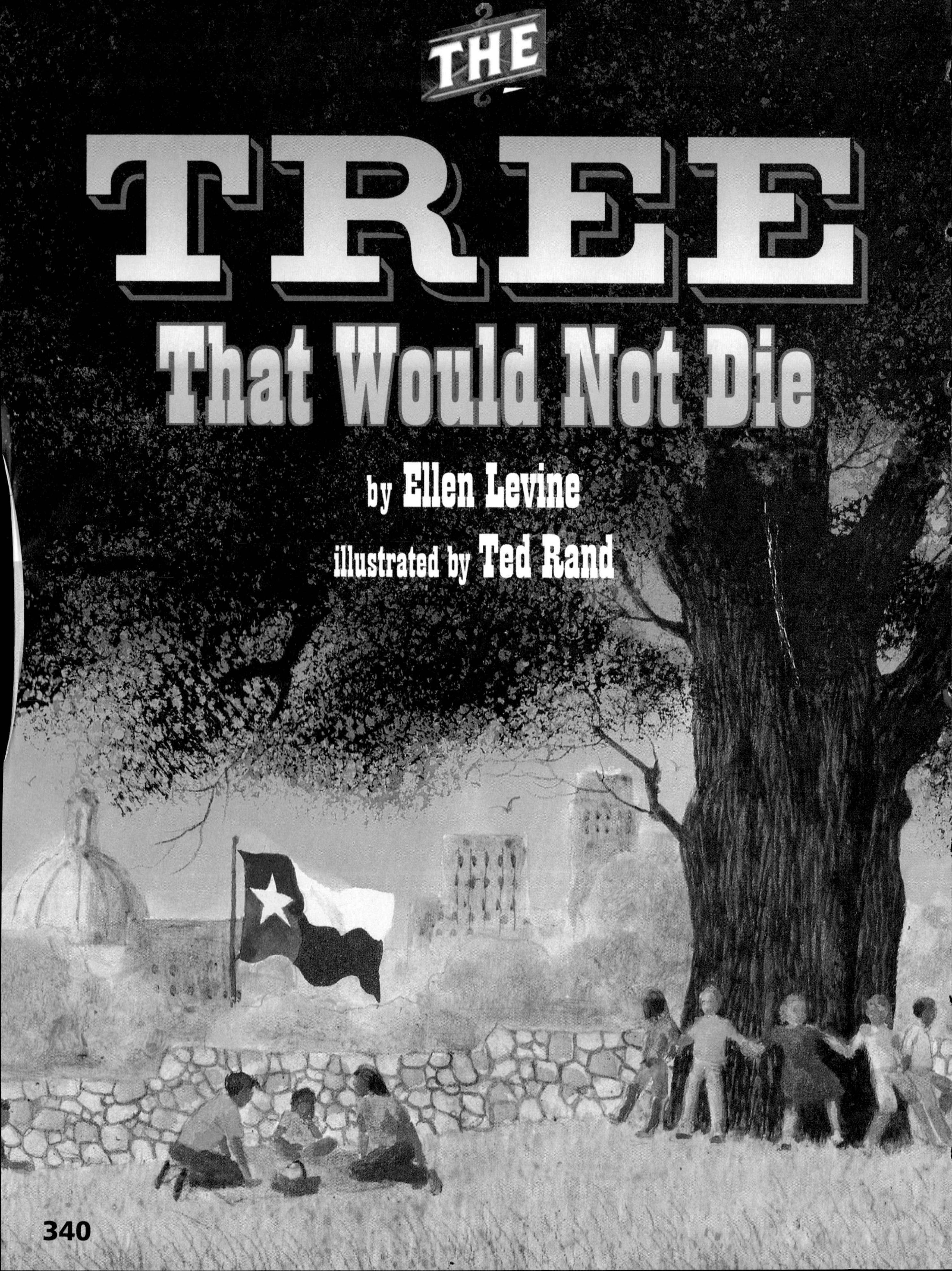

Read a Story

Genre

Historical fiction is a story based on real events. The writer adds events that could happen.

Character

The main character in this story is a special tree in Texas. The tree uses "I" and "me" to tell about events from its point of view.

Tree

Setting

The story happens in Texas, near what is now the capital city of Austin. The tree tells a story that begins 500 years ago.

Austin, Texas

Selection Reading

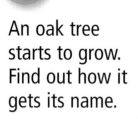

An oak tree
starts to grow.
Find out how it
gets its name.

acorn

One morning hundreds of years ago,
an acorn fell and grew in the earth. And that was me.

And I grew.

And as I grew, I saw farther and farther across the land.

When I was eleven and giving shade, I had a good
friend. My friend was a buffalo calf who nibbled grass
nearby. When he'd rub against my trunk, Blue Jay, who
was high up in my branches, complained about the
shaking. "Calf is just using you to scratch an itch," said
Blue Jay. But I knew Calf was also saying hello.

When the buffalo ran, their **hooves** pounded the earth
and **kicked up** dust for miles around. My branches
swayed, my leaves trembled, and my upper roots quivered.
Blue Jay coughed and flew off until things **quieted down**.

---

hooves feet
kicked up made clouds of
quieted down were quiet again

343

And I grew.

Soon I was so big that the First People chose me as a meeting place. The **Comanche, Tejas, Lipan Apache, and Tonkawa** fought many wars among themselves. But when they sat by me, they **laid their weapons down**.

The First People gathered my acorns and leaves and made sweet teas from them. "Come home safely from the hunt," said the young women as the young men sipped my tea.

The people talked about past hunting trips. And they sang about the buffalo whose hides made thick blankets that kept them warm, **moccasins** for their feet, and robes for their backs.

The children climbed my arms and swung in pairs. Never did they cut me with knives. They knew **my bark** was like a buffalo skin, protecting me and keeping me healthy.

They walked softly on the earth around my roots because they knew I couldn't live without them.

Comanche, Tejas, Lipan Apache, and Tonkawa
Native American tribes

laid their weapons down stopped fighting

moccasins shoes

my bark the wood that covered me

And I grew.

One morning, a loud **clanging echoed over the hills** and woke me earlier than usual. The noise was from soldiers who banged their swords against their armor. When their swords were **still**, I could hear the music of their Spanish words.

After a time, more Spaniards came and built churches and **settlements**. They named the land "Tejas," the First People's word for "friendly people."

---

clanging echoed over the hills noise came from far away

still not moving

armor

sword

And I still grew.

One **steamy** day, four First People sat under my **canopy**. They waited for a man named Stephen F. Austin. I myself cannot say if he came because it was a hot afternoon, and I **dozed off**. I do know that ever since that day I have been called " **Treaty** Oak" because the First People and Austin made **peace beneath my tent**.

I was made into a **boundary** , I'm told. The First People agreed to live to the west of me. Austin's people agreed to live to the east of me.

---

steamy hot

canopy wide branches

dozed off went to sleep

peace beneath my tent an agreement to stop fighting as they sat under my branches

Before You Move On

1. **Cause/Effect** Why did the First People use the tree as a meeting place?

2. **Paraphrase** Tell about the agreement the First People and Austin made.

2

More people settle near the tree. What happens to the land around it?

And I grew.

The American settlers came and cleared the land. They cut down many relatives and friends of mine to build their homes and light their fires. I was the "Treaty Oak," so I was **spared**.

The land began to change. Trails became paths, paths became lanes, and lanes became roads. Farmlands were cleared, and crops were planted.

There was a woman who had nine children. She was always washing clothes, **smoking meats, and putting up fruits and vegetables**. Once a week she'd visit and sit in my shade for a while.

And the Tin Man stopped by whenever he **passed through**. He traded pots and pans, and he sharpened knives and scissors. He also shared news about what was happening in every town.

---

spared not cut down

smoking meats, and putting up fruits and vegetables preparing food to eat later during the winter

passed through came there to trade

And I grew.

I was very large when I **got word** that **Sam Houston** and his soldiers had **defeated** the Mexican Army. They captured General Santa Anna while Sam Houston lay **wounded under a relative of mine**.

"Tejas" became a separate country.

Five men rode up one day and rested their horses near me. They were looking for a place to build Austin, the **capital** of this new country they called Texas. The first man pointed to the river flowing nearby. The second stretched out in a field of bluebonnets.

"The surrounding hills are like soldiers guarding the town," said the third.

"Perfect!" cried the fourth, and the fifth agreed. So the **government** came here to Austin.

---

got word heard
Sam Houston the leader of the Americans
defeated won a battle against
wounded under a relative of mine hurt under another tree like me

As I grew, Texas grew, too. It became part of the United States. We were called "The Lone Star State," and the capital stayed right here in Austin.

I grew tall enough to watch the cowboys ride and **rope in a sea of cattle flowing** toward Kansas.

Then the railroads came. Roads covered the grass, and more trees were cut.

I grew, but telephone poles grew, too. Houses **pressed around me**, and buildings grew taller than me. Everybody was very busy.

The owners on whose land I stood talked of cutting me down to make room for a building. For the first time, I was afraid.

Then something changed. People **lost their jobs** and wandered past me at all hours. I had visitors who slept under me every night. The people called it the Great Depression, or the Bad Times. Once again, people talked about selling me or cutting me down.

---

rope in a sea of cattle flowing gather a herd of cattle moving

pressed around me were built closer and closer to me

lost their jobs didn't have jobs

354

Before You Move On

1. **Paraphrase** What did the settlers do? How did that change the land?

2. **Cause/Effect** Why did people build the capital of Texas near the tree?

355

3

The tree is in danger. Find out how children save it.

Still I grew, but for how long, I wondered.

I think it was the children who saved me. They sent pennies and nickels to the city so it could buy me. And the city made a park around me. There were picnics and weddings, games and **get-togethers**, all in my park.

I grew bigger, but the land around me grew smaller. Buildings hid the sky. At least I was safe, I thought.

_____

get-togethers parties

Then late one night a stranger parked his car across the street. He crept into the park and poured a liquid in a circle by my side. At first it felt cool, and I **shuddered**. Later it burned.

I could not grow.

I could not grow!

My leaves turned brown and fell off. The **foresters** and scientists were called. They cleaned the soil around my roots. I was too sick to make food, so they tried to feed me. I lost so many leaves, I burned in the sun. They **shielded me** and sprayed me with a cool mist of water.

I, who had shaded so many, could not shade myself.

They cut my dead **limbs** away. I am smaller now.

The man was caught and punished, but he would not say why he had **poisoned** me.

Will I grow again? I do not know.

---

shuddered shook
foresters people who take care of trees
shielded me protected me from the sun
limbs branches
poisoned tried to kill

I've had many visitors, sometimes a hundred a day. I didn't think so many people cared **whether** I lived or died. They sing to me, dance, pray, and leave **presents**. Many have brought me flowers. Some people have read me poems.

Thousands have written from around the world. "Dear Tree," the letters all begin. One boy wrote, "Please get well. You are too old to die."

Will I grow again? I do not know.

---

whether if
presents gifts

Wait!

I feel new buds pushing off the old leaves. It's spring, and I am growing! My new leaves are **uncurling**. I hope they will last.

But if they don't, my acorns are planted, and they are my children.

---

uncurling growing

▲ Ten years after the Treaty Oak was poisoned, it is healthy. Its acorns have been planted in Texas and other states.

Before You Move On

1. **Details** Name three things people did to help the tree.

2. **Prediction** How long do you think the Treaty Oak will live? Explain.

363

Letters Help Save the Treaty Oak

When the Treaty Oak was very sick, people wanted to help.
Many wrote letters about how to save the great tree.
Here's an example of a letter to a **newspaper editor.**

Austin, Texas
May 24, 1990

Dear Editor:

The Treaty Oak is an important part of our state's history. One legend says that Stephen F. Austin made peace with other leaders beneath the branches of the great oak. I don't believe that we should just forget about this part of our past.

Now that the tree is in trouble, we must **raise funds** to save it. Every **donation** will help pay for doctors to take care of the tree.

The Treaty Oak is not just a tree. It is a hero. We must save it!

Sincerely yours,
Adam Brook

newspaper editor person who prepares articles for a newspaper
raise funds collect money
donation gift of money

When a student read Mr. Brook's letter to the editor, she decided to **get involved**. She wrote a letter to her school.

Austin, Texas
May 30, 1990

Dear classmates,

Remember our field trip to the Treaty Oak? It reminded me of how hard people have worked for our great state.

Well, now that tree is in trouble. Someone tried to poison it! Yesterday I read a letter in the newspaper, and I agree that we must help save the Treaty Oak!

At our school, we should collect money to help care for the tree. We should hold a contest. The class that collects the most money can **present** our gift to the governor.

We must do everything we can to save the Treaty Oak!

Sincerely yours,

Jessica

get involved do something
present give

Before You Move On

1. **Author's Purpose** Why did Mr. Brook write his letter? Did he do a good job?

2. **Paraphrase** Tell about Jessica's plan to help save the tree.

365

Think and Respond

Strategy: Cause and Effect

Some stories, like "The Tree That Would Not Die," tell what happens and why it happens. In these stories, look for causes and effects.

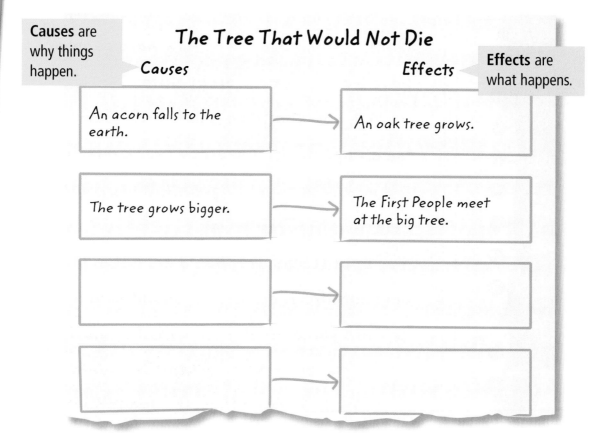

Causes are why things happen.

The Tree That Would Not Die

Causes

An acorn falls to the earth.

The tree grows bigger.

Effects

Effects are what happens.

An oak tree grows.

The First People meet at the big tree.

Make a cause-and-effect chart for "The Tree That Would Not Die."

Retell the Story

Retell the story with a partner. One of you tells an effect. The other tells what caused it.

Talk It Over

 Personal Response Was the story exciting? Why or why not? What makes a story exciting?

 Opinion Is "The Tree That Would Not Die" a good title for this story? Why or why not?

 Author's Purpose Why do you think the author told the story from the tree's point of view? How would the story be different if a person told it?

4 **Conclusion** Did letters like the ones from Mr. Brook and Jessica help save the Treaty Oak? How do you know?

Compare Themes

Both "The Tree That Would Not Die" and "Hello, Fish!" have messages. What are they? Are they the same?

Content Connections

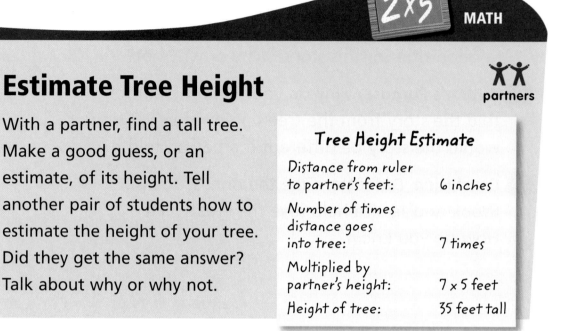

MATH

partners

Estimate Tree Height

With a partner, find a tall tree. Make a good guess, or an estimate, of its height. Tell another pair of students how to estimate the height of your tree. Did they get the same answer? Talk about why or why not.

Tree Height Estimate

Distance from ruler to partner's feet:	6 inches
Number of times distance goes into tree:	7 times
Multiplied by partner's height:	7 x 5 feet
Height of tree:	35 feet tall

SOCIAL STUDIES

small group

Research State People

Internet

Find out about an important person from your state.

1. Write what you already know.

2. Write questions you have.

3. Find the answers and write what you learn.

4. Do you have more questions now? Write those down, too.

Juliette Gordon Low
Savannah, Georgia
Founded Girl Scouts of America

Make a Video

small group

What do people care about in your city
or state?

1. Choose one problem you care about.

2. Make a video to get people to help.

3. Show the video to your class.

Talk about which videos made you
want to help.

Our city has hundreds of
homeless animals. Please
give one a good home.

Write to Persuade

partners

Find articles about your state. Write about
one you think other people should read.
Choose the best form to persuade:

- a letter

- a review

- an ad

Does your writing sound right for
your audience?

March 10, 2004

Dear Editor:
    I just read an article
about a new senator in our
state. Your newspaper
should write about her, too,
and her plans for our state.

Past Tense Verbs

Listen and chant.

Chant

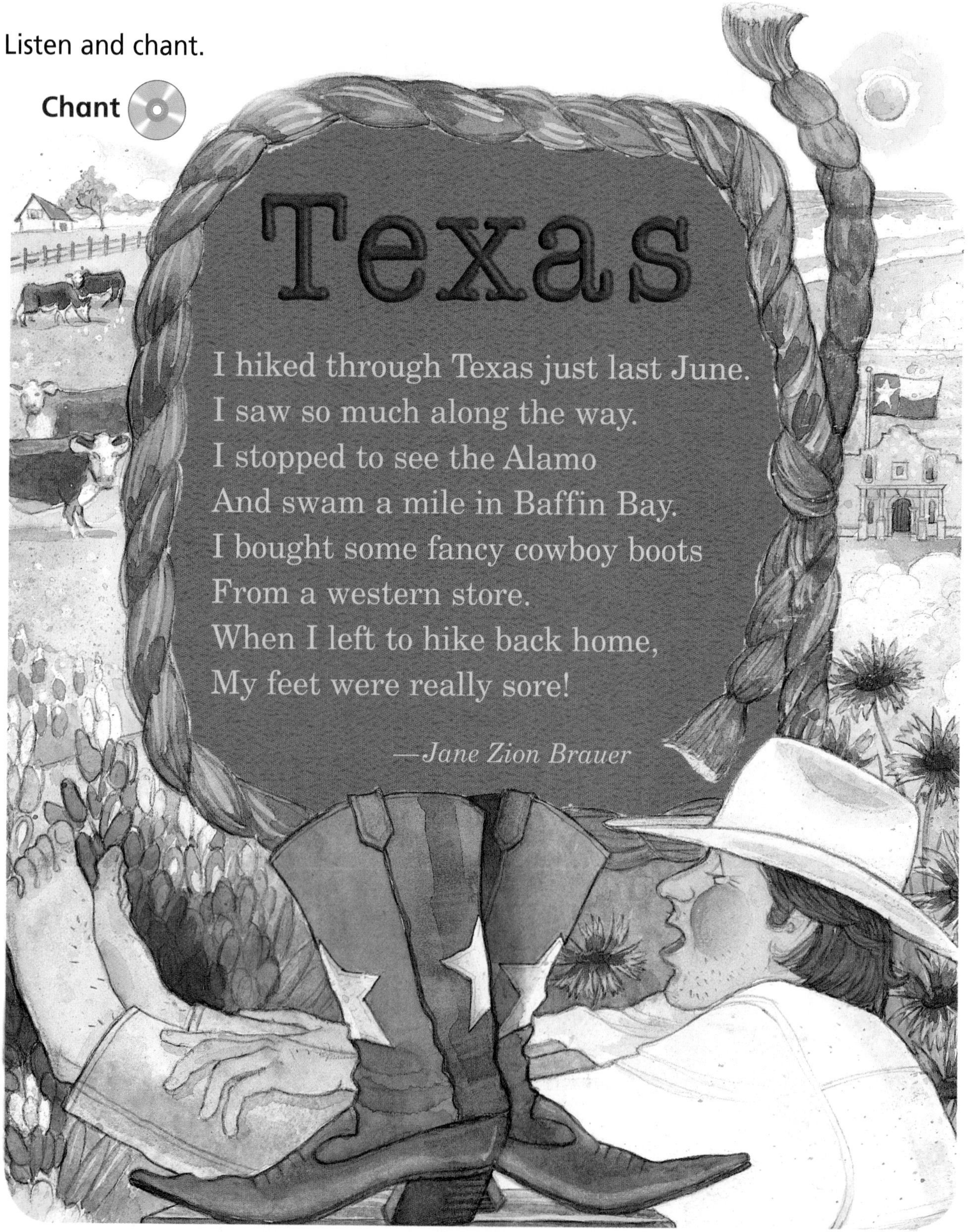

Texas

I hiked through Texas just last June.
I saw so much along the way.
I stopped to see the Alamo
And swam a mile in Baffin Bay.
I bought some fancy cowboy boots
From a western store.
When I left to hike back home,
My feet were really sore!

—Jane Zion Brauer

How Language Works

The **verb** in a sentence shows when the action happens.

Past Tense Verbs	Examples:
■ You can add **-ed** to many verbs to tell about the past.	Verb: **hike** In the Past: I **hiked** through Texas.
■ Other verbs have a special form to tell about the past.	Verb: **take** In the Past: We **took** photos.

Practice with a Partner

Study the verbs in the box. Change each underlined word to tell about the past.

1. The settlers <u>come</u> to a new land.
2. Tall trees <u>grow</u> near a wide river.
3. The settlers <u>build</u> log houses.
4. They <u>plant</u> crops.
5. They <u>work</u> hard.
6. "This is our new home," they <u>say</u>.

Now	In the Past
build	built
come	came
go	went
grow	grew
ride	rode
run	ran
say	said
see	saw

Put It in Writing

Write about a special place in your state or town. Tell about its history. When you edit your work, make sure you used the correct form of the verb.

Early settlers built this house. The first mayor lived here.

Show What You Know

Talk About Your State

In this unit, you read many things about state history. Look back at this unit. Which event was most interesting to you? Tell your group why it interested you.

Make a Mind Map

Work with a partner. Make a web to show what you learned about your own state.

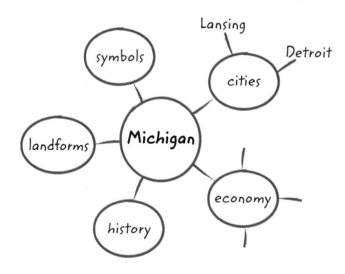

Think and Write

Write the most surprising thing you learned about your state or another state during this unit. Add this writing to your portfolio. Also include work that shows what you learned about other states.

Read and Learn More

Leveled Books

Hawaii and Alaska: Apart, But Still a Part
by Daphne Liu

Your Great State
by Daphne Liu

Theme Library

Celebrate the 50 States!
by Loreen Leedy

The Scrambled States of America
by Laurie Keller

Internet

Go to: www.hbavenues.com

U.S. Facts

State Games

U.S. Mint

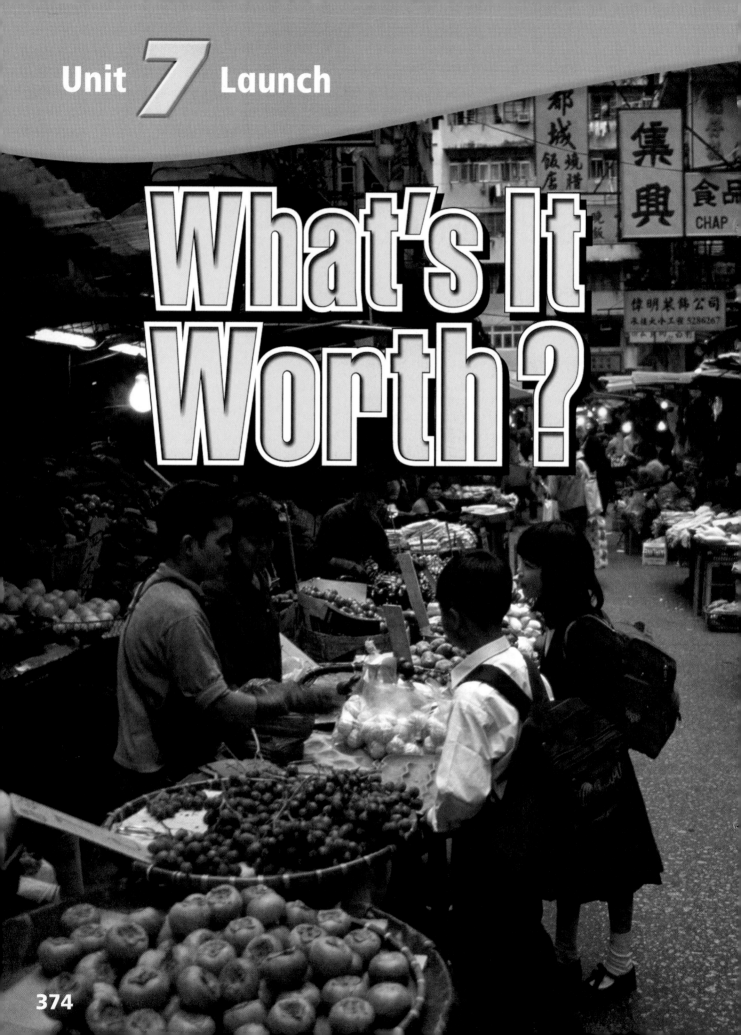

What's It Worth?

Make a Trade

1. Look in your desk. Check your pockets. Find something that you want to trade.
2. Look around you. Who has something you want? Ask your classmate to trade with you.
3. Make the trade. Did you get what you wanted?

The Economic Cycle

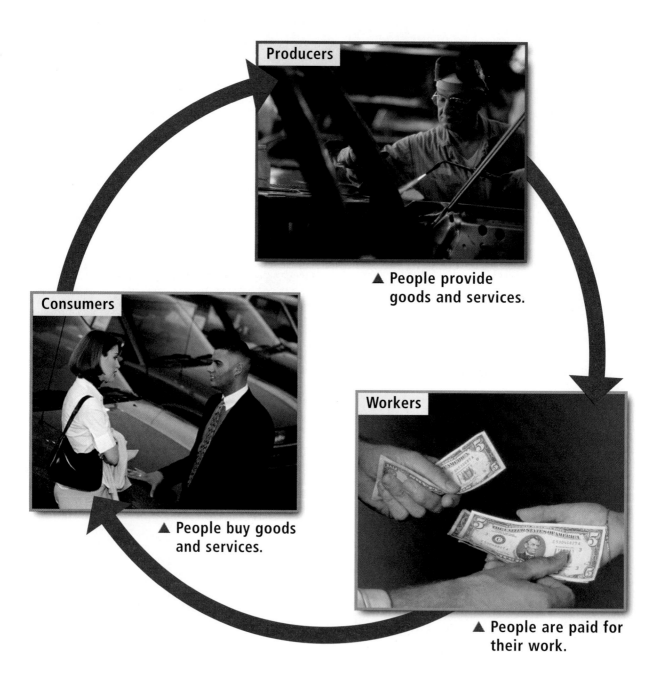

Producers

▲ People provide goods and services.

Consumers

▲ People buy goods and services.

Workers

▲ People are paid for their work.

Advertising

Producers use advertising to get consumers to buy their goods or services.

Bandwagon

▲ This ad wants you to believe that everybody is using the product.

Star Power

▲ This ad uses a famous person to get people to buy the product.

Strong Feelings

▲ This ad wants you to believe that the product will make your family happy.

Amazing Features

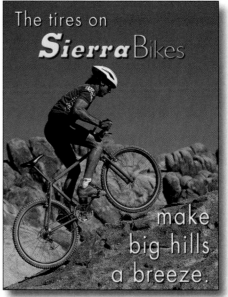

▲ This ad tries to make people believe that the product can do amazing things.

Vocabulary

Market Day

Every Saturday there is a **market**. Farmers take **loads** of boxes from their trucks. They arrange the **goods** on tables.

The **determined** customers push through the crowds. They don't want to be **disappointed** and not find what they need!

Sellers and buyers both get a **reward**. Sellers leave with **coins** and buyers leave with fresh food.

Key Words

market

load

goods

determined

disappointed

reward

coin

MY ROWS AND PILES OF COINS

by **Tololwa M. Mollel** ~ illustrated by **E . B. Lewis**

Read a Story

Genre

Sometimes an author uses events from his or her own life to tell a story. In this **autobiographical fiction** story, the author tells about a time he saved his money to buy something very special.

Characters

Saruni

Murete,
his father

Yeyo,
his mother

Setting

This story happens in a small village in Tanzania, Africa.

Tanzania, Africa

▲ village in Tanzania

Selection Reading

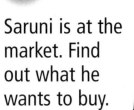

Saruni is at the market. Find out what he wants to buy.

After a good day at the **market**, my mother, Yeyo,
gave me five whole ten-cent **coins**. I **gaped** at the money
until Yeyo **nudged me**. "Saruni, what are you waiting for?
Go and buy yourself something."

---

gaped stared with my mouth open
nudged me pushed me softly

I rushed into the market. I saw roasted peanuts, **chapati**, rice cakes, and **sambusa**. There were wooden toy trucks, kites, and marbles. My heart beat excitedly. I wanted to buy everything, but I **clutched** my coins tightly in my pocket.

---

chapati fried bread (in Swahili)

sambusa dough filled with meat and vegetables and cooked (in Swahili)

clutched held

At the edge of the market, I stopped. In a neat sparkling row stood several big new bicycles. One of them was decorated all over with red and blue.

That's what I would buy!

For some time now, Murete, my father, had been teaching me to ride his big, heavy bicycle. If only I had a bicycle of my own!

A gruff voice startled me. "What are you looking for, little boy?"

I turned and bumped into a tall skinny man, who laughed at my confusion. **Embarrassed**, I hurried back to Yeyo.

A gruff voice startled me An unfriendly voice scared me

Embarrassed Feeling bad because he laughed at me

That night, I dropped five ten-cent coins into my secret money box. It held other ten-cent coins that Yeyo had given me for helping with market work on Saturdays. By the dim light of a lantern, I **feasted my eyes on** the money. I couldn't believe it was all mine.

I emptied the box, arranged all the coins **in piles** and the piles in rows. Then, I counted the coins and thought about the bicycle I **longed to** buy.

---

feasted my eyes on looked happily at
in piles into small groups
longed to really wanted to

Every day after school, when I wasn't helping Yeyo to prepare supper, I asked Murete if I could ride his bicycle. He held the bicycle steady while I rode around, my toes barely touching the pedals.

Whenever Murete let go, I **wobbled**, fell off, or crashed into things and among coffee trees. Other children from the neighborhood had a good laugh watching me.

"Go on, laugh," I thought, **sore** but **determined**. Soon I would **be like a cheetah on wheels**, racing on errands with my very own bicycle!

---

wobbled moved unevenly from side to side
sore hurt
be like a cheetah on wheels ride my bike as fast as a cheetah, the fastest cat

Before You Move On

1. **Details** How does Saruni earn his money?

2. **Goal** What does Saruni want to buy?

Saturday after Saturday, we took **goods** to market,
piled high on Yeyo's head and on my squeaky old wooden
wheelbarrow. We sold dried beans and **maize**, pumpkins,
spinach, bananas, firewood, and eggs.

My money box grew heavier.

I emptied the box, arranged the coins in piles and the
piles in rows. Then, I counted the coins and thought about
the blue and red bicycle.

---

maize corn

After several more lessons, Murete let me ride **on my own** while he shouted instructions. "Eyes up, arms straight, keep pedaling, slow down!" I enjoyed the breeze on my face, the pedals turning smoothly under my feet, and, most of all, Yeyo's proud smile as she watched me ride. How surprised she would be to see my new bicycle! How **grateful** she would be when I used it to help her on market days!

---

on my own all by myself
grateful thankful

The heavy March rains came. The ground became so muddy that nobody went to market. Instead, I helped Yeyo with **house chores**. When it wasn't raining, I helped Murete on the coffee farm. We **pruned** the coffee trees and put fallen leaves and twigs around the coffee stems. Whenever I could, I practiced riding Murete's bicycle.

It stopped raining in June. Not long after, school closed. Our harvest of fresh maize and peas, sweet potatoes, vegetables, and fruits was so big that we went to market on Saturdays <u>and</u> Wednesdays. My money box grew heavier and heavier.

I emptied the box, arranged the coins in piles and the piles in rows. Then, I counted the coins and thought about the bicycle I would buy.

---

house chores jobs around the house like cleaning

pruned cut off small parts of

A few days later I grew confident enough to try to ride a **loaded bicycle**. With Murete's help, I **strapped** a giant pumpkin on the carrier behind me. When I **attempted** to pedal, the bicycle wobbled so dangerously that Murete, alongside me, had to grab it.

"All right, Saruni, the **load** is too heavy for you," he said, and I got off. Getting on the bicycle to ride back to the house, he sighed tiredly. "It is also hard on my bones, which are getting too old for pedaling."

I practiced daily with smaller loads, and slowly I learned to ride a loaded bicycle. No more pushing the squeaky old wheelbarrow, I thought. I would ride with my load tall and proud on my bicycle, just like Murete!

---

loaded bicycle bicycle with heavy items on it
strapped tied
attempted tried

Before You Move On

1. **Inference** Why does Saruni want to learn how to ride a loaded bicycle?

2. **Character** What kind of person is Saruni? How do you know?

391

Saruni returns to the market. Will he get what he wants?

On the first Saturday after school opened in July, we went to market as usual. Late in the afternoon, after selling all we had, Yeyo sat talking with another trader.

I **set off** into the crowd. I wore an old coat Murete had handed down to me for chilly July days like today.

---

set off walked

My **precious** coins were
wrapped in various bundles inside
the **oversize** pockets of the coat.

"I must be the richest boy in
the world," I thought, feeling like
a king. "I can buy anything."

---

precious very important
oversize large

The tall skinny man was polishing his bicycles as I came up. "I want to buy a bicycle," I said, and brought out my bundles of coins.

The man whistled in wonder as I unwrapped the money carefully on his table. "How many coins have you got there?"

Proudly I told him. "Three hundred and five."

"Three hundred and . . . five," he **muttered**. "That's thirty **shillings** and fifty cents." He **exploded with laughter**. "A whole bicycle . . . for thirty shillings . . . and fifty cents?"

His laugh followed me as I walked away with my bundles of coins, deeply **disappointed**.

---

muttered said in a low voice

shillings coins worth less than one dollar

exploded with laughter laughed very hard and loud

Before You Move On

1. **Details** What makes Saruni feel like a king?

2. **Inference** Why does the bicycle man laugh about Saruni's money?

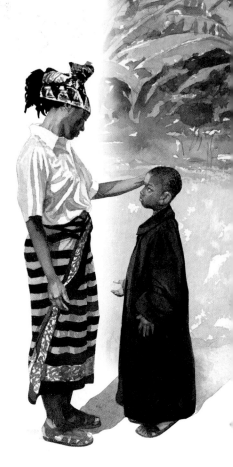

4

Find out about two surprises for Saruni.

On our way home, Yeyo asked what was wrong. I had to tell her everything.

"You saved all your money for a bicycle to help me?" she asked. I could tell she was amazed and **touched**. "How nice of you!" As for the tall skinny man, she said angrily, "Oh! What does he know? Of course you will buy a bicycle. One day you will."

Her kind words did not cheer me.

The next afternoon, the sound of a *pikipiki* filled the air. *Tuk-tuk-tuk-tuk-tuk*. I came out of the house and stared in surprise. Murete was sitting on top of an orange motorbike.

He **cut the engine and dismounted**. Then, laughing at my excited questions about the *pikipiki*, he headed into the house.

---

touched filled with strong feelings
pikipiki motorbike (in Swahili)
cut the engine and dismounted turned off the motor and got off the bike

When Murete came out, Yeyo was with him, and he was **wheeling** his bicycle. "I want to sell this to you. For thirty shillings and fifty cents." He winked at me.

Surprised, I stared at Murete. How did he know about my secret money box? I hadn't told him anything.

Then, suddenly, I realized the wonderful thing that had just happened. "My bicycle. I have my very own bicycle!" I said, and it didn't matter at all that it wasn't decorated with red and blue. Within moments, I had brought Murete my money box.

Murete gave Yeyo the box. Yeyo, in turn, gave it to me. **Puzzled**, I looked from Yeyo to Murete and to Yeyo again. "You're giving it . . . back to me?"

Yeyo smiled. "It's a **reward** for all your help to us."

"Thank you, thank you!" I cried **gleefully**.

---

wheeling pushing
Puzzled Confused
gleefully happily

The next Saturday, my load sat tall and proud on my bicycle, which I walked importantly to market. I wasn't riding it because Yeyo **could never have kept up**.

Looking over at Yeyo, I wished she didn't have to carry such a big load on her head.

"If only I had a **cart** to pull behind my bicycle," I thought. "I could **lighten her load**!"

That night I emptied the box, arranged all the coins in piles and the piles in rows. Then, I counted the coins and thought about the cart I would buy. . . .

---

could never have kept up could not walk as fast as I could ride

cart small wagon

lighten her load help carry some of the load for her

Before You Move On

1. **Outcome** Does Saruni get his very own bicycle? Explain.

2. **Prediction** What will Saruni be like when he grows up?

Meet the Author

Tololwa M. Mollel

Tololwa M. Mollel enjoyed all kinds of stories as a child in Tanzania, Africa. Mr. Mollel knows that stories come from where people live, what they do, and what they hope for. "See what makes the world around you interesting," he says, "and then tell your own story."

The pictures in *My Rows and Piles of Coins* remind Mr. Mollel of his childhood, especially the one that shows Saruni counting his coins in the lamplight. "We had no electricity in my home," Mollel remembers. "The dim glow of the lamp in a sea of darkness is just how I remember it."

Think and Respond

Strategy: Goal and Outcome

Some stories tell how a character reaches a goal.
In these stories, look for the goal, the events,
and the outcome.

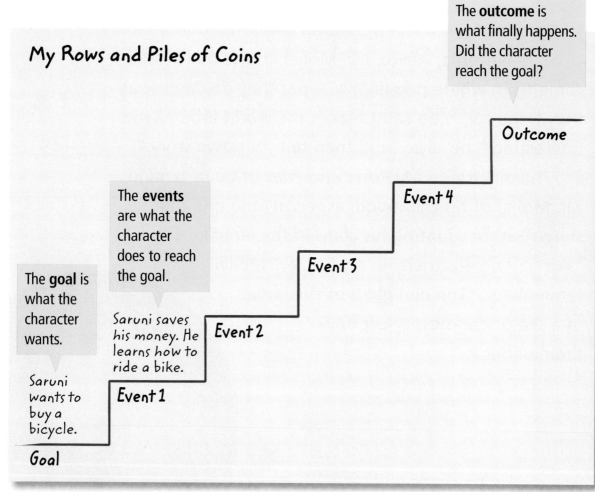

My Rows and Piles of Coins

The **outcome** is what finally happens. Did the character reach the goal?

Outcome

Event 4

Event 3

The **events** are what the character does to reach the goal.

Event 2

The **goal** is what the character wants.

Saruni saves his money. He learns how to ride a bike.

Event 1

Saruni wants to buy a bicycle.

Goal

Make a story map. Show Saruni's goal, the events,
and the outcome.

Interview a Character

Pretend your partner is Saruni. Ask Saruni how he
feels during each event. Use your story map.

Talk It Over

 Personal Response Would Saruni be a good
friend? Why or why not? Give an example from
the story.

 Comparison How are Saruni and Murete alike?
How are they different?

3 **Opinion** Was it a good idea for Yeyo to give
Saruni the reward? Why or why not?

4 **Speculate** How would this story be different if
Yeyo or Murete told it?

Compare Characters

A motive is the reason a character
does things. Compare Saruni's
motives with another character's
motives.

Content Connections

Role-Play a Conversation

partners

Pretend you are Saruni and your partner is Yeyo. Tell Yeyo what happened at the market. Listen to Yeyo's answer. Talk about how Saruni and Yeyo felt.

The bicycle man laughed at me.

---

2 × 5   MATH

Plan a Budget

partners

What do you want to save money for? Create a budget. Tell how your budget will help you get the thing you want.

Jerome's Budget for Summer Vacation

Money In

allowance	$8.00
mowing lawns	$5.00
Total	$13.00

Money Out

movies	$6.00
snacks	$4.00
savings	$3.00

Create Ads

Internet

small group

1. Choose a product to advertise.

2. Think of different ways to get people to buy the product.

3. Choose one way and create an ad.

Which ad makes the most students want to buy? Why?

Mountain Top Raisins

Eat a box of Mountain Top Raisins and climb the highest mountain!

WRITING

Write to Persuade

on your own

What service can you provide for a classmate?
Write something to persuade a classmate to hire you.
Choose the best form to persuade:

- an ad

- a review

- a letter

Check your details. Will they help persuade your audience?

Natalie's Bike Repair Shop

Natalie's Bike Repair Shop has the best bike service in the area. It offers complete bike repair and cleaning for all types of bikes. If you have a bike that needs to be fixed, then Natalie's is the place to go!

Form Generalizations

A **generalization** is a statement that tells about many situations. To form generalizations:

✔ Think about the facts the writer gives.
✔ Use the writer's examples to make a general statement. The words *many, some,* or *usually* can help you make a generalization.
✔ Make sure your statement applies to more than one situation.

Try the strategy.

New Things

Several of my friends just bought new things. Andre just got a new scooter. He bought it with money he earned mowing lawns. Sergio's parents paid him for jobs around the house. He used the money to buy a new video game. Mai just bought a stereo. She gets paid to babysit. She saved her money for the stereo.

This paragraph talks about things people bought with money they earned. I can make the general statement that you can save the money you earn to buy new things.

Practice

Take this test and **form generalizations**.

Read the article. Then read each item. Choose the best answers.

Every country has special designs on its money. An Australian bill shows Queen Elizabeth II. Many U.S. bills have pictures of American presidents. The leader Mahatma Gandhi is pictured on Indian money. Several Mexican bills show Mexican leaders.

One bill from Cyprus shows a famous church. A bill from the Dominican Republic features the National Theatre. One Japanese bill pictures a gate to a famous castle.

1   **Which is the best generalization for the first paragraph?**

   A   Most countries have queens and presidents.

   B   Every country uses paper money.

   C   Many countries show important leaders on their money.

2   **Which is the best generalization for the second paragraph?**

   A   Many people in Japan like castles.

   B   Many countries show important buildings on their money.

   C   Countries usually put churches, theaters, and castles on their money.

> ✓ **Test Strategy**
>
> Look for important words like *not, which,* and *best* in the questions. They will help you find the correct answer.

Vocabulary

FAIR EXCHANGE

I have a problem I need to solve.
I am a farmer, but I have no shed.
Maybe a builder will **exchange**
His **service** for the **value** of grain.

I have a problem I need to solve.
I am a baker, but I have no meat.
Maybe the butcher will **barter** with me.
I'll **trade** my service happily.

—*Maria Del Rey*

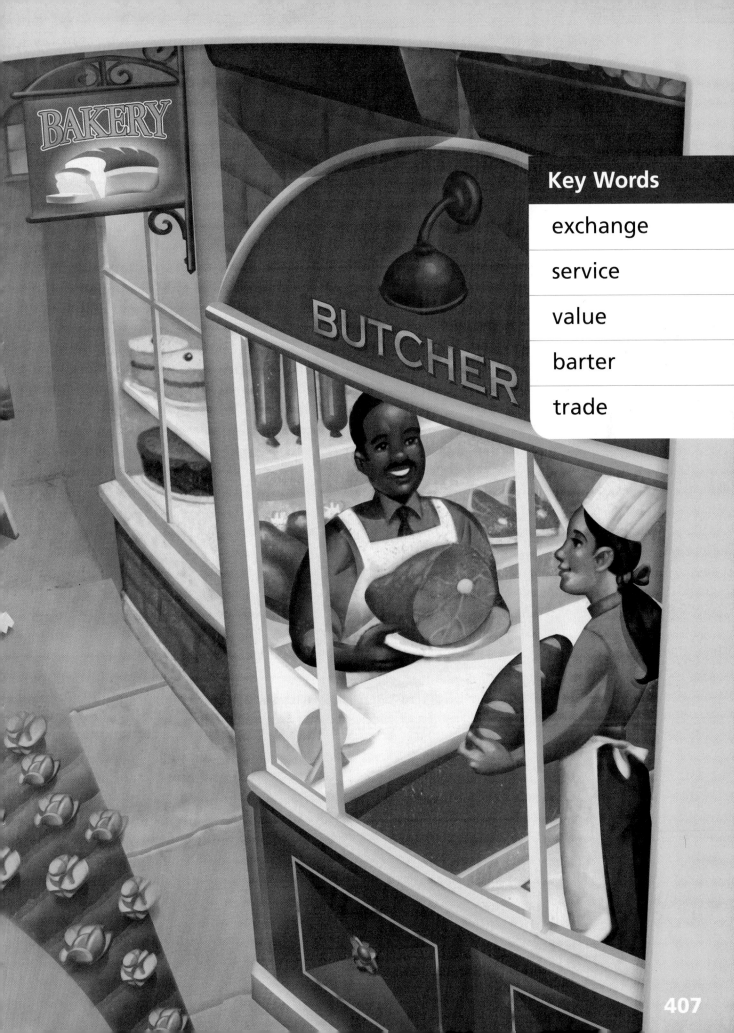

Key Words

exchange

service

value

barter

trade

407

Read a History Article

A **history article** is nonfiction. It often tells who, what, when, where, and why things change over time.

✔ Look for photographs of real objects, or **artifacts**. They show what things were like in the past.

artifacts

▲ Nuggets of gold, silver, and bronze were made into coins.

✔ Read the **captions** and **labels** to learn how things changed.

Selection Reading

MONEY

by **Adele Richardson**

Everyone Needs Money!

Money is important to people all over the world. It's used to buy food, clothing, cars, games, and just about anything. **Its appearance** and its **value** change, **depending on** the country in which it is made. However, one thing is for sure. Everyone needs money!

Its appearance The way it looks
depending on because of the way things are in

▲ **This woman uses money to pay a cab driver.**

This girl uses money to buy jewelry. ▶

▼ People use money to buy food.

Many Ways to Trade

Before money was invented, people couldn't just go to a store and buy something. They had to **trade** the things they owned for other things they wanted or needed. This **practice** is called bartering. In order for bartering to work, the objects two people are trading must be of some value. For example, a farmer who grows grain might trade with someone who raises chickens. This way both families could have grain to make bread and meat to cook.

---

practice way of doing things

▼ People **exchange** objects to get things they want or need.

412

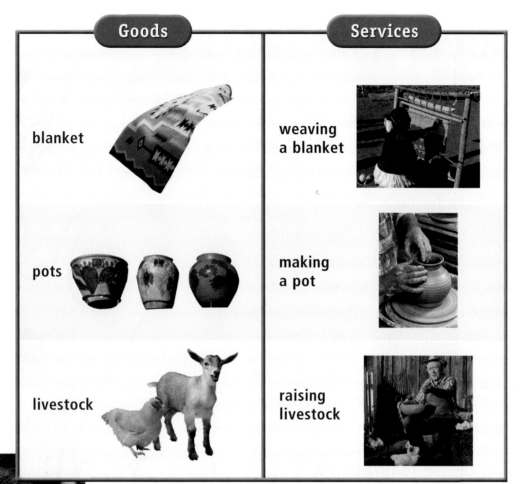

Goods	Services
blanket	weaving a blanket
pots	making a pot
livestock	raising livestock

Bartering has never been limited to trading food. People traded other goods, too. A person who made warm blankets could find a lot of people to **barter** with when the weather turned cold. Others may have traded a **service** for food or clothing. For example, a person who knew how to build a barn could be very **valuable** to someone who raised **livestock**.

---

valuable important
livestock animals

Before You Move On

1. **Paraphrase** What is bartering? Give one example.

2. **Graphic Aids** Compare goods and services. How are they different? Alike?

Objects as Money

It was not always easy to trade things back and forth. Many times people did not agree on the value of an object because their needs and wants were different. Sometimes people could not find anyone to trade with. One orange grower certainly wouldn't want to trade with another orange grower. If a grower's fruit was left to spoil, it **became worthless**. People felt that there had to be a better way.

After people **realized** how hard bartering could be, they **developed a medium of exchange**. To develop a medium of exchange, they agreed on the value of an object and used it to pay for goods or services. Depending on the culture, a medium of exchange can be a piece of gold, a goat or sheep, or even stones.

Objects like beads, musket balls, fishing hooks, and nails were once used as money in many countries. ▶

---

became worthless had no value

realized understood

developed a medium of exchange agreed to use certain objects to pay for goods and services

The **ancient Chinese** used smooth shells found in warm water oceans, called cowrie shells, as money. In Mongolia and western Asia, tea was very valuable. It was made into bricks and used as a form of money. In Africa, blocks of salt were considered forms of money. Other items used for money around the world were seeds, beads, livestock, and feathers.

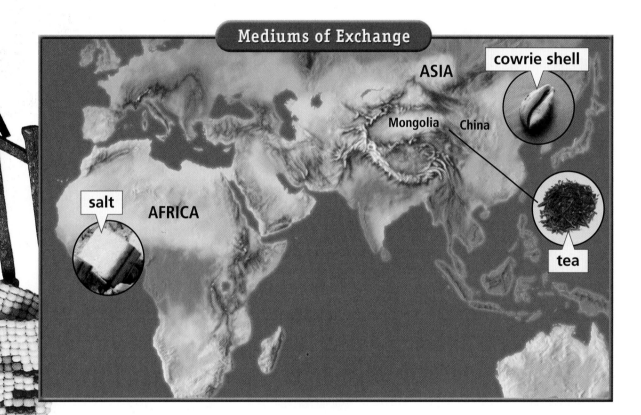

Mediums of Exchange

ASIA

cowrie shell

Mongolia   China

AFRICA

salt

tea

There was still a problem, though. Many of these mediums of exchange could be easily damaged. A shell could break. A cow could get sick. Seeds and feathers could blow away. Food could spoil or be eaten! People needed something that was small, valuable, and tough as a medium of exchange. The answer to this problem was metal money.

---

ancient Chinese people who lived in China long, long ago

Before You Move On

1. **Details** Name three objects that people have used as money.

2. **Problem/Solution** Why was using objects as money a problem?

Metal and Paper Money

There is no record in history to prove when metal money was first used. Some believe it was over 5,000 years ago in Mesopotamia. There are records that prove the people of Greece made and used coins around 700 B.C.E. Greek coins were gold, silver, and bronze nuggets that were **flattened and stamped** with a picture or design. Each coin had to be stamped by hand with a hammer.

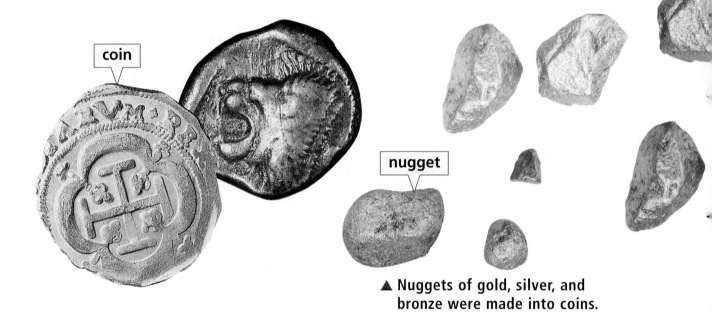

coin

nugget

▲ Nuggets of gold, silver, and bronze were made into coins.

Metal money became a better medium of exchange than feathers or seeds, but there were problems with it, too. If a person carried too much, the coins could be very heavy. This problem was solved with the creation of paper money.

---

flattened and stamped made flat and marked

◀ Chinese notes were some of the first paper money ever made.

The Chinese were the first people known to use paper money around 1300. During the 1700s, many small banks and business owners all over the world started to make bank notes. Bank notes were promises to give gold or silver to the customer in exchange for the notes.

In 1861, the United States government decided to stop the practice of using bank notes and to print its own paper money. The **bills** were called greenbacks because their backs were printed in green ink. Some banks were still allowed to issue money, but by 1877 the government had stopped the practice.

◀ After 1877, only greenbacks printed by the United States government were **legal money**.

---

bills pieces of paper money
legal money money allowed by law

Before You Move On

1. **Details** Why were U.S. bills called greenbacks?

2. **Graphic Aids** What can you tell about metal money from the artifacts?

417

Money Around the World

Countries around the world have different kinds of money. Even if the money has the same name, it may have a different value. Whenever people travel to another country, they must exchange their money for the kind of money used in that country. Large banks and airports around the world usually have places where exchanges can be made.

Travelers can get an idea of what their money is worth in another country by looking at a **foreign exchange rate table**. The exchange rate is listed in many major newspapers and is available at any bank. The rate changes often. What a United States dollar is worth in Mexico one day will probably be different the next week.

Exchange Rates for March 26, 2002

In this part of the world:	$1 of U.S. money was worth:	
Australia	1.89 dollars	
Canada	1.59 dollars	
Europe	1.14 euros	
Japan	132.73 yen	
Mexico	9.02 pesos	

foreign exchange rate table table that tells how much one country's money is worth in another country

Countries That Use the Euro

Countries using
the euro in 2002

Finland

Ireland

The Netherlands

Germany

Belgium

Luxembourg

Austria

France

Portugal

Spain

Italy

Greece

▲ Between 1999 and 2002, many European nations
began to use the same money, the euro.

Before You Move On

1. **Inference** Why did so
   many European nations
   decide to use the euro?

2. **Graphic Aids** On March 26,
   2002, how many pesos was
   a U.S. dollar worth?

United States Money

United States coins are made by machines in mints. Today's coins are made of materials that are less valuable than gold and silver, such as zinc, copper, and nickel. Melted metals are poured and rolled into sheets. After the metal hardens, the shapes of the coins are cut out of the sheet and stamped with the proper design.

ridge

Pennies and nickels are polished and sent through a machine that gives them **a raised rim**. Dollar coins, quarters, and dimes are milled coins. The edges of milled coins have rough ridges. These also go through special machines that do all the work.

---

a raised rim an edge thicker than the rest of the coin

◀ **The "D" on this coin shows that it was made in the Denver mint.**

raised rim

By law, all coins in the United States must show the date they were made and have the word "Liberty" on them. Letters on the right side of the faces on United States coins can tell you where the coins were made: Denver (D), New Orleans (O), Philadelphia (P), or San Francisco (S). It's a law in the United States that the design of a coin be kept for at least 25 years.

Pennies are made partly of copper. This metal gives pennies their red color.

The 5-cent coin is named for the metal originally used to make it, nickel.

The word "dime" comes from a Latin word that means one-tenth. A dime is worth one-tenth of a dollar.

A quarter is named after its value. It is worth one quarter, or one-fourth, of a dollar.

Before You Move On

1. **Steps in a Process** Tell how U.S. coins are made.

2. **Graphic Aids** Why is a U.S. 25-cent coin called a quarter?

421

Can you find 13 arrows, 13 leaves, and 13 stars on this part of a U.S. dollar bill? ▶

All paper money made in the United States is printed in Washington, D.C., at the Bureau of Engraving and Printing. United States bills are printed with a secret formula ink that never completely dries. A one-dollar bill in the United States lasts for an average of 18 months before it **wears out**.

On the back of a United States one-dollar bill is an eagle that **represents the 13 original colonies**. One claw holds 13 arrows, the other holds an olive branch with 13 leaves. There are also 13 stars over the eagle's head.

---

wears out tears or falls apart

represents the 13 original colonies reminds people of the first 13 settlements in America

Money is always moving all over the world. Every day someone pays yen for soup while someone else gives dollars for shirts. Someone receives euros for babysitting while someone else gets pesos as a gift. People use other mediums of exchange every day, too. Friends trade CDs, sandwiches, and books. Wherever there are people, the exchange of money, goods, and services goes on and on.

▼ euro coins

Before You Move On

1. **Inference** Why are all U.S. bills printed with secret formula ink?

2. **Summary** Explain how people exchange goods every day.

Think and Respond

Strategy: Problem and Solution

Make a problem-and-solution chain. Show the problem with each form of money and how it was solved.

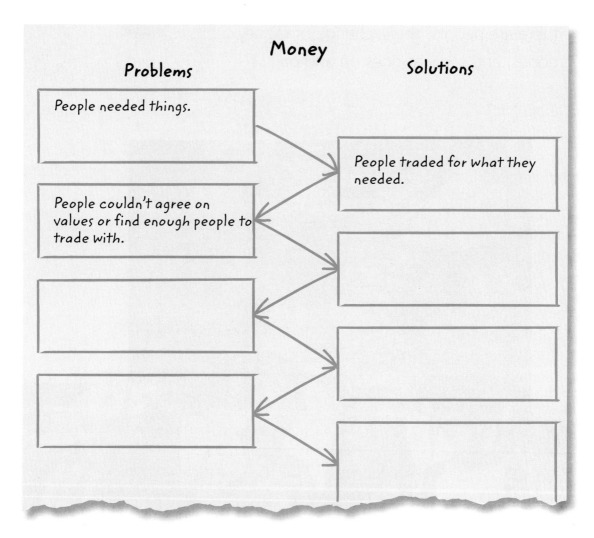

Money

Problems | Solutions

People needed things.

People traded for what they needed.

People couldn't agree on values or find enough people to trade with.

Form Generalizations

Talk about your problem-and-solution chain with a partner. What can you say is true about money throughout its history?

Talk It Over

 Personal Response What is the most interesting fact you learned about money?

 Conclusion Is it easier to buy and sell goods and services today than it was in the past? Explain.

3 **Inference** Why is there a law that a coin design must be kept for 25 years?

4 **Speculate** Do you think money will change again in the future? Explain.

Compare Ideas

How are "Money" and "A Quarter's Worth of Fame" alike? How are they different?

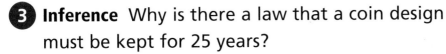

In "Money," I learned about money all around the world. "A Quarter's Worth of Fame" was about just one coin in the United States.

Content Connections

Role-Play History

large group

Choose a time period in history from the selection. Pretend you want to buy something then. What could you buy? How would you pay for it? Role-play buying the item.

I will trade this bag of shells for a cart.

SOCIAL
STUDIES

Make a Product Map

partners

Where in the world were your clothes made?

1. Look at your shoes and clothes. Find the "Made in" information.

2. Draw a picture of each item on a card. Write where it was made.

3. Place your cards on a class world map.

4. Study the map. Show the results on a graph.

What does the graph tell you?

U.S.A. 25%

Mexico 25%

Sri Lanka 12%

China 38%

Shop at a Class Store

1. Choose one kind of product and find three different brands of it.

2. Write the amount in each package and its price on a card.

3. Display the cards in a class store.

4. Find the best values for each product.

Tony's Homemade Pasta

Price: $3.50
Amount: 64 ounces

Write a Letter

Write a letter to an advice column. Ask a question or tell about a problem with money. Tell why you need help. Trade letters with a partner and write a reply. Read your reply to your partner.

Dear Buck,
    Help! I am 10 years old and need a computer. How can I earn money to buy one?

                Sincerely,
                Need Money
                in Tennessee

Helping Verbs

Listen and sing.

Song 🔘

Going Into Town

We are going into town
To buy a bike for Jenny.
We have earned
The money we need.
And never borrowed a penny.

—Jane Zion Brauer

Tune: "Jack and Jill"

How Language Works

Some verbs are made up of more than one word. The last word is the **main verb**. The verb that comes before is the **helping verb**. The helping verb agrees with the subject.

One	More Than One
<ul><li>Luis **was** **trying** to save money.</li><li>He **is earning** money now at the pet shop.</li><li>He **has** also **earned** money from jobs at home.</li></ul>	<ul><li>Luis and I **were** **trying** to save money.</li><li>We **are earning** money now at the pet shop.</li><li>We **have** also **earned** money from jobs at home.</li></ul>

Practice with a Partner

Read each sentence. Add the correct helping verb.

has / have **1.** Luis _____ saved fifty dollars so far.

has / have **2.** Our parents _____ given us some jobs.

was / were **3.** They _____ helping us earn money.

is / are **4.** Luis _____ working hard. So am I!

is / are **5.** We _____ trying to save money for a telescope.

Put It in Writing

Think of someone you know who wants to earn money. Write a sentence. Tell what that person is doing or has done.

Ben has raked the leaves every week. He is saving money for a bike.

Show What You Know

Talk About Money

In this unit, you read a story and a social studies article about money. Choose one new money word you learned from this unit. Find a partner who picked the same word. Talk about what it means.

Make a Mind Map

Work with a partner. Make a web to show what you learned about money.

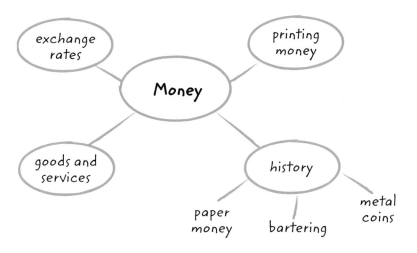

Think and Write

Write a paragraph about one problem people have with money today and how people might solve that problem in the future. Add this writing to your portfolio. Also add other work that shows what you learned about money.

Read and Learn More

Leveled Books

What Is It Worth?
by Susan Buntrock

The Monster Money Book
by Loreen Leedy

Theme Library

Yoshi's Feast
by Kimiko Kajikawa

Money
by Adele Richardson

Internet

Go to: www.hbavenues.com

Exchange Rate Calculator

Money Games

More Money Games

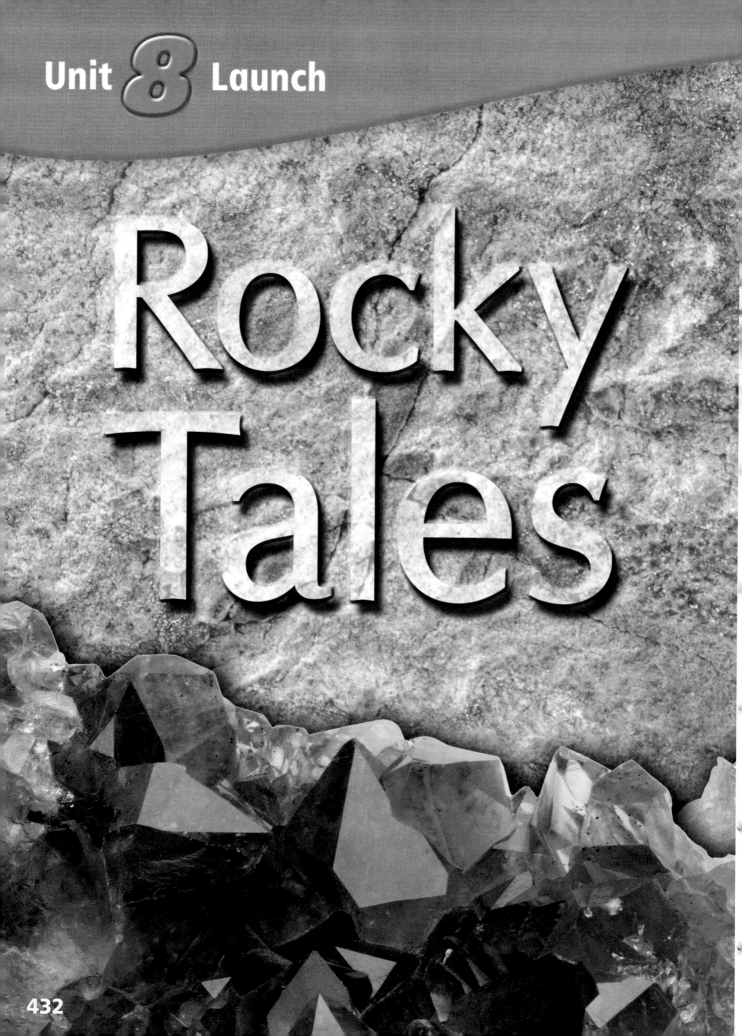

Rocky Tales

Put Rocks into Groups

1. Look at some rocks with a partner.
   What differences do you see? Are some rocks heavier
   than others? Are the colors the same?
2. Put rocks that are alike in the same group.
3. How many groups can you make? Label each group
   of rocks.

sharp edges

stuck together

smooth edges

Properties of Rocks

Shine	Color	Hardness
▲ sandstone	▲ quartz	▲ talc (very soft)
▲ schist	▲ emerald	▲ fluorite (soft)
▲ galena	▲ ruby	▲ topaz (very hard)
▲ gold	▲ tourmaline	▲ diamond (hardest)

Rocks in the Solar System

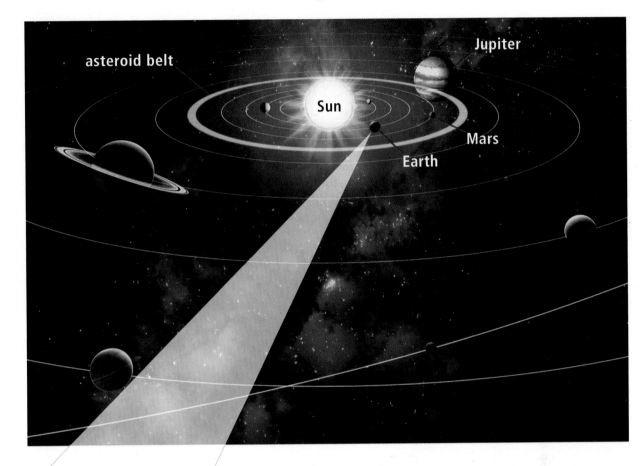

asteroid belt

Sun

Jupiter

Mars

Earth

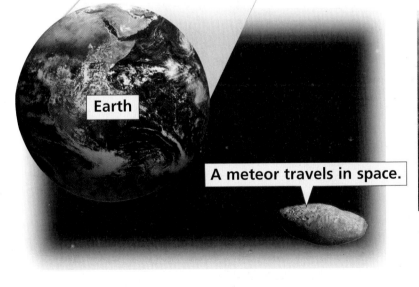

Earth

A meteor travels in space.

crater

▲ Meteors that hit Earth are called meteorites. Sometimes they create large craters.

A ROCK FROM SPACE

We found a strange rock. It looked so lonely by itself. We didn't want to walk away and abandon it, so we lifted it onto our wagon. "Let's take it to Ms. Tran at the museum," I said.

Ms. Tran strained to pick up the heavy rock. "What is this enormous thing?" she asked.

Finally she said, "You have found a **meteorite**!" This rock made a long **journey** from somewhere in space. Let's keep it in the museum so people can see it."

Now our rock does not seem lonely any more!

Key Words

lonely

abandon

lift

museum

strain

enormous

meteorite

journey

CALL ME AHNIGHITO

by Pam Conrad
illustrated by Richard Egielski

Read a Fantasy

Genre

A **fantasy** includes events that could never happen in real life. In this story, a meteorite named Ahnighito tells how he became famous.

Character

A meteorite named Ahnighito tells about his life. He tells the story from his own point of view.

Ahnighito

Setting

The story begins in Greenland and continues in New York City. The events happen over several hundred years.

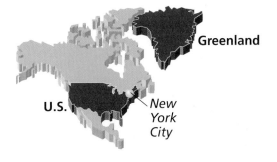

Greenland

U.S.

New York City

Selection Reading

1

Ahnighito sits alone in Greenland. Find out how he feels.

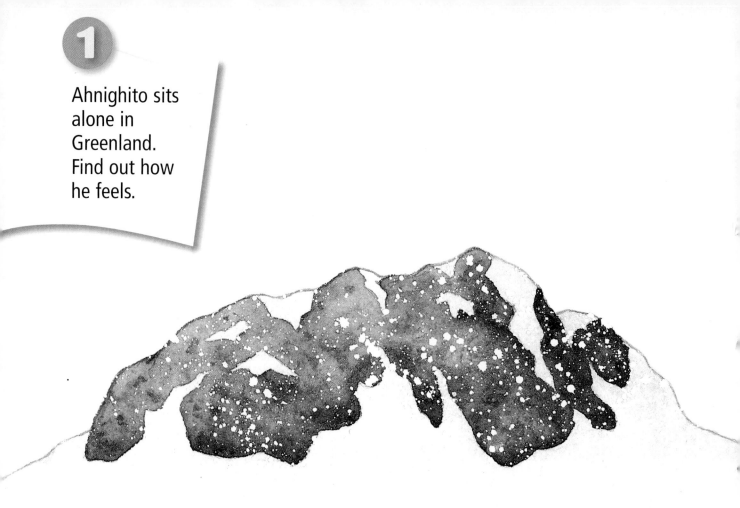

THEY CALL ME AHNIGHITO. They tell me I am made of star stuff, but I don't remember my birth. I remember only the cold Arctic days when I sat for **centuries**, freezing cold and half buried in the hard and **bitter earth**. I sat and I waited and wished that something would happen to me. Nothing did, though.

Nothing much ever happens in the Arctic. The Greenland sun comes up for a while, then **sinks** for a longer while. The ice begins to melt and then freezes again. For years and years, full of days and days, I saw nothing but the Greenland sky.

---

centuries hundreds of years
bitter earth cold ground
sinks goes down

Then one day, the snow people came and gathered around me. I thought, "At last, something is happening."

They began to **hammer at my sides and chip away** little pieces of me. **Imagine**! Little pieces of me! I worried that I would be chipped away to nothing.

Hundreds of melting summers passed, and the snow people kept hammering away.

---

hammer at my sides and chip away   hit me with tools and break off

Imagine! Think about it!

Soon they brought other people. These new people began to dig in the earth around my mighty sides. I thought they would chip away still bigger pieces of me and **scatter** me across the Arctic snows. Instead, they **prodded and probed**. Then, **grunting** and <mark>straining</mark>, they rolled me into the sun.

What joy I felt, free at last!

---

scatter throw pieces of

prodded and probed poked and looked very closely at me

grunting making low noises

I hoped these new people would take me with them, away from the cold and dark, but they did not. They were worried about the ice **closing in on** their boat, and they **abandoned** me.

I watched their ship sail south.

I thought I had been cold before. Now the wind blew across me, and the snow touched places it had never touched before. I lay open, **exposed**, and so alone.

---

closing in on getting too close to
exposed out in the weather

Before You Move On

1. **Character** How does Ahnighito feel when he is in the sunlight?

2. **Prediction** Do you think the people will return?

The people work hard to move Ahnighito. Find out where he goes.

I spent two long **lonely** winters, wishing they would come back.

They finally returned. I watched them come sailing back into the bay. They sailed through the **ice floes**. I was sure they were coming back to get me.

They began to work day and night with axes and picks and hydraulic jacks. They banged and pounded and tried to **lift** me. They laid me on steel rails. Carefully, they rolled me along toward their ship. They **called me stubborn**, not knowing how I strained to help them.

chain block

hydraulic jack

rail

cable

ice floes large pieces of ice floating on the water
called me stubborn said I didn't want to move

Inch by inch, I went forward. I was pushed by jacks and pulled by chain blocks and steel cables. I crushed everything in my path. The rocks **sparked beneath me as I flattened them**. I bent the steel rails as the days grew colder and colder. They called me a monster as the snow began to **swirl** around them. With only inches to go, only inches, I tell you, a **gale** began. It was the winter's first blizzard, and they abandoned me once again.

Would they ever return?

I **wept mightily** as I watched them sail off without me. I never stopped looking for them. I <u>never</u> stopped.

sparked beneath me as I flattened them made hot flashes of light under me as I crushed them

swirl move quickly in circles

gale strong wind

wept mightily cried very hard

In time, when the sun was at its warmest, they came again. They sailed toward me through a **soggy** snowstorm. I sat very still. Patiently, I waited.

They landed and built a bridge for me. It was a bridge of giant oak timbers spiked with iron rails. They greased the rails and steadied the ship. Finally, the tide was exactly right so that the ship was at the perfect height. They tossed a flag across my back and, with **mighty winches** and groaning jacks, began to shove me forward through the fog.

Inch by inch, they moved me across the gangplank. I dared not look down into the water. If the timbers had not held, or if a wave had rocked the ship, I would have **plunged** into the bay and spent the rest of my days beneath the sea.

---

soggy wet
mighty winches strong machines
plunged fallen

Suddenly, a little child ran forward, and I froze in fear. I waited to see if we would **topple** into the water, but she broke a bottle against my side. When the men laughed and cheered, she called out, "I name you Ahnighito!"

At that moment the sun broke through the fog, showing blue patches of sky. The sun **streaked from its low midnight place and lit me like a jewel**.

Ahnighito.

They pushed me the rest of the way and eased me into the ship's hold. My **bulk** settled into the ship. "Ahnighito," I thought. "A most wonderful name."

---

topple fall

streaked from its low midnight place and lit me like a jewel came out and shone on me so I looked like a shiny diamond

bulk weight

For days I heard the ship **plowing into icebergs and floating ice floes**, trying to cut her way out of the bay into the open sea.

Once at sea, the men were upset with me because all the ship's **compasses** pointed at me and at nothing else. I listened to the Arctic waves and **savage** wind beat at the creaking ship. It was a long and troubling **journey**.

plowing into icebergs and floating ice floes hitting large pieces of ice in the water

compasses tools used to find directions

savage very strong

In nearly a month's time, we were in a warmer place, a bright place. The men tied up to a busy dock and, with the help of a giant **crane** and a **sling of** thick chains, I was lifted **from the deep hold** of the ship and laid out in the sun.

Soon I learned I was in the Brooklyn Navy Yard. Everyone who passed wondered what on Earth I was.

"What's this rock doing here?" they would ask.

"Call me Ahnighito," I thought. "I am Ahnighito." But, of course, no one knew.

---

crane machine used to lift heavy things
sling of basket made of
from the deep hold out of the bottom part

Before You Move On
1. **Details** How is the journey dangerous?
2. **Character** What words tell you how Ahnighito feels on the journey?

3

Ahnighito sits in the Brooklyn Navy Yard. Will he stay there?

For seven long years I sat on the dock of the Brooklyn Navy Yard. I grew **dull** and uninterested in the ships that came in and out. One boat was like the next, until one day a huge **barge** pulled up alongside me, and again the chains were slapped around me and cranes were **pressed into use**.

I was lifted up and placed on the barge, which groaned beneath my weight. I was frightened. Would they take me back to Greenland? Would they force me to return to those Arctic nights?

---

dull tired of being there
barge boat with a flat bottom
pressed into use used

Slowly, the barge made its way up the East River. **Tugboats** blew their horns at me, and **yachts** tooted. Soon we tied up at a different pier. I was lifted again, swaying and **enormous** in the sunlight, and gently placed on a huge cart drawn by twenty-eight horses. Together we were a block long, and we made our way slowly across the island of Manhattan.

Children ran beside us, trying to touch me. Men held onto their **derbies**, and women waved their gloves. It was a most **splendid procession**. At the end, I found my home.

Tugboats Strong boats that pull other boats
yachts large boats
derbies hats
splendid procession wonderful parade

Now, **I am at my most glorious**. I am displayed in the center of a warm room with mirrors above me so that people can admire me from all sides. There are signs telling all about me so that I can be understood.

I am no longer lonely. Everyone knows my name. They call me Ahnighito.

It's a good life, being a famous old **meteorite**. Sometimes, late at night, when the bright lights are **dimmed** and the guard has gone home, I **bask** in the soft warmth of the **museum** and think about my life.

I even think sometimes that maybe, if I were to try very hard, I might remember my birth, and how I was made of star stuff.

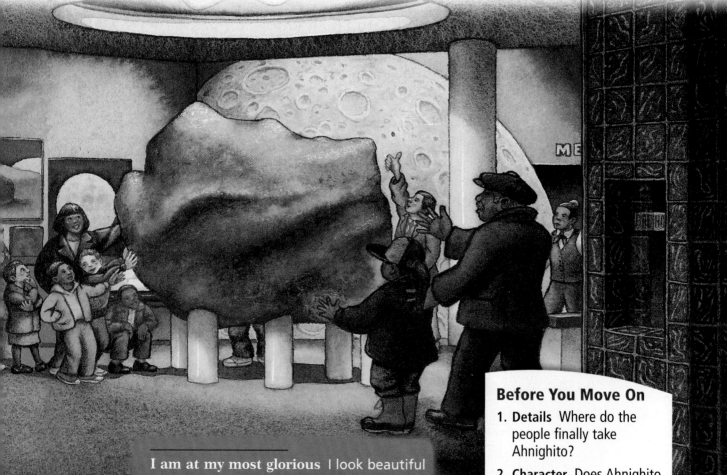

I am at my most glorious I look beautiful
dimmed turned down
bask relax and enjoy myself

Before You Move On

1. **Details** Where do the people finally take Ahnighito?

2. **Character** Does Ahnighito like his new home? How do you know?

Meet the Author

PAM CONRAD

When she was a young girl, **Pam Conrad** saw Ahnighito in the American Museum of Natural History. She was amazed by the huge meteorite and thought about its journey in space. "I imagined this gigantic piece of rock hurtling through space. It was only as an adult that I discovered the rest of the story." Her book *Call Me Ahnighito* tells the meteorite's story just the way a child might imagine it.

Think and Respond

Strategy: Analyze Character

You can understand some stories better if you think about how a character changes. In these stories, look for:

- ✔ how the character feels at the beginning
- ✔ actions or events that change the character's feelings
- ✔ how the character feels at the end.

Make a character chart for "Call Me Ahnighito." Tell how Ahnighito's feelings changed and why.

Call Me Ahnighito

	How Ahnighito feels	Why Ahnighito feels that way
pages 440–442	lonely	Ahnighito sits in the Arctic all day. Nothing happens there.
	scared	People begin to chip away at him.
	free	People roll Ahnighito into the sun.
pages 443–445		

Tell Fantasy from Reality

Some events in the story could never happen because they are fantasy. Other events in the story could happen in real life. Retell the story to a partner. Tell only the events that could really happen.

Talk It Over

1 **Personal Response** What questions do you have after reading this story?

2 **Speculate** What might happen the next time people discover a meteorite? How do you know?

3 **Conclusion** What do you think people can learn from a meteorite like Ahnighito?

4 **Judgment** Was it right to move Ahnighito from Greenland? Why or why not?

Compare Issues

Was it worth the money to move Ahnighito and to save the Treaty Oak? Why or why not?

Content Connections

Report the News

small group

Pretend you and your group are news reporters. Choose one part of Ahnighito's life. You could choose his arrival on Earth or the day he arrived in New York City. Tell what, where, how, and why. Tell what you think will happen next.

> Ahnighito just arrived in New York after a long journey.

Research Meteorites

partners

Find out about other meteorites. Look in books or on the Internet. Create a fact sheet and put it in a class meteorite book.

The Peekskill Meteorite

Location: Peekskill, NY

Size: 12.37 kg

The Peekskill Meteorite crashed into a car! Red paint from the car is still on it.

Play a Directions Game

Pretend Ahnighito goes on tour.

1. Choose a U.S. city, but don't tell what it is.

2. Use a road map. Give driving directions from Ahnighito's last stop to your city.

3. Have another group follow your directions to the city.

Did the group find the city?

Follow Ahnighito
1. Go west on I-78 for 100 miles.
2. Go south on I-95 for 50 miles.

Write to Entertain

Pretend that you are Ahnighito. Write something about your journey before you landed on Earth. Choose the best form to entertain:

- a journal entry

- a letter

- a story

Use different kinds of sentences. Can you combine two sentences?

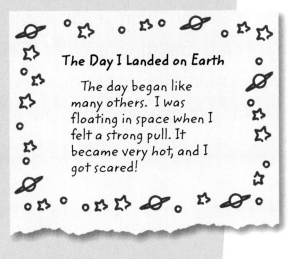

The Day I Landed on Earth

The day began like many others. I was floating in space when I felt a strong pull. It became very hot, and I got scared!

Make and Revise Predictions

When you guess what will happen next in a story, you **make a prediction**. To make predictions:

✔ Read carefully and look for story clues.
✔ Think about what you already know.
✔ Make a guess about what will happen next.
✔ Continue reading to find out if your prediction is right.
✔ Change your prediction if you find new information.

Try the strategy.

from CALL ME AHNIGHITO

Then, grunting and straining, they rolled me into the sun.

What joy I felt, free at last!

I hoped these new people would take me with them, away from the cold and dark, but they did not. They were worried about the ice closing in on their boat, and they abandoned me.

> The people worked very hard to move Ahnighito. So, I predicted that they would take Ahnighito with them. When I read the last sentence, I changed my prediction.

Practice

Take this test and **make and revise predictions** about Ahnighito.

> **Read the new story about Ahnighito. Then read each item. Choose the best answer.**
>
> I was so happy in the museum. Many people came to see me every day and tell me how special I am. Some people even came to measure me.
>
> Then one day a lot of people came, and they closed all the doors around me. They covered me with a huge sheet. What was going to happen to me?
>
> **1 What prediction can you make about Ahnighito?**
>
> **A** People are going to chip off more pieces of Ahnighito.
>
> **B** People are going to move Ahnighito some place new.
>
> **C** The museum doesn't want Ahnighito. They will take him back to the Arctic.
>
> ✔ **Test Strategy**
>
> Read all of the answer choices before you choose an answer.
>
> Every day there were loud noises. The floor shook as people pounded something. I felt something light like dust fall on me.
>
> Every night it was quiet. I hoped someone would lift my sheet to let me see.
>
> Finally, they uncovered me. There was a new display case around me! I was so proud!
>
> **2 Revise your prediction.**
>
> **A** People cleaned Ahnighito.
>
> **B** People moved Ahnighito to a new building.
>
> **C** People built a new display case around Ahnighito.

THE LIFE STORY of a ROCK
by Phyllis Edwards

Chant

ROCK CHANT

From **magma**, or lava,

To cold, **solid** rock,

I turn into **layers**

Of rock upon rock.

solid rock

liquid lava

layers

magma

Erosion breaks me

And moves me along.

Years of **weathering**

Wear me down.

Under the **pressure**

Of rock upon rock,

My **cycle** continues.

I don't ever stop.

—*Phyllis Edwards*

Key Words

magma

solid

layer

liquid

erosion

weathering

pressure

cycle

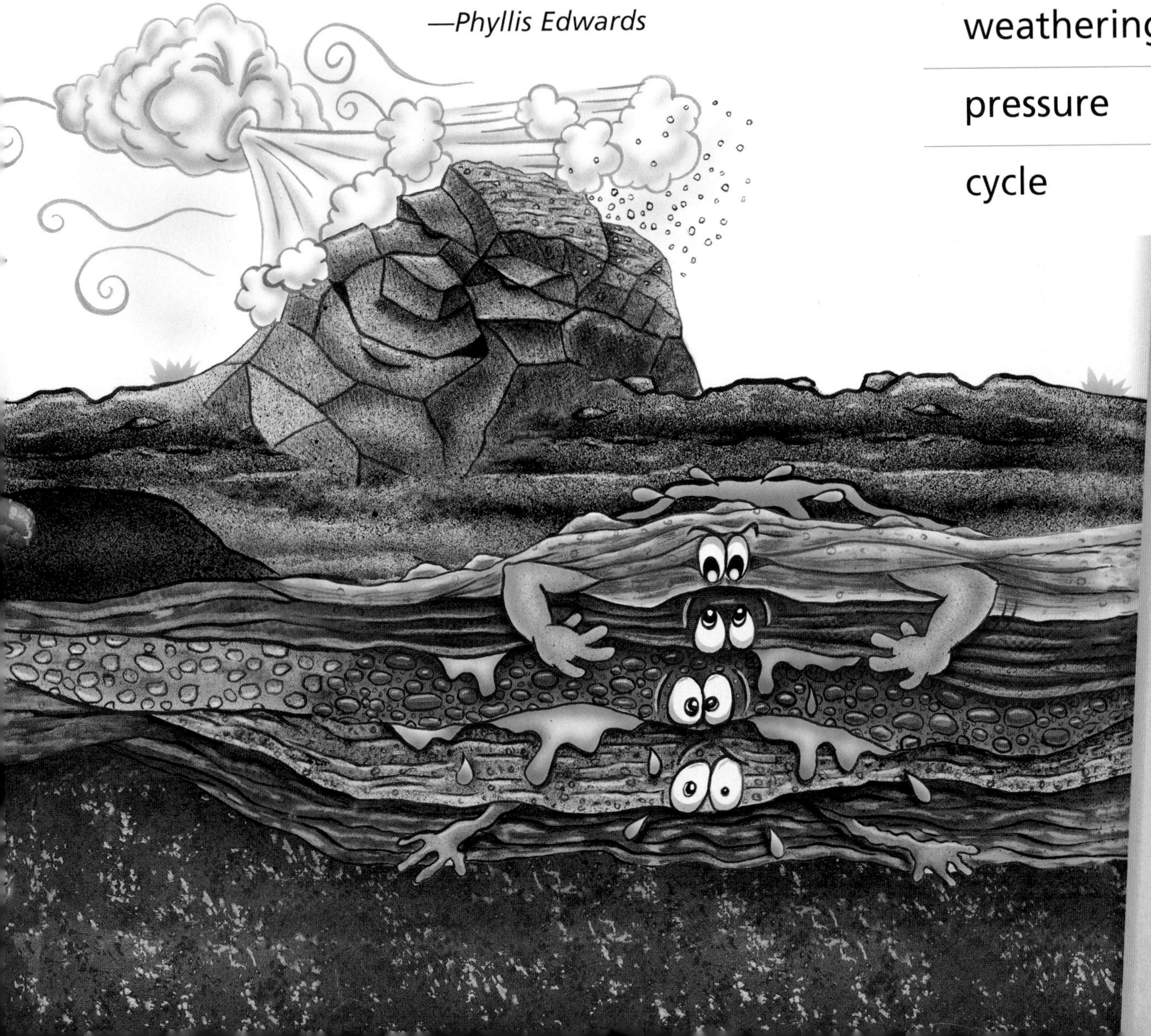

Read a Science Article

A **science article** is nonfiction. It often tells how things work and what things are like.

✔ Look for **diagrams** with **labels** that show you the parts of something.

diagram

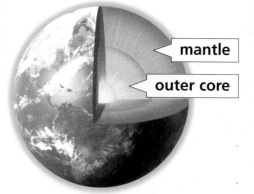

mantle

outer core

✔ Look at **photographs** and **captions** to find out more facts.

Selection Reading

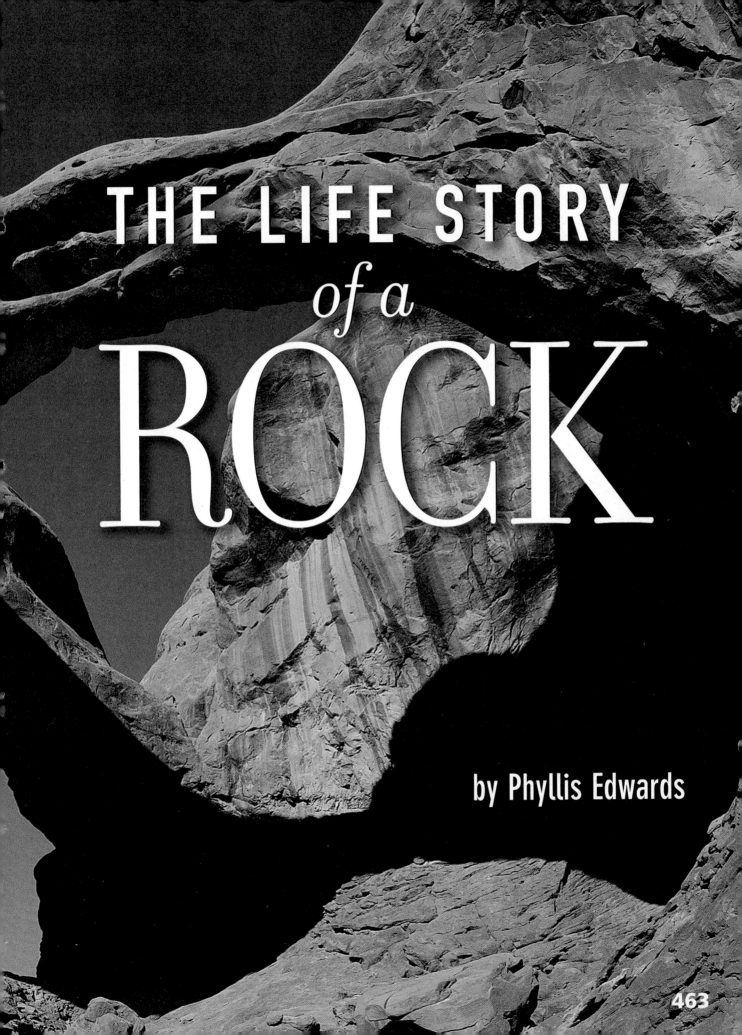

THE LIFE STORY
of a
ROCK

by Phyllis Edwards

Set Your Purpose

Find out how different kinds of rocks form and what they are like.

A Rock Is Born

Some rocks, like Ahnighito, come from space. Other rocks are born inside the Earth. This is the life story of an Earth rock.

From where we stand, the Earth seems like one, big, **solid** rock. In fact, the Earth is made of several **layers**. The thin outer layer that forms the continents and ocean floors is solid. It is called the crust. Part of the next layer, called the mantle, is soft like jelly. Another layer, called the outer core, is extremely hot **liquid** rock. The deepest layer, the inner core, is solid rock.

The **birthplace of a new rock** is a very uncomfortable place. Deep inside the Earth, it is so hot that rocks melt. Underground molten, or melted, rock is called **magma**. When a volcano erupts, magma reaches the **surface**. It is then called lava. The hot, runny lava comes out of a vent in the volcano and **flows** down its sides. There it cools into solid rock. This type of rock is called igneous rock. *Igneous* means "made by fire."

birthplace of a new rock place where a new rock is formed

surface outside of the Earth's crust

flows moves

ocean floor

464

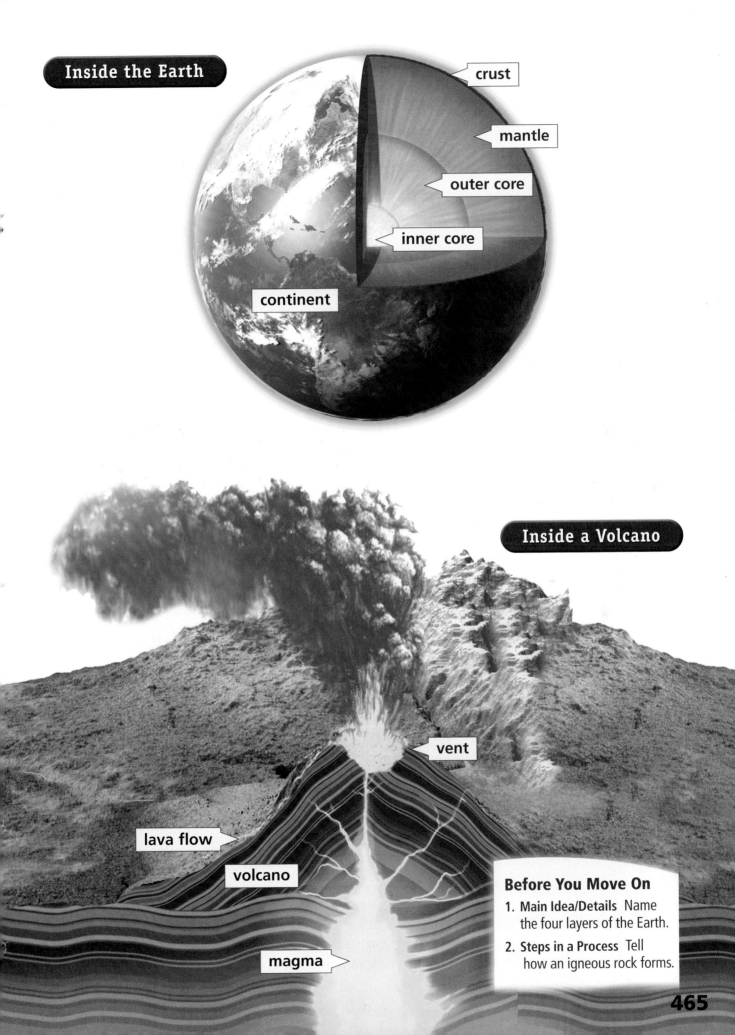

Inside the Earth

crust

mantle

outer core

inner core

continent

Inside a Volcano

vent

lava flow

volcano

magma

Before You Move On

1. **Main Idea/Details** Name the four layers of the Earth.

2. **Steps in a Process** Tell how an igneous rock forms.

465

iron pyrite

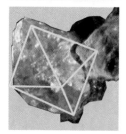

diamond

quartz

Some igneous rocks are crystals with beautiful shapes. The **atoms** of each kind of crystal always arrange themselves in the same way. Because of these arrangements, each kind of crystal has its own regular shape and a specific number of flat sides. If the rock cools quickly, the crystals will be small. If the rock cools slowly, the crystals will be larger. Sometimes igneous rocks contain metals, such as gold. Most metals and many crystals are **embedded in** other kinds of rock.

▲ **Gold embedded in quartz crystals**

---

atoms very tiny parts
embedded in stuck together with

A Rock Changes

A rock may seem permanent, but it is constantly changing. On rainy days, water pounds on the new rock and breaks off tiny **particles**. Some of the rain fills a crack in the rock. During cold nights, the rainwater freezes and **expands**. This can cause the rock to split into smaller pieces. Wind also blows sand against the rock and breaks off tiny particles. These changes are called **weathering**.

▲ Water made these rocks smooth.

▲ Ice broke these rocks apart.

▲ Wind and water changed the shape of this rock.

---

particles pieces
expands gets larger

Before You Move On

1. **Cause/Effect** What causes different sizes of crystals?

2. **Paraphrase** Tell a partner how weathering changes rocks.

A Rock Can Travel

A rock can't walk, but it can travel far away from the place it was born. Strong winds blow tiny particles of rock away as sand. Some of the sand rides a river down into a valley. Rivers of ice, called glaciers, break off parts of the rock and slowly push them down the mountain. Soon these pieces of rock reach a new home and begin to become bigger rocks. All of the changes caused by weathering and movement are called **erosion** .

▼ **Rocks ride a river down a mountainside.**

A river carries some pieces into a lake or the sea. There, the sand and **pebbles** settle to the bottom of the water. They are called sediment. As the river brings more sand and pebbles, more and more layers of sediment **pile up**.

Pressure from these layers squeezes the sediment for many, many years until the pebbles and sand stick together very tightly. This makes a new kind of rock called sedimentary rock. *Sedimentary* means "settled down."

sedimentary rock ▶

---

pebbles small rocks
pile up settle on top of each other

How Sedimentary Rock Is Made

1. Pebbles and sand go to the bottom of a lake.

2. Layers of sediment pile up.

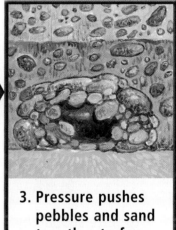

3. Pressure pushes pebbles and sand together to form sedimentary rock.

Before You Move On

1. **Main Idea/Details** What is erosion?
2. **Graphic Aids** What does the diagram help you see? How?

469

A Rock Changes Again

Now it's time for the rock's life to **heat up** again! More and more layers pile up and push the sedimentary rocks deeper and deeper into the Earth. Inside the Earth, the rocks get hotter and hotter. Heat and pressure change the shapes and colors of the rocks. These new rocks are called metamorphic rock. *Metamorphic* means "changed."

---

heat up get hot

▲ **Granite shaped by heat and pressure**

The Cycle Repeats

A rock may look like it does not have a life, but a rock's life story never really ends. Its **cycle** repeats and repeats, again and again, for thousands and thousands of years.

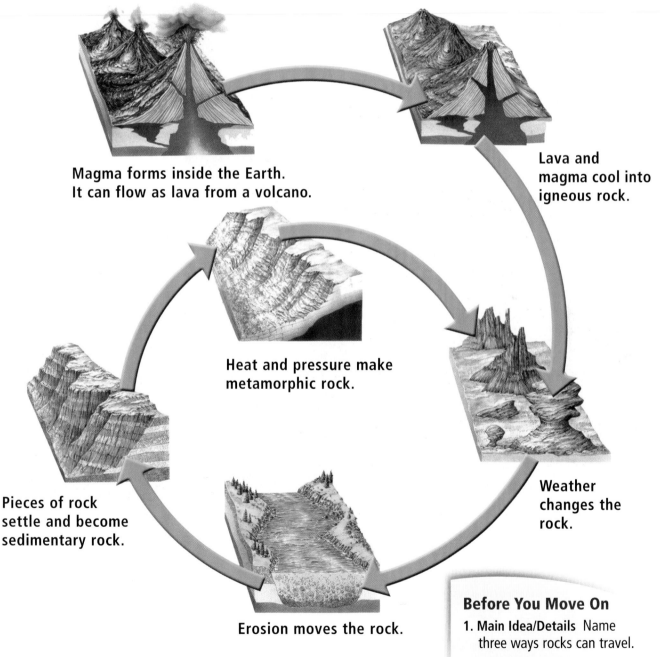

The Rock Cycle

Magma forms inside the Earth. It can flow as lava from a volcano.

Lava and magma cool into igneous rock.

Heat and pressure make metamorphic rock.

Weather changes the rock.

Pieces of rock settle and become sedimentary rock.

Erosion moves the rock.

Before You Move On

1. **Main Idea/Details** Name three ways rocks can travel.

2. **Paraphrase** Describe the rock cycle to a partner.

Rocks Are Very Useful!

Day to day, rocks are useful in our world. Rock caves provide shelter for animals that need places to hide or rest. On a windy day, underground rocks give trees a place to hold on tight.

◀ **A cougar finds shelter in a cave.**

▼ **Concrete highways connect cities across the United States.**

People use rocks **in all kinds of construction**. Rocks help make concrete for sidewalks, highways, and **skyscrapers**. Rocks can make a strong wall. Thin pieces of rock can make a pretty floor in a house.

---

in all kinds of construction to make many different kinds of things

skyscrapers very tall buildings

472

Rocks are also important for plant growth. In the topsoil, small particles of rock mix with rotted plant parts to provide minerals and other **nutrients** for the plants. The subsoil gives the roots of a plant something to hold onto. Bedrock holds the subsoil together.

---

nutrients food

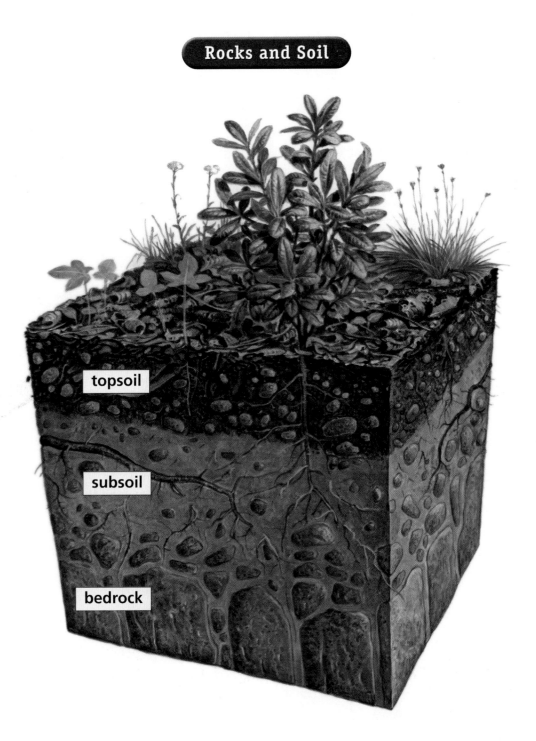

Rocks and Soil

topsoil

subsoil

bedrock

Rocks add to the beauty of our world. Many people love to explore sparkling crystal caves and colorful canyons.

A scientist studies the rocks in Crystal Cave in Missouri.

Great artists carve **magnificent** statues from rocks. We even wear rocks as jewelry.

Rocks have been around since Earth began, and they will continue their endless cycles far into the future. All in all, rocks are pretty wonderful!

---

magnificent beautiful

ROCKY FACT

The Hope Diamond, the world's largest deep blue diamond, is more than a billion years old! It was found in India, crossed oceans and continents, and finally arrived in the United States. Every year, millions of people visit the Hope Diamond in the Smithsonian Institution in Washington, D.C.

Before You Move On

1. **Details** Name two ways rocks help plants.

2. **Personal Experience** How are rocks used where you live?

Think and Respond

Strategy: Main Idea and Details

Make an outline of "The Life Story of a Rock."

Write the **main idea** of each part of the article.

The Life Story of a Rock

I. Rocks are born. (pages 464-466)
   A. Earth has layers.
   B. Volcanoes form igneous rocks.

Write **details** that tell more about, or support, each idea.

II. Rocks change and move. (pages 467-471)
   A. _____
   B. _____
   C. _____
   D. _____

III. Rocks are useful. (pages 472-475)
   A. _____
   B. _____
   C. _____
   D. _____

Summarize

Use your outline to summarize the article. Tell only the main ideas and supporting details. Remember to keep your summary short.

Talk It Over

1 **Personal Response** What do you think are the most interesting facts about rocks?

2 **Opinion** The author says, "All in all, rocks are pretty wonderful!" Do you agree? Why or why not?

3 **Conclusion** Are new rocks being born today? How do you know?

4 **Judgment** Is it important to learn about the inside of the Earth? Why or why not?

Compare Nonfiction

"The Life Story of a Rock" and "Money" are both nonfiction articles. How are they alike? How are they different?

Both articles have photographs of real things. "The Life Story of a Rock" has more diagrams.

Content Connections

Interview a Rock Hound

small group

Listen to a rock hound, a person who is very interested in rocks. Find out about different kinds of rocks. Compare what you hear about rocks with what you already know. Talk with your group about what you learned from the rock hound.

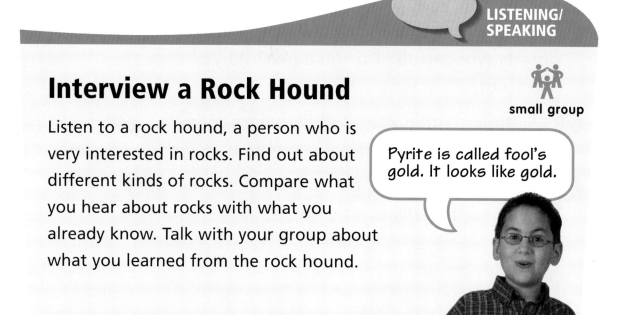

Pyrite is called fool's gold. It looks like gold.

Research Rocks Around the World

partners

Internet

1. Use the Internet to view rock stamps from all over the world.

2. Choose one that interests you.

3. Find out why that rock is important to that country.

Show the stamp and explain what you learned to the class.

Brasil 77 1,30
PORTUCALE 7

The Emerald Stamp
Brazil has an emerald stamp. Brazil produces more emeralds than any other country.

478

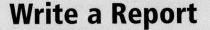
partners

Experiment with Rocks

Design an experiment to test the hardness of rocks or answer another question about rocks. Use the scientific process. Explain the results to your class.

Question:	Guess:
What does weathering do to rocks?	It breaks rocks down and makes them softer.
Materials:	**Steps:**
2 pieces of chalk jar with lid water	1. 2. 3.

WRITING

on your own

Write a Report

1. In a chart, write what you know about volcanoes.

2. Write what you want to learn.

3. Watch a video or read a book.

4. Write what you learned and what questions you still have.

Use your chart to write a report.

Some eruptions end quickly, but others last many years. Volcanic eruptions are really amazing!

Mount St. Helens

Join Sentences

Listen and sing.

Song

TRAVELS OF A ROCK

The rain and the wind
Washed a rock down the hill,
And it dropped into a stream.
When the rain ended,
The rock still moved on
Until it reached the sea

— *Jane Zion Brauer*

Tune: "I Love the Sun"

How Language Works

Use a **conjunction** to put two sentences together.

and	Use when ideas are alike.	A volcano erupts. Lava shoots into the air. ↓ A volcano erupts, **and** lava shoots into the air.
but	Use when ideas are different.	A volcano erupts. No one is hurt. ↓ A volcano erupts, **but** no one is hurt.
or	Use when the ideas are choices.	Volcanoes can erupt. They can be quiet for years. ↓ Volcanoes can erupt, **or** they can be quiet for years.
when	Use to relate ideas in time.	Rocks wear away. Wind pounds against them. ↓ Rocks wear away **when** wind pounds against them.
because	Use to tell why something happens.	Rocks change shape. Water wears them down. ↓ Rocks change shape **because** water wears them down.

Practice with a Partner

Use the red conjunction to put the two sentences together.

because	**1.** I like rocks. They are interesting.
when	**2.** I collect rocks. I go hiking.
and	**3.** I pick the best rocks. I put them in a sack.
but	**4.** The sack gets heavy. I keep walking!
or	**5.** I keep the rocks in a jar. I put them on a shelf.

Put It in Writing

Draw a new rock you have discovered. Write about it. Put some of your sentences together.

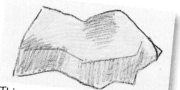

This new rock has sharp points. It hurts when you touch it.

481

Show What You Know

Talk About Rocks

In this unit, you read a fantasy and a science article about rocks. Look back at this unit. Do you think it is important for people to understand rocks? Use pictures from the unit to tell why or why not.

Make a Mind Map

Work with a partner. Make a summary chart to show what you learned about rocks.

What I Know About Rocks

Kind of Rock	Summary
meteorite	A meteorite is a space rock that hits Earth.
igneous	
sedimentary	
metamorphic	

Think and Write

Where do you see rocks every day? Write a paragraph that tells about rocks in your world. Include a picture. Add this writing to your portfolio. Also add other work that shows what you learned about rocks.

Read and Learn More

Leveled Books

What Is It?
by Shirleyann Costigan

The Coolest Rock
by Sherilin Chanek

Theme Library

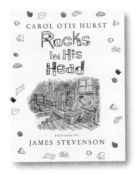

Rocks in His Head
by Carol Otis Hurst

How Mountains Are Made
by Kathleen Zoehfeld

Internet

Go to: www.hbavenues.com

Rocks and Minerals

Meteorite Movie

Volcano Videos

Picture Dictionary

The definitions are for the words as they are introduced in the selections in this book.

Pronunciation Key

Say the sample word out loud to hear how to say, or pronounce, the symbol.

Symbols for Consonant Sounds

b	box	p	pan	
ch	chick	r	ring	
d	dog	s	bus	
f	fish	sh	fish	
g	girl	t	hat	
h	hat	th	Earth	
j	jar	th	father	
k	cake	v	vase	
ks	box	w	window	
kw	queen	wh	whale	
l	bell	y	yarn	
m	mouse	z	zipper	
n	pan	zh	treasure	
ng	ring			

Symbols for Short Vowel Sounds

a	hat
e	bell
i	chick
o	box
u	bus

Symbols for Long Vowel Sounds

ā	cake
ē	key
ī	bike
ō	goat
ū	fruit
yū	mule

Symbols for R-controlled Sounds

ar	barn
air	chair
or	corn
ur	girl
ir	fire

Symbols for Variant Vowel Sounds

ah	father
aw	ball
oi	boy
ow	mouse
oo	book

Miscellaneous Symbols

shun	fraction	$\frac{1}{2}$
chun	question	?
zhun	division	$2\overline{)100}^{50}$

Parts of an Entry

The **entry** shows how the word is spelled.

The **pronunciation** shows you how to say the word and how to break it into syllables.

The **picture** helps you understand more about the meaning of the word.

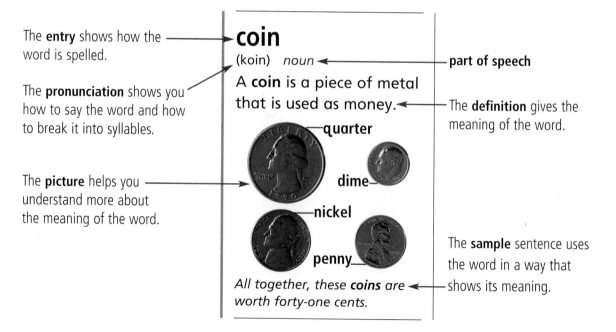

coin

(koin)   *noun*

A **coin** is a piece of metal that is used as money.

quarter

dime

nickel

penny

*All together, these **coins** are worth forty-one cents.*

part of speech

The **definition** gives the meaning of the word.

The **sample** sentence uses the word in a way that shows its meaning.

abandon
(u-**ban**-dun) *verb*

You **abandon** something when you leave it and do not plan to return to it.

*The sailors **abandon** the sinking ship.*

adjust
(u-**just**) *verb*

When you **adjust** to something, you get used to it.

*This family must **adjust** to a new life in the United States.*

agree
(u-**grē**) *verb*

People **agree** when they have the same idea about something.

*The girls **agree** that the book is funny!*

arrive
(u-**rīv**) *verb*

When you **arrive** at a place, you get there.

*The passengers **arrive** at the train station.*

B

backbone
(**bak**-bōn) *noun*

The **backbone** supports, or holds up, the body. It is made up of many small bones.

backbone —

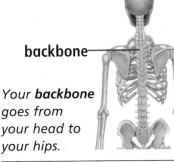

*Your **backbone** goes from your head to your hips.*

backward
(**bak**-wurd) *adverb*

Something is **backward** if it points to the back instead of to the front.

frontward   backward
*Look at the duck with its feet on **backward**! Which way will it walk?*

barter
(**bar**-tur) *verb*

When you **barter**, you trade things. You don't use money.

*This woman **barters** strawberries for eggs.*

better future
(**bet**-ur **fyū**-chur)   *noun*

A **better future** means things will be nicer in the time to come.

*This mother hopes for a **better future** for her daughter.*

blend
(blend) *verb*

A thing **blends** in when it looks like the rest of the things around it.

*It is hard to see the fish because it **blends** in.*

485

blizzard

(**bliz**-urd)   *noun*

A **blizzard** is a heavy snowstorm with strong, cold winds.

Snow piles high during a **blizzard**.

bloom

(blūm)   *noun*

The flower of a plant is a **bloom**.

This plant has many **blooms**.

boldness

(bōld-nis)   *noun*

You show your **boldness** when you are brave and not afraid.

Maria's **boldness** helped her jump from the plane.

boundary

(**bound**-u-rē)   *noun*

A **boundary** is where one place stops and another place starts.

The Mississippi River is the **boundary** between Missouri and Illinois.

brand-new

(brand-nū)   *adjective*

Something that is **brand-new** has not been used yet.

I wear **brand-new** jeans to a party, but I wear old jeans to paint.

camouflage

(kam-u-**flawzh**)   *noun*

Camouflage is a way some animals hide. Their colors and patterns look like the things around them.

The cheetah's colors and markings are good **camouflage** in a grassy area.

capital

(**kap**-i-tul)   *noun*

The government of a country or a state is located in its **capital**.

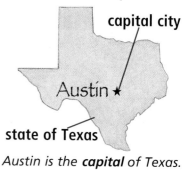

Austin is the **capital** of Texas.

capture

(**kap**-shur)   *verb*

You **capture** something when you catch it and keep it.

I used a net to **capture** the butterfly.

cellar

(**sel**-ur)   *noun*

A **cellar** is a room that is under the ground.

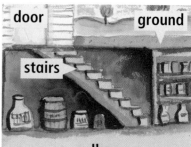

People can hide in a **cellar** to keep safe from a storm.

chief
(chēf) *noun*

A **chief** is the leader of a group of people.

chief

*The **chief** leads the members of his tribe.*

coin
(koin) *noun*

A **coin** is a piece of metal that is used as money.

quarter
dime
nickel
penny

*All together, these **coins** are worth forty-one cents.*

cold front
(kōld frunt) *noun*

A **cold front** is a place where cold air meets warm air.

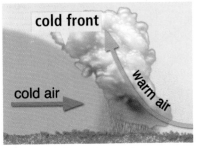
cold front
cold air
warm air

*The **cold front** brought stormy weather.*

come from
(kum-frum) *verb*

The place that you **come from** is the place where you were born.

before
now

*I **come from** Maine, but now I live in Florida.*

communicate
(ku-**myū**-ni-**kāt**) *verb*

When you **communicate**, you share your thoughts and feelings.

*Mom and José **communicate** by telephone.*

contest
(**kon**-test) *noun*

A **contest** is something you try to win. It shows a person's skills.

starting line

*Who will win this **contest**?*

creature
(**krē**-chur) *noun*

A **creature** is a living person or animal.

bird
dog
goldfish

*All these **creatures** live with the boy.*

culture
(**kul**-chur) *noun*

A group's **culture** is made up of its beliefs, arts, traditions, and way of life.

*This dance is part of the Mexican **culture**.*

curious
(**kyoor**-ē-us) *adjective*

When you are **curious**, you really want to know about something.

*These kids are **curious** about how this engine works.*

cycle
(sī-kul) *noun*

A **cycle** is something that happens over again in the same order.

spring summer
fall winter

*It takes one year for the seasons to complete a **cycle**.*

damage
(dam-ij) *noun*

Damage is harm to places or things. It makes things less useful.

*Look at the terrible **damage** from the storm!*

dangerous
(dān-jur-us) *adjective*

Something that is **dangerous** can hurt you.

*Be careful crossing this street. It is **dangerous**.*

deadly
(ded-lē)
adjective

A **deadly** thing can kill a person, an animal, or a plant.

*This dirty water is **deadly** to the fish.*

defense
(di-fens) *noun*

A **defense** is something that helps you not get hurt.

quills
porcupine fox

*The quills of this porcupine are a **defense** against the fox.*

design
(di-zīn) *noun*

A **design** is a drawing that shows how something will look.

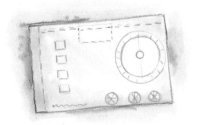

*This is the **design** for the new playground.*

determined
(di-tur-mind) *adjective*

When you are **determined**, you keep trying as hard as you can.

*Kate is **determined** to make a basket. She tries again and again.*

basketball

disappointed
(dis-u-**point**-ed) *adjective*

When something does not happen the way you hope, you are **disappointed**.

*Frank is **disappointed** with the gift. He wanted a puppy!*

discover
(dis-kuv-ur) *verb*

You **discover** something when you find it for the first time.

hikers lake
trail

*The hikers **discover** a lake by the trail.*

488

E

emperor
(**em**-pur-ur) *noun*

An **emperor** is a man who rules, or controls, a country.

*Julius Caesar was the **emperor** of the Roman Empire.*

enormous
(i-**nor**-mus) *adjective*

An **enormous** thing is very, very big.

*These are **enormous** trees.*

erosion
(i-**rō**-zhun) *noun*

Erosion happens when parts of things break off and are carried away.

wave

*Waves cause **erosion** of the land.*

exchange
(eks-**chānj**) *verb*

You **exchange** when you trade one thing for another.

teller
customer

*I **exchanged** a pot for a blanket.*

experience
(ek-**spēr**-ē-uns) *noun*

An **experience** is something that you did or that happened to you.

*The roller coaster ride was an exciting **experience**.*

F

forecaster
(**for**-kast-ur) *noun*

A **forecaster** tells what the weather will be like.

*The **forecaster** says that today's weather will be cool.*

forgot
(fur-**got**) *verb*

If you **forgot** something, you did not remember it.

shoelaces

*In the present: Sally **forgets** to tie her shoes.*

*In the past: Sally **forgot** to tie her shoes.*

frame
(frām) *noun*

The pieces of wood or metal that hold up a house are the **frame**.

frame

*The **frame** for this tipi is made of wooden poles.*

G

goods
(goodz) *noun*

Goods are things that can be bought, sold, or traded.

*We buy and sell **goods** at the market.*

government

(**guv**-urn-munt) *noun*

The **government** is the group of people that makes laws for a country, a state, or a city.

*These people are part of the **government** of the United States.*

hail

(hāl) *noun*

Hail is small round pieces of ice. Hail falls from the sky like rain or snow.

*During the storm, **hail** hit the ground like little rocks.*

hand-me-down

(**hand**-mē-**down**) *adjective*

Hand-me-down clothes belonged to someone else first.

hand-me-down shirt

new shirt

*My brother gives me his **hand-me-down** clothes.*

honor

(**on**-ur) *verb*

When you **honor** a person, you thank that person and show your good feelings.

police officer

plaque

*They **honor** this police officer when they give her a plaque.*

howling

(**how**-ling) *noun*

Howling is a loud, crying sound that the wind makes during a storm.

*The terrible **howling** of the wind scares me.*

imagination

(i-**maj**-u-**nā**-shun) *noun*

Pictures and ideas you form in your mind are your **imagination**.

*I use my **imagination** to make up stories.*

journey

(**jur**-nē) *noun*

A **journey** is a trip.

*Many families made the **journey** from their homelands to the United States.*

layer

(lā-ur) *noun*

A **layer** is one thickness of something.

*It took thousands of years to form the **layers** in this cliff.*

lift

(lift) *verb*

When you **lift** something, you pick it up.

*Jane **lifts** the box.*

lightning

(līt-ning) *noun*

Lightning is a flash of light in the sky.

***Lightning** flashes in the sky during a storm.*

liquid

(lik-wid) *adjective*

Something **liquid** moves easily. It is not a solid or a gas.

*Hot, **liquid** lava raced down the side of the volcano.*

load

(lōd) *noun*

A **load** is something that is carried.

*The horse pulls the **load** of hay.*

lonely

(lōn-lē) *adjective*

When you are **lonely**, you feel sad because you are alone.

*Chad is **lonely** because everyone went home.*

lotus

(lō-tus) *noun*

A **lotus** is a plant with flowers. It grows in the water.

*This **lotus** has a beautiful pink flower!*

magma

(mag-mu) *noun*

Magma is melted rock that is under the ground.

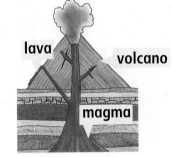

*A volcano erupts when **magma** shoots out of it.*

market

(mar-kit) *noun*

A **market** is a place where food and other things are sold.

*You can buy fruits and vegetables at an outdoor **market**.*

mass
(mas) *noun*

A **mass** is a large amount of something in one place.

A **mass** of clouds moves in over the valley.

material
(mu-**tir**-ē-ul) *noun*

You can use **material** such as grass or wood to build a house.

Native Americans used **materials** from nature to build their homes.

meteorite
(**mē**-tē-u-**rīt**) *noun*

A **meteorite** is a piece of rock from space that hits the ground.

This **meteorite** hit Earth.

mind
(mīnd) *verb*

❶ If you **mind** something, you care about it.

Chen does not **mind** getting wet.

noun

❷ Your **mind** is the part of you that thinks, learns, and feels.

Shevum uses his **mind** to think.

museum
(mu-**zē**-um) *noun*

A **museum** is a building people visit to see and learn about special things from nature or history.

There are models of animals at the natural history **museum**.

mysterious
(mi-**stēr**-ē-us) *adjective*

Something that is **mysterious** is hard to explain or understand.

What is this **mysterious** sign?

N

nation
(**nā**-shun) *noun*

A **nation** is a group of people that shares the same heritage and traditions.

The people of the Inuit **nation** live in the Arctic region.

Native peoples
(**nā**-tiv **pē**-pulz) *proper noun*

The first humans to live in a place are called **Native peoples**.

Native peoples have lived in North America for thousands of years.

notice

(**nō**-tis) verb

You **notice** something when you pay attention to it.

*The students **notice** the different colors of the snake's skin.*

opportunity

(**op**-ur-**tyū**-nu-tē) noun

An **opportunity** is a good time to do something.

*When the pond froze, we had the **opportunity** to go ice-skating.*

outgrown

(**owt-grōn**) verb

When you have **outgrown** something, you have gotten too big for it.

*He has **outgrown** his baby clothes.*

*In the present: The children **outgrow** their clothes fast.*

*In the past: I **outgrew** that shirt last year.*

peace

(pēs) noun

There is **peace** when there is no war or fighting.

dove

olive branch

*A dove with an olive branch is a symbol of **peace**.*

permanent

(**pur**-mu-nunt) adjective

When something is **permanent**, it lasts a long time.

*She will have her **permanent** teeth for many years.*

pole

(pōl) noun

A **pole** is a long piece of wood or metal.

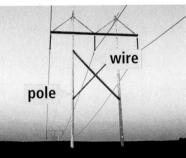

wire

pole

*The telephone **pole** holds up the telephone wires.*

pressure

(**presh**-ur) noun

When one thing pushes or squeezes against another, it causes **pressure**.

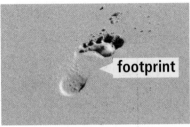

footprint

*The **pressure** from a foot makes a footprint in the sand.*

pride

(prīd) noun

You have **pride** when you feel good about someone or something.

*The parents of these children have a feeling of **pride**.*

promise

(**prom**-is) verb

When you **promise** to do something, you say that you will do it.

*Sam **promised** to feed the birds every week.*

493

proudly

(prowd-lē) *adverb*

You act **proudly** when you show that you feel good about yourself.

*Chen **proudly** accepts the first-place ribbon for his science project.*

publish

(pub-lish) *verb*

You **publish** a book, newspaper, or magazine when you print it for people to read.

*My school **publishes** a newspaper every month.*

push up

(poosh-up) *verb*

When you **push up** on something, you move it higher.

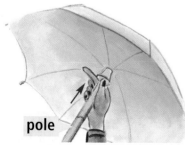

pole

*You **push up** on the pole to open this umbrella.*

---

refuse

(ri-fyūz) *verb*

When you **refuse** something, you do not take it.

*Some people **refuse** to take money from friends.*

region

(rē-jun) *noun*

A **region** is an area that has similar features.

Midwest Region

*The Midwest is a mostly flat **region** of the United States.*

---

remember

(ri-mem-bur) *verb*

When you think about something that happened in the past, you **remember** it.

*They **remember** when John was a little boy.*

remind

(ri-mīnd) *verb*

When something **reminds** you, it makes you think about a person or thing.

*This hat **reminds** me of my grandmother.*

reply

(ri-plī) *verb*

When you **reply**, you use words or actions to answer someone or something.

*Tonya likes to **reply** to a letter from her friend right away.*

reward
(ri-**word**) *noun*

A **reward** is a gift for doing something good or helpful.

*They get a **reward** for their hard work.*

S

safety
(**sāf**-tē) *noun*

Safety is when you are free from danger or harm.

helmet

*A helmet gives you **safety** because it protects your head.*

secret
(**sē**-krit) *adjective*

When something is **secret**, few people know about it.

birthday present

*Tony has a **secret** hiding place for Mom's birthday present.*

service
(**sur**-vis) *noun*

A **service** is an activity that provides something people need.

mail
postal worker

*This postal worker provides mail **service**.*

settlement
(**set**-ul-munt) *noun*

A **settlement** is a small group of homes in one place.

*Jamestown, Virginia, was the first British **settlement** in the United States.*

shelter
(**shel**-tur) *noun*

Shelter is a place that covers you and keeps you safe from harm or danger.

*This dog house gives **shelter** for the dogs.*

signal
(**sig**-nul) *noun*

A **signal** is a word, a thing, or an action that tells you what to do.

*This flag is a **signal** to start the race.*

silent
(**sī**-lunt) *adjective*

It is **silent** when there is no noise.

*Snow falls in the **silent** woods.*

sketch
(skech) *noun*

A **sketch** is a quick drawing.

sketch

painting

*I made a **sketch** before I made this painting.*

solid

(**sol**-id) *adjective*

A **solid** object has the same hard material all the way through.

*This log is **solid** wood.*

special

(**spesh**-ul) *adjective*

Something **special** is nicer or more important than other things.

*Mom uses the **special** dishes when my grandparents visit.*

strain

(strān) *verb*

When you **strain**, you work very hard to do something.

*The horse **strains** to pull the heavy wagon.*

style

(stīl) *noun*

A **style** is a type of clothing that people wear at a certain time.

1902   2004

*The **style** of clothes for boys has really changed!*

talent

(**tal**-unt) *noun*

When you do something well, you have a **talent** for it.

dancing

singing

playing music

playing sports

*Each of these children has a different **talent**.*

temperature

(**tem**-pur-u-chur) *noun*

Temperature is a measurement of how hot or cold something is.

freezing point

Fahrenheit scale

Celsius scale

Temperature may be measured in degrees Fahrenheit or Celsius.

temporary

(**tem**-pu-**rer**-ē) *adjective*

When something is **temporary**, it lasts only for a short time.

permanent home

temporary home

*Walt stays in this **temporary** home until his permanent home is ready.*

throne

(thrōn) *noun*

A **throne** is a special chair for a ruler.

*The king sits on his **throne**.*

thunder

(**thun**-dur) *noun*

Thunder is the loud noise that comes after a flash of lightning.

*Did you hear that boom of **thunder**?*

thunderstorm

(**thun**-dur-**storm**) *noun*

A **thunderstorm** is a storm with rain, thunder, and lightning.

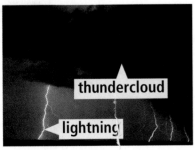

*A **thunderstorm** moves across the land.*

tornado

(tor-**nā**-dō) *noun*

A **tornado** is a powerful storm with winds that spin in a funnel-shaped cloud.

*The **tornado** moves through a town.*

trade

(trād) *verb*

People **trade** when they give each other something they need or want.

*These kids **trade** toys.*

traditional

(tru-**dish**-u-nul) *adjective*

Something that is **traditional** has been done for many generations.

*Some Native people in Florida have built these **traditional** homes for hundreds of years.*

treaty

(trē-tē) *noun*

A **treaty** is an agreement between two governments or groups.

*These men signed the **treaty** that ended World War I.*

tribe

(trīb) *noun*

A **tribe** is made up of people who share the same language, traditions, and ancestors.

*These people are members of the Hopi **tribe** in Arizona.*

497

twister
(**twis**-tur) *noun*

A **twister** is a spinning, funnel-shaped cloud.

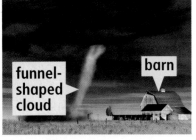

funnel-shaped cloud

barn

*The **twister** goes toward the barn!*

value
(**val**-yū) *noun*

The **value** of something is what it is worth or how important it is.

*What is the **value** of this jewelry?*

village
(**vil**-ij) *noun*

A **village** is a small group of houses.

*Many years ago, Native people lived together in this **village**.*

weathering
(**weth**-ur-ing) *noun*

Changes that happen because of water, temperature, and wind are called **weathering**.

before weathering

after weathering

***Weathering** by the wind changed the shape of this rock.*

Acknowledgments, continued

Victor Cockburn and Judith Steinbergh: "Something New." All rights reserved. Text and audio copyright © 1993 by Victor Cockburn and Judith Steinbergh. Used by permission of the authors. "Where I Come From" from *Where I Come From! Songs and Poems from Many Cultures*, lyrics by Victor Cockburn and music by Judith Steinberg. Copyright © 1991 by Judith Steinbergh and Victor Cockburn. Used by permission.

Crabtree Publishing Company: *Native Homes* by Bobbie Kalman. Copyright © 2001 by Crabtree Publishing Company. Reproduced with permission of Crabtree Publishing Company.

The Creative Company: "Money" reprinted by permission of The Creative Company. Material selected from "Money" originally published by Creative Education, 123 Broad Street, Mankato, MN 65001.

Dr. Sylvia Earle/National Geographic Image Collection: *Hello, Fish!* By Dr. Sylvia Earle. Text copyright © 1999 by Sylvia A. Earle. Photographs copyright © 1999 by Wolcott Henry. Reprinted by permission.

Farrar, Straus and Giroux, LLC.: *Twister* by Darleen Bailey Beard, illustrated by Nancy Carpenter. Text copyright © 1999 by Darleen Bailey Beard. Illustrations copyright © 1999 by Nancy Carpenter. Reprinted by permission of Farrar, Straus and Giroux, LLC.

Harcourt, Inc.: Cover from *Baseball in April and Other Stories* by Gary Soto. Illustration copyright © 1990 by Barry Root. Reprinted by permission of Harcourt, Inc. Cover from *Canto Familiar* by Gary Soto. Illustration copyright © 1995 by Annika Nelson. Reprinted by permission of Harcourt, Inc. *The Lotus Seed* by Sherry Garland. Text copyright © 1993 by Sherry Garland. Illustrations copyright © 1993 by Tatsuro Kiuchi. Reprinted by permission of Harcourt, Inc.

HarperCollins Publishers: "I imagined this gigantic piece of rock. . ." from Pam Conrad *Call Me Ahnighito* (Author Notes). Text copyright © 1995 by Pam Conrad. Used by permission of HarperCollins Publishers. Used with permission of Sarah Conrad and Maria Carvainais Agency, Inc.

Houghton Mifflin Company: *My Rows and Piles of Coins* by Tololwa M. Mollel. Text copyright © 1999 by Tololwa M. Mollel. Illustrations copyright © 1999 by E. B. Lewis. Reprinted by permission of Clarion Books, a division of Houghton Mifflin Company. All rights reserved.

Ramson Lomatewama: "Cloud Brothers" from *Silent Winds: Poetry of One Hopi* by Ramson Lomatewama. Copyright © 1981 by Ramson Lomatewama. Reprinted by permission of the author.

Penguin Putnam Inc.: Cover of *Chato's Kitchen* by Gary Soto. Illustrations copyright © 1995 by Susan Guevara. Used by permission of G.P. Putnam's Sons, an imprint of Penguin Putnam Books for Young Readers, a division of Penguin Putnam Inc. All rights reserved. Cover of *The Earth Under Sky Bear's Feet* by Joseph Bruchac. Illustrations copyright © 1995 by Thomas Locker. Used by permission of Philomel Books, an imprint of Penguin Putnam Books for Young Readers, a division of Penguin Putnam Inc. All rights reserved. *If the Shoe Fits* by Gary Soto. Text copyright © 2002 by Gary Soto. Illustrations copyright © 2002 by Terry Widener. Published by arrangement with G.P. Putnam's Sons, an imprint of Penguin Putnam Books for Young Readers, a division of Penguin Putnam Inc. All rights reserved. *Pushing Up the Sky* by Joseph Bruchac and illustrated by Teresa Flavin. Text copyright © 2000 by Joseph Bruchac. Illustrations copyright © 2000 by Teresa Flavin. Used by arrangement with Dial Books for Young Readers, a member of Penguin Putnam Inc. Cover from *Snapshots from the Wedding* by Gary Soto. Copyright © 1997 by Gary Soto. Used by permission of G.P. Putnam's Sons, an imprint of Penguin Putnam Books for Young Readers, a division of Penguin Putnam Inc. All rights reserved. Cover from *The Talking Eggs* by Robert D. San Souci. Pictures copyright © 1989 by Jerry Pinkney. Used by permission of Dial Books for Young Readers, a member of Penguin Putnam Inc. Cover from *Too Many Tomales* by Gary Soto. Illustrations copyright © 1993 by Ed Martinez. Used by permission of G.P. Putnam's Sons, an imprint of Penguin Putnam Books for Young Readers, a division of Penguin Putnam Inc. All rights reserved.

Random House, Inc.: Cover of *The Lizard and the Sun* by Alma Flor Ada. Used by permission of Random House Children's Books, a division of Random House, Inc. Art from *The Secret Footprints* by Julia Alvarez. Illustrations copyright © 2000 by Fabian Negrin. Used by permission of Alfred A. Knopf, an imprint of Random House Children's Books, a division of Random House, Inc.

Marian Reiner: "Wind Song" from *I Feel the Same Way* by Lilian Moore. Copyright © 1967 by Lilian Moore. Used by permission of Marian Reiner for the author.

Scholastic Inc.: "Quarter Kids" from *Scholastic News*, March 20, 2000. Copyright © 2000 by Scholastic Inc. Reprinted by permission. *The Tree That Would Not Die* by Ellen Levine. Text copyright © 1995 by Ellen Levine. Illustrations copyright © 1995 by Ted Rand. Text and audio reprinted and used by permission of Scholastic Inc.

Simon & Schuster Children's Publishing Division: *The Big Storm* by Bruce Hiscock. Text copyright © 1993 by Bruce Hiscock. Excerpted, adapted and reprinted with the permission of Atheneum Books for Young Readers, an imprint of Simon & Schuster Children's Publishing Division.

Susan Bergholz Literary Services: Text of *The Secret Footprints* by Julia Alvarez. Copyright © 2000 by Julia Alvarez. Published by Alfred A. Knopf, a division of Random House. Reprinted by permission of Susan Bergholz Literary Services, New York. All rights reserved.

Photographs:

Jay Adeff Photography: p123 (time capsule, ©Jay Adeff Photography), p311 (building, ©Jay Adeff Photography).

Alexander Photography, Bryan & Cherry: p204 (polar bear snow cave).

AP/Wide World Photos: p187 (Paris, Texas), p191 (snow storm), p268 (escape war), p268 (job fair), p330 (Xander Kotsatos at unveiling), p479 (Mt St. Helens) p184 (watching the weather).

Artville: p378 (vegetable stand), p409 (one dollar bill), p418 (pesos), p420 (dime-L), p420 (penny, dime-B, penny), p421 (nickel, quarter, dime-B, back of quarter, back of nickel, cash register), p422 (one dollar face and back, quarter, penny back), p487 (coins), p493 (telephone poles), p493 (footprint).

Austin Convention & Visitor Bureau: p363 (Treaty Oak tree), p478 (postage stamp of Brazil, Courtesy Busch, Richard).

Batista Moon: p12 and p49 (Gary Soto).

Doug Bekke: p496 (thermometer).

Richard Busch: p478 (emerald stamp of Brazil 48k, Courtesy Richard Busch @ http://stampmin.home.att.net).

Sue Carlson: p486 (Texas).

Cartesia: p487 (girl).

Corbis: p497 (thunder cartoon, Gianni Dagli) Orti, p486 (cheetah, Mary Ann McDonald), p490 (government), p490 (journey, Bettmann), p489 (roller coaster, Buddy Mays), p487 (Native Americans, Gunte Marx Photography), p496 (1902 clothing, H. Armstrong Roberts), p495 (doghouse, Julie Habel), p491 (hay wagon, Richard A. Cooke), p492 (hieroglyphics, Richard T. Nowitz), p493 (boy feeding birds, Tom Stewart), p497 (Hopi, Underwood & Underwood), p489 (market, Wolfgang Kaehler).

Corel: p485 (fish).

Dr. John Crossley: p474 (Canyon wall).

Digital Stock: p491 (lightning), p491 (volcano), p491 (lotus), p492 (elephant).

Environmental Protection Agency: p497 (treaty signing) Still Pictures Branch, National Archives at College Park.

Getty Images: p5 (Rocky Mountains National Park/Greg Probst), p5 (golden eagle/John Downer), p5 (clouds), p6 (lightning), p6 (tornado, Eric Meola), p6 (winter tree), p8 (girl, Terry Vine), p8 (Rajasthani textile, Carlos Navajas), p11 (Quartz), p14 (computer, fax machine, and touch tone telephone), p42 (red t-shirt, and jeans), p70 (golden eagle, John Downer), p70 (clouds), p96 (spiral note book, Carl Glover), p128 (tornado on horizon, Eric Meola), p129 (lightning), p138 (breezy, gale, and hurricane), p249 (starfish), p176 (snow flake), p177 (rain drops), p180 (storm over mountains, Michael K. Nichols), p181 (snowy winter scene), p183 (barometer and thermometer), p189 (hail on ground), p206 (sand and sea shells, Burke/Triolo Productions), p206 (beach house, Rod Long), p206 (starfish stamp), p209 (island, Mike Molloy), p244 (octopus, David Fleetham), p266 (Rajasthani Textiles, Carlos Navajas), p268 (family, Sylvain Grandadam), p269 (dance, Sylvain Grandadam), p270 (family portrait, Stewart Cohen), p270, p271, and p308 (lotus flower, Giantstep), p270 (landscape, Steven L. Raymer), p292 (boy in class, Ian Shaw), p293 and p294 (girl from Buenos Aires, Terry Vine), p293 and p300 (rice, Francisco Ontanon Nunez), p313 (technology), p322 (Mayflower), p377 (riding up a hill), p378 (Vendor, David Lees), p379 (Fruits and Money), p403 (bike), p408 (gold nuggets), p410 (paying the cab, Ron Chappel), p410 (teen girls), p411 (Vietnam market, Oliver Benn), p413 (raising livestock and pots, Paul Chesley), p415 (tea leaves, Batista Moon), p415 (cowry, Jim Linna), p416 (gold, C-Squared Studios), p423 (woman selling handmade silk, Paul Chesley), p423 (lemonade stand), p423 (extracting money from wallet, Alberto Incrocci), p432 (quartz), p434 (emerald, Luis Veiga), p435 (meteor headed for earth, Peter Sherrard), p462 and p479 (natural arch), p472 (freeway), p472 (cliff tree, Martial Colomb), p497 (trade, Alan R. Moller/Stone), p489 (tepees, EyeWire), p489 (waves, Gary Vestal/Stone), p487 (race, Mike Powell/Allsport Concepts), p489 (redwood trees, V.C.L./Taxi).

Peter Grosshauser: p488 (seasons).

Scott Hanson: p9 and p310 (North America made with license plates).

Grant Heilman: p486 (butterfly net, Runk/Schoenberger).

500

Hutchings Photography: p266 (photo shoot: woman stitching a multi-cultural star quilt, Hutchings Photography).

The Image Works: p486(shoveling snow, F. Pedrick).

Index Stock Imagery: p72 (crafts, Barry Slaven), p205 (running cheetah, John Dominis), p480 river, Mark Windom, p498 (jewelry, Arni Katz).

Masterfile: p117 (wood & bark, Gloria H. Chomica), p117 (mud, Daryl Benson), p118 (sunset over field, Daryl Benson), p138 (drizzle, Lloyd Sutton), (rain, Zoran Milich), p290 (background, R. Ian Lloyd).

Dick Milligan: p79 (story pole).

Paul Mirocha: p487 (cold front diagram).

Museum of History & Industry, Seattle, WA: p78 (William Shelton) National Geographic Society, Wolcott Henry p240 and p245 (moray eel), p242, p246, and p264 (damselfish), p244, p258 and 260 (coral reef), p247 (clownfish & anemone), p248 (rainbow scorpionfish), p249 (stargazer), p250 (spotted stingray), p251 (brown goby), p252 (frogfish), p254 (silvertip shark).

National Center for Atmospheric Research/University Corporation for Atmoshperic Research/National Science Foundation: p182 (blizzard).

NCDC Satellite Services Group/NOAA: p190 (Satellite Image Map, NOAA).

NPS/Appomattox Court House: p313 (Appomattox, Appomattox Court House National Historic Park).

NYRockman.com: p456 (Peekskill Meteorite, www.nyrockman.com).

North Wind Picture Archives: p495 (settlement), p498 (weathering illustration), p 492 (Native people) p497 (Hopi tribe, N.Carter).

Heather Parsons: p336 (Xander), p331 (Xander), p332 (Xander), p334 (Xander), p334 (Xander).

PhotoDisc: p485 (girls laughing), p486 (orchid blossoms), p488 (dead fish), p491 (boy/lockers), p493 (students), p494 (region), p494 (women), p496 (log), p496 (violinist), p497 (tornado), p498 (village).

PhotoEdit: p493 (ice-skating) Barbara Stitzer, p492 (teepee, Bill Bachmann), p487 (students/engine, Bonnie Kamin), p487 (Mexican dancers), p495 (postal worker, David Young-Wolff), p491 (cliff, Jonathon Nourok), p488 (girl with basketball, Michael Newman), p488 (storm damage, Richard Lord), p490 (hail storm, Robert Brenner), p489 (forecaster), p492 (meteorite, Rudi Von Briel), p490 (police, Tom Carter).

Photo Researchers, Inc.: p183 (storm across the plains, Larry L. Miller), p193 (lightning, Larry L. Miller), p313 (stock market, E.Young), p376 (workers, Novastock), p434 (talc, Ben Johnson/ SPL/Photo), p434 (ruby, Charles D. Winters), p434 (topaz, Mark A. Schneider), p434 (tourmaline, M. A. Schneider), p495(snow on woods, Jim Steinberg), p492 (Inuit people) Lawrence Migdale, p488(traffic, Rafael Macia).

PhotoSpin: p409 (50 note, PhotoSpin), p418 (Euro dollar, PhotoSpin).

PictureQuest: p14 (pager, Corbis), p118 (wood frame, Image Farm), p138 (blizzard, Stockbyte), p204 (frog catching food, Rauschenbach Premium Stock), p248 and p252 (sea sponge, Hal Beral/ Photo Network), p253 (shrimp, Photobank/Pictor International, Ltd.), p256 and 257 (coral, Stephen Frink/ Index Stock Imagery), p267 (rug background, StockByte), p267 (red white and blue fabric, StockByte), p376 (consumer, Skip Nall), p408, 424 and 426 (new coin background, Rob Bartee/Index Stock), p423 (Euro coin, Thomas Craig/ IndexStock), p434 (gold, DigitalVision), p467 (water erosion, Peter Essick/ Aurora), p485 (passengers, C.J. Allen/Stock), Boston Inc.

Random House: p453 (Pam Conrad, Sarah Conrad).

Robert Richardson: p474 (Crystal Cave, Robert Richardson).

Sandra T. Sevigny: p485 (backbone).

Roni Shepherd: p485 (sinking ship), p485 (family arriving), p485 (ducks), p485 (barter), p485 (better future), p486 (boldness), p486 (Mississippi), p486 (painting party), p486 (cellar), p487 (creatures), p488 (porcupine, fox), p488 (playground design), p488 (disappointed), p488 (hikers), p489 (bank), p489 (loose laces), p490 (hand-me-down), p490 (howling wind), p490 (pegasus), p491 (lift), p491 (volcano diagram), p492 (valley), p493 (dove), p494 (photo copy), p494 (umbrella), p494 (refusal), p494 (reminds), p494 (writing letter), p495 (reward), p495 (gift), p495 (finishing race), p495 (sketch), p496 (special dishes), p496 (horse and cart), p496 (tent/home), p497 (thunderstorm), p497 (chickee houses).

Smithsonian Institution: National Museum of Natural History ©2002: p462 and p475 (Hope Diamond).

Gary Soto: p4 (Gary) and p50 (Gary as a boy), p51 (street scene and Gary), p52 (Gary as a teen) p62, 68 (Gary).

Clem Spalding: p4 (girl reading), p48 (boy reading), p54 - p61 (all photos).

Stock Food: p21 (Moussaka, Joy Skipper/Stock Food).

SuperStock, Inc.: p197 (Buenos Aires), p379 (shoppers, Bluestone Productions), p489(emperor, Stock Montage).

Texas Department of Transportation: p365 (Treaty Oak).

TimePix: p412 (Woman examines running shoe, ©Enrique Marcarian/TimePix).

Tom and Pat Leeson: p210 (Lynx chasing rabbit, Tom and Pat Leeson/AGPix).

US Mint: p316 (Quarters, ©US Mint), p317 (Change background, ©US Mint), p319 (Front and back of Quarter (old), © US Mint), p324 (Massachusetts Quarter front, Courtesy of US Mint), p325 (Massachusetts Quarter back, Courtesy of US Mint), p331 (4 new quarters, ©US Mint), p333 (Quarters backgrnd, ©U.S. Mint), p334 (Quarters backgrnd., U.S. Mint), p339 (Georgia, Ohio, Indiana & South Carolina state quarters, Courtesy of US Mint), p372 (Quarter, ©US Mint), p372 (quarter, Courtesy of US Mint).

Visuals Unlimited: p466 (gold in quartz, George Herbeul/Visuals Unlimited), p467 (ice erosion, Martin G. Miller/Visuals Unlimited), p469 (sedimentary rock, Arthur R. Hill/Visuals Unlimited).

Liz Garza Williams: p487 (U.S. map), p487 (woman and man talking on telephones), p491 (market), p492 (boy in rain, boy thinking), p493 (outgrown), p493 (girl), p493 (drama), p494 (1st place ribbon), p495 (girl on bike), p496 (2004 clothing), p496 (dancers, singer), p496 (playing baseball), p490 (girl).

Author and Illustrator Photos:

p39 (Courtesy of Terry Widener), p89 (Michael Greenlar), p119 (R. Lomatewama), p165 (Darleen Baily Beard), p167 (Courtesy of Mauan Reiner), p176 (Courtesy Audrey Baird), p193 (Bruce Hiscock), p231 (Bill Eichner. Reprinted by permission of Susan Bergholz Literary Services, New York. All rights reserved.), p257 (Al Giddings Images, Inc.), p283 (Courtesy of Tatsuro Kiuchi), p329 (Olin Mills), p399 (Courtesy of Tololwa M. Mollel), p453 (Courtesy of Boyds Mills Press).

Illustrations:

BSS: pp102-103 (map), p73 (map), pp294-295 (border), pp296-297 (border), pp298-299 (border), pp300-301 border), pp302-304 (borders); **Annie Bissett:** p15, maps and globes p 79, p131, p176, p180, pp182-183, p186, p189, p191, p209, p243, p273, p313, p341, p381, p439, p494; **Linda Bleck:** p262; **Doug Bowles:** pp132-133; **Ann Boyajian:** p306; **Lynn Chapman:** pp338-339; **Helen D'Souza:** pp166-167; **John Dawson:** p469, p471, p473; **Julie Durrell:** pp300-301, p364 (tree); **Cameron Eagle:** pp460-461; **Teresa Flavin:** p5, pp76-89, pp90-91, pp92-93 (border); **Pam-Ela Harrelson:** p124; **Mary Haverfield:** p370; **Inklink:** p5, pp98-116, p126; **Kveta Jelinek:** p428; **Gideon Kendall:** pp46-47; **Darryl Ligasan:** pp406-407; **John Mantha:** pp72-73; **Michele Noiset:** pp314-315; **Sebastian Quigley:** pp178-179, p185, p188, p415, p419, p435, p462, p465; **Mike Saunders:** pp 238-239; **Mark Shroder:** pp74-75; **Stacey Schuett:** pp174-175; **Susan Spellman:** pp436-437; **Amy Wummer:** p198

The Avenues Development Team

Hampton-Brown extends special thanks to those who contributed so much to the creation of the Grade 3, 4, and 5 Pupil Editions.

Editorial: Janine Boylan, Julie Cason, Lisa Cittadino, Shirleyann Costigan, Phyllis Edwards, Roseann Erwin, Nadine Guarrera, Margot Hanis, Fredrick Ignacio, Cynthia Keith, Phillip Kennedy, Tiina Kurvi, Sheron Long, S. Michele McFadden, Amy Ostenso, Heather Peacock, Sharon Ursino, and Cullen Wojcik.

Design and Production: Renae Arcinas, Katherine A. Butler, Christy Caldwell, Jen Coppens, Sherry Corley, Jeri Gibson , Terry Harmon, Rick Holcomb, Connie McPhedran, Michael Moore, Robert Myles, Russ Nemec, Marian O'Neal, Anthony Paular, Cathy Revers, Augustine Rivera, Debbie Saxton, DJ Simison, Curtis Spitler, Jonni Stains, Debbie Swisher, Vicki Vandeventer, Elvin (JR) Walker, and Bill Smith Studios

Permissions: Barbara Mathewson